La Belle Créole

La Belle Créole

THE CUBAN COUNTESS

WHO CAPTIVATED HAVANA, MADRID, *and* PARIS

Alina García-Lapuerta

CHICAGO
REVIEW
PRESS

Published by Chicago Review Press, Incorporated
814 North Franklin Street
Chicago, Illinois 60610
ISBN 978-1-61374-536-6

Library of Congress Cataloging-in-Publication Data
García-Lapuerta, Alina.
    La Belle Créole : the Cuban countess who captivated Havana, Madrid, and Paris / Alina
García-Lapuerta. — First edition.
        pages cm
    Summary: "The adventurous woman nicknamed La Belle Créole is brought to life in this
book through the full use of her memoirs, contemporary accounts, and her intimate letters.
The fascinating María de las Mercedes Santa Cruz y Montalvo, also known as Mercedes, and
later the Comtesse Merlin, was a Cuban-born aristocrat who was years ahead of her time
as a writer, a socialite, a salon host, and a participant in the Cuban slavery debate. Raised
in Cuba and shipped off to live with her socialite mother in Spain at the age of 13, Mercedes
triumphed over the political chaos that blanketed Europe in the Napoleonic days, by charming
aristocrats from all sides with her exotic beauty and singing voice. She married General Merlin
in Napoleon's army and discussed painting with Francisco de Goya. In Paris she hosted the
city's premier musical salon where Liszt, Rossini, and great divas of the day performed for
Rothschilds, Balzac, and royalty. Celebrated as one of the greatest amateur sopranos of her day,
Mercedes also achieved fame as a writer. Her memoirs and travel writings introduced European
audiences to 19th-century Cuban society and contributed to the debate over slavery. Mercedes
has recently been rediscovered as Cuba's earliest female author and one who deserves a place in
the canon of Latin American literature"— Provided by publisher.
    Includes bibliographical references and index.
    ISBN 978-1-61374-536-6 (hardback)
    1. Merlin, María de las Mercedes Santa Cruz y Montalvo, comtesse de, 1789-1852.
2. Countesses—Spain—Biography. 3. Countesses—Cuba—Biography. 4. Spain—Court
and courtiers—Biography. 5. Socialites—France—Paris—Biography. 6. Socialites—
Spain—Madrid—Biography. 7. Socialites—Cuba—Biography. 8. Women authors,
Cuban—Biography. 9. Slavery—Political aspects—Cuba—History—19th century.
10. Cuba—History—1810-1899—Biography. I. Title.
    DP202.M5G37 2014
    972.91′2405092—dc23
    [B]

                                                                                    2014018302

See www.alinagarcialapuerta.com for additional information and references.

Interior design: Monica Baziuk
Map design: Chris Erichsen

Printed in the United States of America

5   4   3   2   1

To my parents: José Manuel and Mireya,

and to all the other Cubans who left her shores

but never forgot their beloved "Cuba bella."

CONTENTS

AUTHOR'S NOTE

*W*riting about a woman who was born in the late eighteenth century, lived in three countries, and published in two languages presented a few challenges—and choices. To ease the reader's way a little, here are some explanations.

The phrase "creole" often puzzles the modern reader. Many think that creole or *criolla* (in Spanish) means a person of mixed race from the former slave-owning states or the Caribbean. However, the word merely indicates that someone was born in a colony, generally of European descent. In Cuban terms, *criolla/criollo* can be used for anything from food to customs, and distinguishes the colonies from the Spanish peninsula. Mercedes and her family most certainly considered themselves creoles, and when people in Europe called her La Belle Créole, they were referring to her Cuban birthplace.

Names are also problematic. Throughout the book I use the original spelling for Spanish or French names—both for individuals and places. There are three exceptions: Havana, Napoleon, and Wellington. La Habana is the Spanish name of Cuba's capital but since the English version is so well-known I have used it throughout. For similar reasons, it seemed pointless to add an accent to such a famous name as Napoleon. I have also called him Napoleon throughout, although strictly speaking, he was only called that as emperor. Likewise, Wellington is always Wellington, even though Arthur Wellesley did not receive his dukedom until the end of Europe's Peninsular War. Also related to titles, I have translated the titles *comte*, *conde*, and so on, in an attempt to simplify matters. The one exception is *marqués/marquesa* or marquis/marquise. I felt that the English equivalent (marquess and marchioness) are less well known and probably as confusing as the originals. I have kept the original names that go with the titles. Where appropriate, I have also kept the honorific *don* or *doña* as there is no adequate translation. The honorific was placed before the first name and in Mercedes' day was only used for the white population.

María de las Mercedes Santa Cruz y Montalvo is a rather long name. But the double last name is not an aristocratic styling; rather, all Spanish-speaking countries follow this usage. Men and women have two last names: paternal first and maternal second. The parents each pass on their first (paternal) last name. Mercedes Santa Cruz y Montalvo is the daughter of Joaquín de Santa Cruz y Cárdenas and Teresa Montalvo y O'Farrill, therefore her name Santa Cruz comes from her father and Montalvo from her mother. And so it goes.

Another source of confusion is that Cuban and Spanish women never lose their maiden name—even after marriage. Therefore, all such women in the book continue to be called by their original names. They do accept their husbands' titles, however! Again, there is an exception: Madame Merlin. Since Mercedes married a Frenchman and lived in France, in the British and French press, she was sometimes called Madame Merlin.

Finally, despite the profusion of names and titles—María de las Mercedes, María Merced, María de la Merced, Mercedita, Condesa de Merlin, Comtesse Merlin—I have chosen to call her Mercedes throughout. It seems a touch more personal, and after so many years immersed in her life, I feel as though I know her.

La Belle Créole

PROLOGUE

On the fifteenth of April in 1840, the *Great Western* steamship set sail from the English port of Bristol bound for New York City. This was only the second year that the new steamships made regular Atlantic crossings, beginning the transformative age of steam. It was a world away from the days of the sailing ships, of the caravels, galleons, sloops, and brigs that had sailed the world and helped to create the great colonial empires. On this triumphantly modern ship, one passenger embarked on a voyage in reverse, retracing the path she had taken as a child. María de las Mercedes Santa Cruz y Montalvo, the Comtesse Merlin of the Rue de Bondy in Paris, was returning to her birthplace of Havana, Cuba. Armed with her family contacts, her memories, and her letter writing desk, she journeyed to Cuba for the first time since she had left the island colony with her father, the Count de San Juan de Jaruco.

The ocean seemed as vast as ever, and the splash of the waves against the ship still broke the silence of the open sea, but the second crossing could not have been more different. Thirty-eight years earlier, in 1802, her ship had been part of an official squadron of the Spanish navy commanded by Admiral Gravina. The Spanish fleet, laden with men, gold, and supplies, had crisscrossed the seas, from

America to Spain, for three hundred years. On that first sea voyage, she was the thirteen-year-old-daughter of an important passenger: the sub-inspector general of Cuba's royal forces. Mercedes had not seen her mother since infancy, and she would not see her birthplace again for almost four decades. This thirteen-year-old had just escaped life cloistered in a Havana convent, but would never again experience the previously cherished freedom of running wild on her family's plantations. Still, she looked toward the future and the longed-for reunion with her mother—the beginning of a new life.

On the second crossing, Mercedes, now aged fifty-one and widowed but still full of life, sought the renewal of her fortunes among the remnants of her past. Although she traveled for personal and legal reasons, she used the sights and sounds gathered on this second voyage to write an account of Cuban life and customs for her European friends. This account, *La Havane*, would confirm her place in Cuban history as its first female author and chronicler of nineteenth-century colonial life. She would often be referred to as the "elegant, Havana-born Comtesse Merlin from Paris," cited in countless Cuban histories and coffee table books for her glamorous life and for her descriptions of upper-class colonial society.

These twin journeys each represented one half of her story— the naïve Cuban youth and the worldly adult European writer. In between, Mercedes underwent a different sort of journey. A young girl with a wild and free spirit was educated, socially polished, and turned into a member of the Borbón Spanish royal court, then into the young wife of a conquering French-Bonapartist general. Escaping as a fugitive from Spain after Wellington's triumph over Napoleonic forces, she finally emerged as the exotic creole hostess of a brilliant Parisian salon, enthralling all with her exquisite voice. Forced by her family's decisions to rebuild her life, she seized the chance to carve her own place in those turbulent times.

Fashion and political tastes change, and Mercedes' story faded with the crumbling of Cuba's colonial past. Now her singular experience lies hidden as though guarded behind a long-shuttered window in a decaying Havana palace. But reopening the window reveals a dazzling panorama.

PART I

Cuba

ISLAND OF
CUBA

·⟨✦⟩·

CIRCA 1800

Straits of Florida

LA HABANA

Pinar del Río   Matanzas

Santa Clara

⑦④③② ⑤⑥ ①

●(now Cienfuegos)

Bay of Jagua

100 miles

Puerto Príncipe (Camagüey)

Holguín

● Bayamo   Guantánamo

Caribbean Sea

Santiago de Cuba

Joaquin's Major Properties

1. Palos, Bagaes, and Santa Margarita (near Nueva Paz)
2. Jaruco—entailed lands
3. Jesús Nazareno (now Nazareno)
4. San Antonio de los Baños—founded by Cárdenas family
5. Las Delicias (Alquízar)
6. Seybabo and Río Blanco (near San Antonio de las Vegas)
7. Cafetales Neptuno and Minerva (near Artemisa)

PLACES OF INTEREST

1. One of Joaquín's homes, near La Punta
2. *Palacio* of the Counts de San Juan de Jaruco
3. *Palacio* of the Marqués de San Felipe y Santiago, where Joaquín died 1807
4. *Casa de Mateo Pedroso*, home of Juan Montalvo in 1840
5. *Casa de la Obra Pía*
6. Convent of Santa Clara
7. *Real Casa Cuna* (Foundling home)
8. Convent of the Ursalines

Castillo de la Punta

PASEO DEL PRADO

CUARTELES

CHACÓN

Plaza de la Catedral

Castillo de la Fuerza

Plaza de Armas

Havana Extramuros

OBISPO

OBRAPÍA

CUBA

SAN IGNACIO

MERCADERES

OFICIOS

AMARGURA

Plaza de San Francisco

Plaza Vieja

CUNA

Havana Bay

MURALLA

SOL

LUZ

ALAMEDA DE PAULA

1/4 mile

N
W E
S

THE WALLED CITY
HAVANA
·※·
IN MERCEDES' DAY

HAVANA

A CITY OF SEA AND LIGHT

A traveler arriving in the city of San Cristóbal de La Habana in the winter of 1789 would have easily found the city's cathedral. The huge building sat in one of Havana's main plazas— La Plaza de la Catedral—its surprisingly plain, asymmetrical towers and contrastingly ornate facade made in part of pale grey coral rock from the nearby sea. The sea could also be sensed in the undulating baroque curves of the cathedral's facade, reminiscent of breaking waves, interrupted by three great wooden doors. Along the cathedral square, the magnificent family palaces of the Pedroso, the Peñalver, and the Marqués de Aguas Claras stood with their arcades offering shady paths against the sun. The plaza was a central meeting point in Havana, and all day long the different people of the city would pass by—merchants, artisans, soldiers, slave traders, aristocrats and slaves—going about their daily business as the great bells of the cathedral marked the passing of the day. The cathedral's beauty and grace would have stood out even in the days of ornate buildings. A later Cuban writer would call it "music set in stone."

On that winter day of February 16, 1789, the cathedral's thick walls obscured the light and sounds of the tropical street life while Havana's vicar general, Don Luis Peñalver y Cárdenas, solemnly baptized a ten-day-old infant girl, María de las Mercedes Josepha Teresa Bárbara Luisa de Jesús Santa Cruz y Montalvo. Mercedes took her place as the latest link in the chain of an intricately related creole aristocracy. The aristocracy was creole in the Spanish sense of the word, meaning born in the empire's colonies but tracing its lineage back to Spain. Blessed with young and wealthy parents, a beautiful mother, and powerful relatives, Mercedes seemingly had a sparkling, preordained destiny. The baby's maternal and paternal lines, both firmly entrenched in Cuba's economy and administration, would play a critical role in the transformation of the island from a lesser Spanish possession into the sugar powerhouse of the nineteenth century.

But Cuba in 1789 was not quite what most people would have imagined; even the cathedral had only replaced the decrepit old main parish church in 1779. Indeed, the building only received the rank of cathedral in 1788 when Havana was promoted to a diocese, rather late for a capital city founded in the early sixteenth century. Cuba had been one of Columbus's earliest discoveries, and he had praised it extravagantly as "of such marvelous beauty that it surpasses all others…as the day doth the night in lustre," having claimed it under the name Juana for Spain and *los Reyes Católicos*, Fernando and Isabel. But this beautiful island with its rich mahogany-filled forests, valleys covered in royal palms, and white beaches, had quickly been eclipsed by the later conquests of the Aztec and Inca empires. Cuba had only made its mark as a critical staging post for the most amazing and rich treasure fleets ever to sail the transatlantic routes. The gold and silver of Peru, Mexico, and Colombia all sailed to Spain on the fleets that stopped in Havana's deep-water port. To protect the port and the treasure route, the Spaniards built forts or *castillos* all around Havana, and it remained a walled city into the nineteenth century.

Havana is a city of sea and light. The city sits on the northern coast of the island of Cuba, the largest island of the Caribbean, which spreads out like a lizard in the sun. Cuba's position in the Caribbean controls the entrance to the Antilles, and both the Spanish conquistadores and their colonial challengers quickly realized it was the key to controlling the new world: *la Llave del Nuevo Mundo*, as the royal decree of 1634 named it. The original old city, founded in 1519, faced the harbor, a protected bay with a pincerlike narrow outlet to the sea that facilitated military defense. Walled on its inland boundaries for protection, with two sea-facing fortresses at its entrance and three more along both sides of its bay, it was a fortress city. The oldest fortresses, La Punta, La Fuerza, and El Morro, were made of coral rock or limestone known locally as *piedras conchíferas*. Small bits of sea creatures can still be seen in their massive bases, and the stone cannot be cleanly carved or polished. The sea seems to exist in their very walls, which take on a luminescence in soft early morning and late evening light.

The need for these monumental city defenses had been quite real—pirates had burned the first settlements to the ground and killed many of the early inhabitants in 1538 and again in 1555. Within living memory, the British forces of Lord Albemarle had laid siege to it, captured it, and held it for a year in 1762. During that year, the great monastery church of San Francisco de Asís was used for Protestant worship, the bishop of Cuba was deported, and slaves and goods poured in in huge numbers as the British opened Cuba to free trade. Spanish trading restrictions resumed with Spanish rule in 1763, but Havana's yearlong British sojourn helped begin the transformation of Cuba from a small sugar producer, in the shade of the fabled Sugar Islands of Barbados, Jamaica, and St. Domingue, into the Queen of Sugar by the 1820s.

The families attending Mercedes' christening in the new cathedral represented some of the main landowners of Cuba who together owned most of the estimated five hundred sugar mills, including the nine mills on Mercedes' grandfather's huge estate. Their family names appear over and over in the list of civic officials and officers of the local militias: Beltrán de Santa Cruz, Cárdenas, Montalvo, O'Farrill, Herrera, Chacón, Calvo de la Puerta, Peñalver, Nuñez del Castillo,

and Castellón. They had married with the descendants of older settlers, including the original founders of Havana and first city officials:
Sotolongo, Recio, Pérez Barroto, Guilizasti. The original conquistadores and settlers, arriving in Havana with the Governor Diego de
Velázquez de Cuéllar, built their first homes in the humblest of materials, emulating the native Arawaks by using mud and the branches and
bark of royal palms to make little thatched huts or *bohíos*.

In those early days, the sound of thousands of crabs coming up
from the sea in search of food was a nightly occurrence, and the
settlers' landholdings were dedicated to raising cattle and pigs for
food and hides. The streets were not paved, and when night fell only
moonlight broke the otherwise absolute darkness. The future Plaza
de la Catedral was merely a swampy area regularly flooded by the
bay. The many fruit trees planted by the early settlers led to infesta-
tions of mosquitoes, described by one visitor in 1598 as ferocious.
The adult Mercedes immortalized these vicious insects after her celebrated 1840 visit, recalling how she bathed her arms in *aguardi-
ente* distilled from sugarcane to repulse the insects. With her arms
soaked in the cane spirits, she would sit writing her letters while
being fanned by a young slave girl.

Despite these challenges, those early settlers seemed beguiled by
the richness of the land. Havana's terrain was incredibly fertile, with
much of the land covered in forests with huge ceiba trees spreading
their enormous canopies, and rich cedars and mahogany along with
granadillos and *jaguas*. Throughout the area, indeed throughout the
whole island, the majestic royal palms rose straight and tall above
all other trees. The Cuban forests would provide one of the first
important exports for the newly arrived Spaniards. Cuban-sourced
mahogany and other tropical hardwoods would initially be used to
repair ships carrying gold and silver from Mexico and Peru, then as
material for Philip II's Escorial palace and monastery back in Spain,
and finally to build the great ships of the Spanish navy or armada in
the eighteenth century.

The pirate raids of the sixteenth and early seventeenth century
eventually led to the building of the city walls, although that project

took over one hundred years to complete. The original single-street settlement clinging to the water's edge had expanded considerably by 1789, and the buildings were no longer made from various bits of royal palms. From the late sixteenth through the early eighteenth century, handsome houses began to appear along with churches and plazas. However, many streets remained narrow and crowded, following the instructions laid down by the Laws of the Indies, which demanded narrow streets in the tropics to offer shelter from the relentless sun. The unappealing smell of *tasajo*—the dried meat supplied in huge quantities to visiting ships of the Flota de Indias—filled these claustrophobic streets. Even in 1800, the naturalist Alexander von Humboldt would describe walking through congested streets knee-deep in mud.

Busy streets were not surprising given Havana's role as the meeting point of Spanish fleets and home to a major shipyard. Mercedes' great-grandfather, Lorenzo Montalvo, had directed the building work for the royal shipyard, the Real Arsenal. The Real Arsenal was the largest shipyard in the world at the time, and produced great ships such as the towering 136-gun *Santísima Trinidad* (1769). So important were the shipyards that in 1763, after the departure of the British, Carlos III of Spain created a naval office in Havana and named Lorenzo Montalvo as its *intendente general*. The Havana shipyards employed all sorts of craftsmen and laborers who resided year-round in the city. The sailing of the Spanish fleets, however, brought a major influx of visitors that swelled the local population. Spanish treasure ships would sail from the mainland ports of Veracruz (Mexico), Cartagena de Indias (Colombia), and Portobelo (Panama). Veracruz also received the cargo carried overland from Acapulco, the destination of the Pacific-based Manila galleons. The cargoes would include more than just gold and silver; they would also include spices, porcelain, and silk from the Philippines and China. Ships would meet in Havana to form great convoys to Sevilla and later to Cádiz, the main Spanish ports for the Indies. The Flota de Indias continued sailing until 1776, but even after its official end, ships continued to round El Morro and enter Havana's harbor in growing numbers.

As a port city, Havana had numerous taverns, boarding houses, gaming dens, and brothels. Most of its disreputable venues were concentrated in the poorer southern area of the city. The sailors who poured into Havana for weeks at a time made great use of its amenities—even in those early days, the city had a reputation for licentiousness that lives on through the present day. Havana also had a reputation for contraband. The Spanish crown had maintained a strict monopoly on all trading activity to its New World possessions through its port of Cádiz, but the aftermath of the British takeover saw the liberalization of trade with other Spanish ports in 1765. Both before and after 1762, the local need for slaves and their ready availability in nearby British Jamaica made the contraband trade an open secret, adding to Havana's dubious reputation.

Slavery, unfortunately, played an important role in the city's economic life. The first slaves had arrived in the New World in 1505, sent by Fernando of Aragón to the island of La Española (the Dominican Republic and Haiti). Slavery was quite common in Spain at the time, having also flourished under the Moors, so it was not strange for the Spanish crown to send slaves to its new possessions. As with commercial trade, Spain restricted the slave trade through the use of licenses, which awarded monopoly rights to specific companies. The British won the concession from 1713 to 1739 through the Treaty of Utrecht, which ended the War of the Spanish Succession. The license was granted to the London-based South Sea Company with Havana as the entry port for all Cuban slave traffic. After 1790, Cuba's first proper newspaper, *El Papel Periódico de la Havana*, carried advertisements for individual slaves. These ads lie scattered amid more mundane ones for used *volantes* (carriages), clavichords, and recently arrived European books: stark evidence of the eighteenth century's perspective of slaves as a mere commodity. This trade in humans initially brought Mercedes' great-great-grandfather, Richard O'Farrill y O'Daly, from the British island of Montserrat to Havana as the first representative of the South Sea Company. O'Farrill settled in Cuba, becoming a Spanish subject and marrying a well-connected widow, María

Josefa de Arriola. He remained active in the slave trade but also invested in sugar plantations after the concession changed hands.

As a fortress city, Havana also housed countless soldiers. Not only were there fixed regiments from the Spanish army stationed in Havana, there were also locally raised creole militias with regiments of whites and free blacks. Cuba after the British-controlled year of 1762 was a thoroughly militarized society. Even the most prominent citizens were fully integrated into military operations, with almost all the families having various members who were militia commanders or officers in the Spanish army. Many held membership in prestigious military orders such as those of Santiago, Calatrava, or Montesa. Whatever their landholding and commercial interests, the creole elite served the king's armies and his civil services because in the Spanish Empire, all authority and power centered on the king and royal court; all power and all decrees emerged from Madrid. The Spanish government co-opted the leading citizens through quasi-honorary appointments as senior militia officers.

Mercedes' family abounded in military connections, with relatives holding military appointments in the royal forces and militias. Her father, Joaquín de Santa Cruz y Cárdenas, a captain of the white militia of Havana at the time of her birth, would eventually rise to the rank of *mariscal de campo* (field marshal). Mercedes was also the granddaughter of the Count de Casa-Montalvo, Ignacio Montalvo y Ambulodi, a brigadier in the royal army and a colonel of a Cuban regiment of dragoons. Mercedes' female relatives often married military men, in some cases Spanish officers, such as her great-aunt María Manuela de Cárdenas, wife to the then general and later *mariscal de campo* Pedro de Mendinueta. At her baptism, Mercedes' extended family could count some nineteen officers of the royal army including twelve present or future generals and *mariscales de campo*.

The men in Mercedes' family circle also held many of Havana's civic offices. Some of these positions were officially hereditary while others passed along informally within a particular family. In many cases, the Spanish crown sold offices outright. With their dominance in commerce, military, and civic posts, the various families attending the baptism in the Havana cathedral formed a creole oligarchy well placed to lobby for Cuban interests and to benefit from the tremendous economic growth about to transform Cuba. From 1762 to 1792, sugar cultivation grew by 1,500 percent and exports increased tremendously. Spain faced growing pressure to open more ports to Caribbean products and to eliminate the slave trade monopoly. Cuba's population also increased by approximately one hundred thousand from 1774 to 1792, although it was still a relatively racially balanced society compared to the neighboring British and French islands. Sixty-nine percent of Cuba's population in 1792 was free, including a large black and mixed-race component.

While Havana's seamier side might be notorious, the elegant plazas and palaces housing its wealthier citizens appeared a world away. Moving away from the humble *bohíos* of early days, the Habaneros (Havana residents) built masonry homes based on Moorish-influenced Spanish style. The new homes were designed with greater permanence in mind but also sought to protect their occupants from the intense Cuban sun—the sun that influenced so much of daily life. The chronicler from 1598 recalled "the burning rays of an oven-hot sun," and Mercedes later claimed that "throughout the day, one languishes under the heavy weight of the sun." Early creole homes were constructed around a square or rectangular central patio. All rooms would open onto this patio in a manner designed to catch every possible breeze and ensure optimal ventilation. The Cuban desire to benefit from the island breezes became a national characteristic; even now a soft breeze is something to treasure and enjoy. Mercedes captured this longing, recalling the feeling of "voluptuous delicacy" that accompanied the arrival of longed-for breezes.

The homes also employed the typically Spanish details of reddish tiled roofs, intricately pieced wooden ceilings, and wooden doors wide enough for a carriage to pass. The patios would often contain a fountain or central well, and the roofs would carefully funnel rainwater down to hidden cisterns for later use. While the first more permanent structures were only one story, with more wealth came larger homes with a second floor, interior galleries, and outward-facing balconies—all with intricately turned wood window grilles—never any glass. As the seventeenth century gave way to the eighteenth, Habaneros added more elaborate sculptured door ornaments and graceful frescos on the interior walls. Leading citizens requested permission for porticoes and arcades, and entire plazas offered covered walkways. Still, the facades along the side streets were generally simple—the plain wall hiding the lavish interiors favored by wealthy Habaneros.

Impressive houses, some actual palaces, belonging to the aristocratic creole families were concentrated in the area north of the Plaza Vieja. Despite the introduction of a system of house numbering in 1763, Habaneros still referred to most homes by their owners' names and made note of the cross streets. The practice was especially true of the palaces but also would occur with more average residents, as a 1795 advertisement in the *Papel Periódico de la Havana* indicated, directing interested buyers to the "casa de Don Vicente Ponce, Calle de Cuba." A short carriage ride in a typical Cuban *volante*, avoiding the mud and dust, would take the visitor south from the Plaza de la Catedral to the Plaza Vieja along Calle de San Ignacio; if it returned north along Calle de Mercaderes it would pass one of the most beautiful homes in Havana, the Casa de la Obra Pia, with its innumerable arches hidden behind a quiet facade. The graceful home belonged to the family of Mercedes' paternal Cárdenas grandmother. Mercaderes also conveniently housed the particularly high-end shops where Habaneros could purchase luxurious linens, silks, and wools along with fabrics shot with gold and silver. Luxuries were always in demand; Havana's first historian wrote in 1761 that Cuban fashion placed no limit on the delicacy and splendor of clothing.

The immense Plaza Vieja, dating from the sixteenth century, contained no public buildings, only residences, although it featured a lively market in its center. In Havana even the residential homes often had shops in the lower floors, and the bustle was constant. Along one side of the plaza, an altar to Our Lady of the Rosary inspired the name Rosario given to the porticoes of the home of Mercedes' cousin, the Marquesa de Casa-Calvo. Evening rosary processions would make their way from various churches to the Rosario arcade to sing and pray to the Virgin. The plaza also contained the palatial family home of the Counts de San Juan de Jaruco. Imposing arcades with arches and columns marched along the Plaza Vieja, a testament to the importance of the Santa Cruz family. Mercedes' great-great-grandfather Gabriel de Santa Cruz petitioned the Spanish king for a license to build the arcade; the petition records his claim to be one of the leading citizens of Havana and reminds His Majesty of his family's loyal service. In old Havana, arcades equated to privilege and power. Although the house on the Plaza Vieja was the most prominent of the Santa Cruz houses, like many affluent families, the Santa Cruz family had several homes scattered throughout the various streets of Havana. Mercedes' godmother, the actual Countess de Jaruco, owned a spectacular house by the Plaza de Armas, and she too received permission to add *portales* in 1784. Traveling farther east from the Plaza Vieja led to the Plaza de San Francisco, dominated by the church and convent of the same name. That plaza opened up to the harbor and was a bustling hive of activity. Mercedes' maternal great-grandfather, Lorenzo Montalvo, was buried, dressed in the robes of a Franciscan friar, in a chapel adjoining the convent, near the Montalvo family home on Calle de Oficios.

The insularity of Havana's elite became obvious in the tangled web of familial ties that united the city's prominent inhabitants. A quick review of old Cuban parish records and genealogies makes it abundantly clear that the term *intermarriage* is an understatement. Not only did second and third cousins marry with great frequency, but first-cousin unions were remarkably common. What really makes the creole elites stand out, however, is the number of marriages between uncles and nieces—sometimes followed up with a first-cousin marriage in the next generation. The families united at the cathedral had numerous examples in their midst. Mercedes' aunt María Luisa Montalvo y O'Farrill married her own uncle Juan Manuel O'Farrill y Herrera, while another O'Farrill y Herrera sibling, Rafael, married his niece María Luisa O'Farrill y Arredondo. The intricate relationships that resulted from these close intermarriages make these family trees resemble the thick canopies of the majestic native ceiba trees that rise from a single, tall trunk. Frequent early deaths also resulted in remarriages and extended families living together in their palaces, often uniting younger children of a second marriage with grandchildren from the first. Multiple generational living perhaps encouraged more interfamily unions.

Frequent intermarriages reflected the fairly universal desire to retain estates and fortunes within the family or to ensure the future of a younger son or daughter. Creole families often set up entailed estates tied to their titles, and keeping more in the family was an attractive prospect. There was another reason for preferring marriages within a small circle, which was very specific to Spain and its colonies: *limpieza de sangre*. *Limpieza de sangre* translates as "purity of blood," and was prerequisite for certain honors or legal entitlements. As a legal matter, an individual would have to prove a "clean" bloodline free from Jewish, Moorish, or newly converted ancestors for several generations. Strange as it sounds today, it was a concept born from the turmoil of Spain's reconquest of the Iberian Peninsula from the Moors and its later expulsion of Jews and its remaining Moorish subjects. Likewise, some honors required proof of noble lineage. For an eighteenth-century family concerned with maintaining its status and obtaining more honors, marrying a stranger was riskier than marrying a close relative.

While most Cuban aristocratic families shared similar customs, Mercedes' maternal and paternal families seemed strikingly different in their outlook on life. Mercedes' paternal side, the Santa Cruz and Cárdenas families, had arrived in an earlier wave of settlers, particularly the Cárdenas, whose founder arrived in the late sixteenth century. They quickly married into the founding families of Havana, and through their relations inherited the beautiful old home of the Obra Pía charity and its patronage that annually dowered five orphaned girls. The king granted Mercedes' great-grandfather the title of Marqués de Cárdenas de Monte-Hermoso, ostensibly in appreciation for services given in the British invasion. While the Cárdenas served in various civic positions, they don't seem to have been very active in the military. The Beltrán de Santa Cruz family arrived in 1628 when Don Pedro Beltrán de Santa Cruz y Beitia was sent to establish the Real Tribunal de Cuentas (Royal Court of Accounts) in Havana. The Santa Cruz men had previously been conquistadores in the Canary Islands and in Colombia. Like the Cárdenas family, the Santa Cruz family also married into the older families and favored mainly civic service. Both families established "feudal" towns tied to their titles of Cárdenas de Monte-Hermoso and San Juan de Jaruco. These families abounded with religious figures, including the legendary Cárdenas sisters, known for decades as the Beatas (the blessed) Cárdenas because of their piety. In both cases, the overall impression is of a conservative, settled family, and Mercedes' closed-minded grandmother, María Josefa Cárdenas y Santa Cruz (with a Cárdenas father and Santa Cruz mother) personified many of the family's traits.

In contrast to the Santa Cruz-Cárdenas side, Mercedes' maternal line, the Montalvo and O'Farrill families, were relative newcomers, having arrived within twenty years of each other in the first decades of the eighteenth century. The Montalvo and O'Farrill families were closely linked through Richard O'Farrill's wife, the widowed María Josefa de Arriola, mother of Lorenzo Montalvo's second wife, Teresa Ambulodi y Arriola. Hence the O'Farrill children were Teresa Ambulodi's half brother and half sister. Both families shared a strong business sense, and within a generation their respective heirs held extensive landholdings with established entailed estates. Compared to many of their contemporaries, these early generations of O'Farrills and Montalvos seemed more forward thinking and open to new ideas and technologies. Mercedes' grandfather, Ignacio Montalvo, Count de Casa-Montalvo, had sent his two sons to study in Madrid's prestigious Colegio de Nobles and would later place them as cadets in the Spanish Guards. Montalvo himself traveled in 1794 with Francisco Arango, the representative of the Havana council, on an eleven-month fact-finding mission to learn about advancements in efficient sugar production and technologies beyond the Spanish colonies. The enterprising duo visited Cádiz, Portugal,

Britain, Barbados, and Jamaica before dramatically concluding their journey with a shipwreck on the southern coast of Cuba. Ignacio Montalvo, along with his O'Farrill brother-in-law (and son-in-law!), Juan Manuel O'Farrill, was a founding member of the Real Sociedad Económica Amigos del País, which tried to establish a more enlightened society in Cuba by opening schools and the first public library. Arango, Montalvo, and various relatives also helped create the Real Consulado de Agricultura y Comercio that lobbied for a more liberalized economy and commissioned their investigative journey.

The O'Farrills had looked outside of Cuba for opportunities in an even earlier generation. Mercedes' great-grandparents, Juan José O'Farrill y Arriola and Luisa Herrera y Chacón, sent their ten-year-old son Gonzalo for military training in France, starting a career that would culminate in his position as minister of war to Joseph Bonaparte in Spain. The O'Farrills were always ready to help well-connected foreigners, as when Gonzalo O'Farrill, then Spanish minister in Berlin, aided the naturalist Alexander von Humboldt in his scientific journey through the Americas. O'Farrill offered to swap his Cuban income for von Humboldt's Prussian rents, providing the explorer access to local currency while on the island. They were an outward-looking clan, and in her future life Mercedes seemed to take after this maternal line. At the end of her life, Mercedes would be buried next to her great-uncle Gonzalo O'Farrill—two Habaneros lying in the Parisian Père Lachaise cemetery.

A clear visualization of this outward-looking perspective still hangs in Havana's city museum, located in the old Palace of the Captains General. The portrait commemorates the successful journey of the intrepid Ignacio Montalvo. Montalvo, bewigged and dressed in a military uniform, proudly indicates with an elegantly out-held hand the evidence of his grand achievements: a diagram of a steam engine for a sugar mill. It calls to mind another portrait depicting another grand achievement affecting Cuba: Sir Joshua Reynolds's portrait of General William Keppel at the fall of Havana in 1762. Shown in his scarlet British army coat, Keppel looks into the distance and indicates with his hand the far-off Morro fort and a long, snakelike line of redcoats. Keppel's achievement is military, and his painting is by a Royal Academician, while Montalvo's portrait celebrates the acquisition of technology, executed by a provincial painter. Still, side by side, the similarity is startling. Did Montalvo consciously emulate the European style of Keppel's portrait? In his choice one can see how Montalvo viewed his accomplishments, aspirations, and Cuba's position in the world.

Perhaps it would seem surprising that Joaquín de Santa Cruz and Teresa Montalvo, children of very different families, should marry. However, Havana's relatively small society offered limited choices, and the two shared mutual Calvo de la Puerta cousins. Joaquín might also have been attracted to the dynamic Montalvo-O'Farrill clan, since he demonstrated early on his own forward thinking in his business dealings. Passion might even have played a role. Mercedes suggested this last reason, claiming that her father fell in love with her mother, whom she extravagantly described as beautiful as the day and "uniting all the natural charms which heaven in its generosity can bestow upon a mere mortal." Mercedes would always praise her mother to the skies in all her reminiscences, and generally adopted a romantic perspective.

Mercedes' father and mother married young in June 1786, when they were just sixteen and fourteen, respectively. Both shared the early loss of a parent. Teresa's mother, María Josefa O'Farrill y Herrera, had died two years before, while Joaquín had lost his father as a baby. Although young, Joaquín commanded a fortune inherited through his paternal grandparents. Joaquín and Teresa's firstborn son, Manuel María, arrived within two years of their marriage, and Mercedes was born a year later. After Mercedes' birth in 1789, Joaquín would use the Jaruco title in official correspondence with his great-aunt's blessing, though his widowed great-aunt still possessed his great-uncle's title and estates. This third Count de San Juan de Jaruco has been described as an intelligent and restless man, a person looking for more than what was then the status quo of Cuba. His ambition showed in his many business ventures and dealings with the royal court in Madrid. But in 1789, he and his young and bewitching wife seemed merely eager to travel and see the great cities of Europe. Yet another family portrait reveals a clue to these European aspirations and to the family's wealth and position. Painted before Mercedes' birth, this curious painting depicts Teresa, Joaquín, their son and heir Manuel, and Manuel's slave nurse, Agueda. They sit in a European interior, Joaquín every inch the eighteenth-century nobleman: curled and powdered wig, elegant coat, waistcoat, and breeches, holding a tricorne hat in one hand with a gentleman's dress sword at his side. Teresa appears stylishly in a frothy white dress with its bouffant kerchief, fitted bodice, and frilled short sleeves, her hair fashionably teased, and her son Manuel in a lacy dress. Agueda, slightly in the shadows and dressed in a dark version of her mistress's gown, wears a *mantilla* (lace veil) and *peineta* (comb) in her hair, and provides the most exotic element of the portrait. Otherwise, the family could be in Madrid, Paris, or even colonial America—nothing else readily identifies them as a creole family. Other than the slave Agueda, the only clue to the provincial location is the relatively untrained and primitive skill of the anonymous painter. The sitters' proportions are somewhat odd; Teresa's right arm seems enormous, and Joaquín's stockinged legs are fat. Few formally trained painters existed in late-eighteenth-century Havana. Not until the early part of the nineteenth century would the French painter Jean-Baptiste Vermay, a follower of David, take the city by storm, producing more artistically advanced portraits of the ranking families.

The chance to travel to Europe presented itself in the form of a prospective inheritance from one of Joaquín's uncles, an exiled Jesuit priest living in Italy. Since the planned journey was arduous, and the young couple would probably visit various countries, they decided to leave the children behind. The children would be safer with their extended families, and Joaquín and Teresa could wander easily with no responsibilities. The arrangements for their care were somewhat surprising: the children were separated from each other and placed with different family members. Perhaps the strong-willed María Josefa de Cárdenas insisted on caring for the next heir, or other family rivalries existed. Regardless of the reasons, Joaquín and Teresa entrusted the young Manuel to his paternal grandmother, the stern and devout Countess de Casa-Barreto, while baby Mercedes went with her great-grandmother, Luisa Herrera y Chacón, her mother's own grandmother.

At the end of the baptismal rite, the priest, Don Luis, would have urged the infant to keep true to her baptism throughout a blameless life, ready for the coming of the Lord and life everlasting. Don Luis would have concluded with the words: *Vade in pace, et Dominus sit tecum*, Amen. Go in peace, and may the Lord be with you, Amen. With this blessing, the newly christened Mercedes emerged to start her life's journey. But already, her particular path deviated from the standard for most Cuban children. At less than one year old, Mercedes saw her parents sail for Europe on their own journey— one which most thought would end in a year or two. Mercedes later wrote in her memoirs that the separation was predicted to last six months; wishful thinking given the distances involved and the long, dangerous sea crossing. Few would have guessed that she would not see her father until she was almost nine years old, and that it would be a new century before she saw her mother again, and then only in far-off Madrid.

2

MERCEDES
AND MAMITA

oaquín and Teresa sailed away to commence their European adventures, leaving behind one-year-old Manuel and
the infant Mercedes to the tender mercies of their extended family.
For Mercedes, the saving grace of a difficult situation lay in her parents' decision to place her with her maternal Montalvo/O'Farrill
relatives, specifically with the O'Farrill family matriarch, her great-
grandmother Luisa Herrera y Chacón. This forward-looking family's attitudes would steep her earliest childhood days in openness,
affection, and freedom that laid the foundations for her attitudes and
beliefs. Mercedes felt at home in the sparkling O'Farrill world, but
the permissiveness and freedom that she experienced would later
conflict with the sterner Santa Cruz/Cárdenas side.

The O'Farrills were more than a mere Havana family. They were
known as a "clan" because of their notable intermarriages and links
with key families as well as their strong sense of mutual assistance.
The strength of the O'Farrill concept of clan was unique among
Cuban families, and has come down through the ages in histories and
tales of old Havana. Perhaps the key to this strong bond lies in their

Celtic roots, since the O'Farrills traced their line to County Long-ford in Ireland. The first Habanero O'Farrill was Richard O'Farrill y O'Daly. No matter how later generations tried to ennoble him by claiming royal Irish descent, he had been the son of an Irish soldier on the tiny English-owned island of Montserrat—an island that would almost be destroyed by a violent volcanic eruption over two centuries later. There his parents had settled, but the O'Farrills always sought more—more than just life on a speck in the British Empire.

The chance to come to Cuba as the agent for the South Sea Company was a coup in all respects. The position meant trading in human beings, not shocking in the early eighteenth century, unlike today or even the nineteenth century when the abolitionist movement strengthened. At the time, the company merely viewed it as another commercial opportunity in line with a tradition of transatlantic slave trade that had flourished since the beginning of the sixteenth century. Most of the major European nations had participated—indeed even fought for the privilege. But let's be clear, despite his important commercial position as the company's agent, Richard (or "Ricardo") O'Farrill would have been closely involved in the trade and more than a witness to the horrors that accompanied the profits. Whether he ever traveled on a slave ship is unknown, but he certainly would have been present at the arrival of the wretched vessels and their unfortunate cargo. The Spaniards euphemistically called the Africans shipped across as *piezas de India* (pieces of India)—exotic pieces of cargo.

The South Sea Company's license did not last long, but Ricardo had realized that there were many opportunities to be had in Cuba—perhaps in slaves but especially in sugar. Sugar and land seeped into the O'Farrill blood. Before long, Ricardo had married the widowed daughter of the royal treasurer, petitioning the Spanish king for citizenship and permission to bring his property from Jamaica—including 236 slaves. He also bought land and began to cultivate sugar. The O'Farrills were wealthy landowners and members of the Havana elite by the time that Luisa Herrera, daughter of a marqués and bred from a long line of Spanish nobility, married old Ricardo's son, Juan José.

Luisa adored children and was used to managing an enormous household. She came from a family of twelve children, gave birth to twelve of her own, and raised the eleven that survived. She had a talent for creating a nurturing home life. Her son Gonzalo fondly recollected how "one tender look from my mother filled my father's face with joy and serenity." Luisa had worked hard at establishing these eleven children in society and ensuring their fortunes. Most of her children had married or established their own homes by the time Mercedes was born, although in typical Cuban fashion her two youngest daughters still lived with her, and others came and went.

Luisa Herrera was probably in her early sixties by the time Mercedes entered her great-grandmother's home, and her own eldest daughter, Mercedes' grandmother María Josefa, had been dead for five years. Luisa herself had been widowed for almost ten. So perhaps Mercedes offered a final chance for Luisa to cherish a new baby. All the family could see that Mercedes became her special delight. For Mercedes, Luisa Herrera became more than just her great-grandmother; she became her own Mamita.

There is no known surviving portrait of Luisa Herrera, either in youth or in old age. Her great-granddaughter, however, left a vivid sketch in her account of that early Cuban childhood. Luisa, Mercedes wrote, had been a rare and delicate beauty who even in her old age preserved traces of loveliness in her finely drawn features. Almost forty years later, Mercedes could still recall "her snow-white hair gracefully rolled up and pinned up in braids exposing a perfectly formed brow and angelically sweet blue eyes. Her fine and delicate features revealed her entire soul by an ineffable expression of calm and habitual benevolence, just as the barely tinted whiteness of her skin, like a transparent veil, barely covered her small blue veins, and conveyed an almost youthful charm despite her age." Above all, Mercedes remembered a serene character that was both indulgent and cheerful, the very idea of the loving grandmother.

Mamita's serenity extended to every fiber of her being, including her physical aspect and her exemplary toilette. The day's end would find her dressed in her habitual white, as fresh and fragrant as she had started, with every hair in place and her gown still carefully pleated. After reading Mercedes' tender description it is easy to envision a loving spirit gliding through the lives of her extended family, leaving a trail of calmness and goodwill in her wake. This benevolent matriarch was surrounded by the love and respect of all those near to her and even the wider Havana society. Luisa was so highly regarded that at her death in 1806, the bishop of Havana, Don Luis Espada, chose her to be one of the first persons buried in the new city cemetery and officiated at the burial himself, hoping that his personal involvement and her prominence would together inspire other eminent Habaneros to emulate and begin burying their dead there rather than in the city's churches and monasteries.

Cuban grandmothers are legendary for spoiling their grandchildren, feeding them favorite foods, letting them have their way, and drowning them in affection. From what Mercedes herself wrote decades later, the late eighteenth century was no different. Mamita's own children chided her for excessive tenderness toward the motherless girl, but Mamita responded sweetly to the criticism: "What do you want? She embodies the last piece of my soul—let me enjoy her!" Mercedes more than reciprocated the affection, and Mamita's love filled the void left by Mercedes' parents in these early, formative years. Mercedes thrived in the tropical heat of Cuba under the doting eye of Mamita. Mercedes' deep sentiments for Mamita would become the seed for her own emotional growth, encouraging feelings of tenderness and love. She remembered her affection for Mamita as an "awakening to the world." The absence of the child's parents also drew attention from other members of her extended family, and she later wrote that "all...had the right to spoil me and no one had the right to chastise me." Mercedes could only recall being surrounded by love and the tenderest of care. Sitting at the end of a long line of ninety-five relatives at one of Mamita's family celebrations, Mercedes could not help but feel like the "last link in a chain," firmly part of a thriving world.

Mercedes' attachment to the matriarch of the O'Farrill clan would later spur close ties to Mamita's son Gonzalo O'Farrill, the only one of the eleven children who would spend his adult life in Spain and France with Mercedes. The family had sent Gonzalo away to be educated in France at a young age, and he later entered the Spanish army as a career officer, rarely returning to his homeland. He served the king wherever he was needed, from battlefields in North Africa to more glamorous postings in European capitals. But his mother never stopped missing her "little boy" and always longed to see him. So often did Luisa recount his one and only visit to Havana that Mercedes became convinced, in her young mind, that she had been witness to the great event. Years later, meeting the famed great-uncle in Madrid, she was able to tell him with unerring accuracy details of his long-ago Havana sojourn. Gonzalo O'Farrill laughed and laughed when he heard the teenage Mercedes spin her tale, but such had been Luisa's longing for her flesh and blood that she had bequeathed this memory to Mercedes.

Mamita's Havana home was busy, and like most Havana homes—including grand *casas*—it had offices or businesses located on the lower floor. The comings and goings of business associates would only have added to the general household bustle, including those enormous family gatherings. The centrality of the extended family is not just a modern Latin phenomenon, but rather one rooted in a time when family ties were often the most reliable ones, and where family protection was crucial for advancement and security. Blood kin could be trusted, or so was the general belief. For a little girl, far away from her own nuclear family, belonging to this rich tapestry of life would have had a fundamental impact—creating a foundation for which she would always search or wish throughout her life.

Luisa maintained not only a Havana home but also held extensive fincas (country estates or farms) and visited them regularly, as was the custom of wealthy Havana families. In Havana, feminine life was rather constrained, centered on the home with excursions limited to visits to other family homes, regular attendance to church, or an evening outing in a *volante*, the Cuban carriage with two enormous wheels that navigated the narrow streets. The city was full of noise as the famous Cuban street vendors offered their bread, fruits, and milk. Market traders always called out their wares, and there was also the constant sound of the bells from the churches, convents, and monasteries. Mamita, like most wealthy Havana matrons, had her own household chapel or oratory and regularly received her confessor. The Roman Catholic religion was not just part of everyday life in Cuba; it helped shape the flow of the days and months. Feast days were celebrated, processions marked special events, and the family chaplain played an integral part in aristocratic households. For women in particular, including Mamita, attending mass constituted a regular feature of daily life.

City life could seem a bit formal and constrained for a child, perhaps. But the graceful walled houses offered their own sort of entertainment for a little girl. Their shady garden patios, full of flowers, held secret places. The huge interconnecting rooms offered endless space for racing and running, while the marble staircases could be used as slides—sometimes with tearful consequences. The rooms surrounding the enormous gateway—wide enough for a carriage to roll through—held intriguing barrels and containers full of plantation products for storage and sale, and provided entertainment from the daily parade of traders. Mercedes' memoirs suggest she was playful and maybe a bit naughty. Running around the house, up and down the marble stairs, slipping and falling as all children do, and being picked up and taken care of by her mother's old nanny, Agueda, Mercedes must have been somewhat of a devil. She had no thought for studies, preferring games and mischief. She sent her writing master's bonnet flying in the air as he tried in vain to make her learn her lessons. Mercedes' tricks spared no one, and no one really tried to stop her in these first nine years. She always "played by right the central role... no one had the will to use their authority to make me see reason." Only persuasion was ever employed, never punishments. The result, as Mercedes admitted, was the development of a precocious sensibility and an exalted spirit that remained with her all her life. Freedom and indulgence meant a world ruled by her caprices.

Fincas provided even more opportunities to indulge her flights of fancy. The countryside contained a wealth of freedom for an adventurous child. There in the open spaces, Mercedes could explore the unspoiled terrain, rich in flowers, plants, birds, lizards, frogs, and other wildlife. Royal palms stretched across the fields, often lining the paths, and wild, rare orchids grew throughout the island. The royal palms in particular often captured the imagination of foreign visitors, such as the future wife of the writer Nathaniel Hawthorne, who eagerly wrote to her family of her enchantment with these "splendid" trees that were "columns of white marble with a Corinthian capital of green." She also recalled the great ceiba trees, in particular one which "exceeded anything I have ever conceived of in the way of a production of the earth." The great swathes of Cuban forests with their cedar, mahogany, and ebony were full of graceful intertwining vines which for Sophie Peabody had a "melancholy beauty."

The plantation lands contained sugarcane and tobacco fields and coffee and citrus groves, along with beehives producing rich honey and wax. There were also vast pastures for the herds of horses and cattle. The cane fields were full of Cuban crickets and snakes. Colorful birds roamed the skies, including the *zunzún*, the tiniest hummingbird. Later in the day, as the sun set, the *cucullos* (Cuban fireflies) would come out, which children captured and used as lanterns to light the evening shadows.

Mercedes loved the open air and recalled "running in the countryside like a greyhound," where she "knocked the fruits from the trees that were within my reach, or searched to catch the bird's nests which, held by creepers, dangled over my head. Other times, running far away, I tried to ride the young foals grazing in the savannah." She would only head home when the sun was setting, as the herds of horses "still overwhelmed by the heat of the day, their manes ruffled by the evening breeze" drank by the river. Then she would arrive "cheeks rosy, my heart leaping and joyous…my dress hiked up and almost tearing under the weight of the flowers and fruits which I had collected along my way."

Accompanying Mercedes in almost all aspects of her early life were the slaves charged with her care. Like all upper-class Cuban babies, Mercedes had a wet nurse who was also her nanny. Mercedes recalled "Mama Dolores" with great affection, and the feeling was reciprocated. The reward for nursing an infant was freedom, but according to Mercedes, Mama Dolores refused to be parted and stayed on, still a slave, as her nanny. While it could seem farfetched to believe in such a sacrifice, the most intimate household slaves could, in some cases, form a very important part of the Habanero household. In grand Havana palaces, the owners lived and slept on the top floor, with the large, airy interconnected rooms offering some coolness and shelter from the heat. The slaves and the servants lived just below, and the whole household shared relatively close quarters. Aristocratic households abounded with individuals for every domestic task: laundresses, cooks, coachmen, seamstresses, and even, occasionally, someone specialized in curling feathers. The close proximity could create close bonds, and there were very mundane cases where the owners freed a slave in his will, as the first Count de Jaruco did in 1772 when he ordered that "a young black boy called Felipe of the *Arará* nation, who their lordships had reared, should serve the Countess during her life and by her death be freed…and be given the equivalent in money of his value today."

Along with Mama Dolores, Mercedes also had a personal slave, a young girl named Catalina. Many Cuban children had a particular slave child to play with or care for them. Catalina would often soothe Mercedes to sleep, caressing Mercedes while singing her songs or retelling the sad story of Catalina's passage into slavery and the final separation from her brother. Mercedes later recalled that the story, recounted hundreds of times, would always end with both Catalina and Mercedes in tears.

These childhood experiences and ties perhaps colored Mercedes' later seemingly contradictory feeling toward slavery. In many cases, household slaves had a very different life and experience than those who suffered the brutality of the sugar plantation. There could be, in the best of cases, a paternalistic relationship with these servants, something that was more difficult to replicate in the tobacco and coffee plantation and all but impossible in the sugar mills. The detailed inventory of one of Mercedes' father's sugar mills, San Ignacio de

Río Blanco, shows that 24 out of 178 slaves were considered run-aways, having attempted escape at some point in their lives. Mercedes saw some, but not all, the signs of misery. Describing a slave family's burial ground, Mercedes recalled noticing as a child that the slaves rarely grew flowers on their small plots of land, and that there were none on the grave sites. "All that is a pleasure for life is far out of reach and even far from their possible desires." Even with these experiences, however, Mercedes was describing the old-fashioned, still small-scale slavery of the eighteenth century, already in the process of changing. She missed the subsequent explosive growth of slavery in the many years she was away from her homeland.

Mercedes primarily recalled her Cuban days as blissful, a world that revolved around her. But in reality, other aspects were less pleasant to remember. As in all enchanted tales, Mercedes' idyllic childhood contained an evil fairy. In Mercedes' case, it was her paternal grandmother, the virtuous and devout María Josefa de Cárdenas y Santa Cruz. In Mercedes' tales, María Josefa never smiled, never showed affection, and was always consumed with a need to control all around her. The contrast with Luisa Herrera could not have been more striking, but in fairness María Josefa had experienced more than her share of tragedy. Barely seventeen when she married Mercedes' grandfather, she saw her firstborn son and her husband die in the span of two years. Widowed at twenty-two with another baby son, she remarried a man almost thirty years her senior whose evil reputation still resounds in the tourist plaques of *la Vieja Habana*. María Josefa became the wife of Jacinto Barreto y Pedroso, later Count de Casa-Barreto, and had four more children, but her new husband was known as one of the cruelest of Havana slave owners. Part of the Barreto fortune was based on the license granted for the brutal but lucrative occupation of capturing and reselling the run-aways who hid in the hills and caves. One story tells of the count inviting a group of beggars to receive alms but then setting loose his slave-hunting dogs on the defenseless gathering. The pandemonium that ensued left many men wounded, and only then did Barreto distribute his alms—in proportion to the wounds received. The count died in 1791 in the middle of a terrible storm and the final part of the black legend claims that his body was swept away by the storm waters: the devil had claimed his own.

Whatever the facts within these legends, there does seem to have been something dark about the Barreto men, documented in multiple occasions of reneging on legacies or trying to disinherit legitimate heirs.

Mercedes' encounters with her grandmother were not enjoyable. One particular episode left a haunting impression on Mercedes, as she alluded to it twice in her writings. While she changed the location, the key moment remained the same. She credited the moment as the awakening of her moral life, which spurred a lifelong repugnance for the use of brute force.

According to the more detailed description, the incident occurred on a visit to her grandmother's finca, probably when Mercedes was around eight years old. The visit began on an ominous note upon Mercedes' arrival at the plantation, when she was greeted by the severe María Josefa flanked by her household chaplain and her confessor. According to Mercedes, her grandmother could not spend more than forty-eight hours without these two Capuchin priests, since she required daily confessions. María Josefa dominated her household with iron-clad rules under which "every hour had a purpose, and all occurred with strict regularity—the day before the same as the next one. Her daughters, like her slaves, were broken under her authority...and under the force of obedience seemed to have lost the power of free will." Intimidated at first, Mercedes quickly decided to take no notice of these rules, and immediately resumed her "vagabond ways."

As Mercedes recounts it, the first day she was left alone, the second she was reprimanded, and on the third day she encountered her grandmother: "her brows creased, her look severe." Mercedes was told off, and the confessor mumbled threats of locking her away. Rising to the challenge, Mercedes continued her countryside adventures. The punishment came one hot, sunny day. Mercedes found herself locked up in a ground-floor room, with bits of light seeping between the wooden bars of the solitary window. It was the siesta hour and the air, "inflamed by the heat and the light," was oppressive. "All was calm and quiet, and if not for the buzzing of the insects...one could have believed that a magician's wand had lulled Nature." In her account Mercedes completes the scene by noting that, in the overwhelming heat, a serpent outside was spread out voluptuously on the giant banana leaves, and a thieving monkey eyed an ear of corn that it intended to steal at nightfall.*

Accompanying Mercedes in her imprisonment was Conchita, one of her young aunts. The room also contained a large aviary full of colorful and chattering birds. The timid and delicate Conchita, who would one day contemplate entering a convent, was probably the favorite sister of Mercedes' father—the only one he named in his will. A stronger foil for the mischievous Mercedes would have been hard to find. After shedding frustrated and fruitless tears at her imprisonment, Mercedes leaned sadly against the wooden bars of the window and quickly discovered that the wood was worm eaten. Quick as a flash, Mercedes persuaded her young aunt to help pull apart the bars to create an escape route. From that moment, Mercedes was carried away by her passions—as she would often be in the years to come. She seized the moment, oblivious to consequences, and as an extra flourish flung open the bird cage. The tropical birds flew out the window and Mercedes and her aunt followed. In Mercedes' words, they found themselves "in the midst of the fields surrounded by a cloud of beautiful, colorful birds that flew back and forth over our head...as though thanking us for their liberty."

The exhilaration did not last long, however, as they heard the alarm raised in the house and saw the approach of a search party of slaves led by the two family priests. Mercedes immediately realized that her young aunt was terrified. She knew her mother better than Mercedes, and Mercedes recalled how Conchita's "lips trembled"

---

* Mercedes wrote this piece around 1838 with a view to the dramatic narrative—monkeys are not native to Cuba! She often distilled real events into a more romanticized version.

and she could barely breathe. Trapped by the search party, the two escapees were led back "fearful and humiliated."

When they arrived at the door, one of the priests told Conchita that her mother awaited, and Conchita "cast one lost glance around her, almost looking for an escape, but at one glance from the father-confessor, one of the slave women who had accompanied us seized her and disappeared with her." Feeling guilty for causing the predicament of her delicate and graceful aunt, Mercedes tried to follow but was blocked by the slaves and the priests. Mercedes soon heard Conchita's cries in another room, ran in, and was shocked by the spectacle of Conchita "sustained in the air by her feet and shoulders by two slave women." Under the unmoving eye of her mother, Conchita was beaten repeatedly until Mercedes jumped on the back of one of the slave women, sank her nails into her, and caused her to release Conchita.

Mercedes felt an overwhelming sense of indignation at the mistreatment and humiliation of a weaker being. Passionate and protective responses would recur over the course of her life, as would the image of a strong, independent spirit cultivated by the wild nature of her island paradise. The sun, the light, the perfumed air, and the all-encompassing heat were forever seared into her earliest memories. But another aspect of Cuba contrasted with this natural, romantic freedom that Mercedes cherished. The rigidity of a colonial society balanced its tropical, sensual nature.

In Mercedes' case, a rebellion and clash with her grandmother—the ultimate representative of close-mindedness and order—eventually convinced María Josefa of the need to rein Mercedes in and of the danger in Mamita's softness and permissiveness. Mercedes commented that her escape that day cost both her and Conchita tears, but she could not have realized then what price she would ultimately pay for her brief triumph.

3

JOAQUÍN

On the third of February, 1797, the royal mail ship *El Rey* arrived on the eastern tip of the island in the port of Santiago de Cuba, Cuba's second largest city and its former capital. The ship had sailed out of the port of La Coruña in northern Spain three months earlier and had been forced to shelter from heavy weather in the Canary Islands, finally reaching its destination after eluding a division of British warships near Cuban coastal waters. In addition to the mail, *El Rey* also carried the newly minted sub-inspector general of the Royal Armies, who enjoyed the second-highest military rank on the island. The sub-inspector, carrying the rank of brigadier general, was also entrusted by King Carlos IV with a special commission to map the almost uncharted expanse of Guantánamo Bay, to explore the possibilities for settlements, to develop new roads, and to plan a canal in the expanding sugar lands near Havana. The sub-inspector brought engineers, botanists, naturalists, and other staff for what became known as the Royal Guantánamo Commission.

The royal commission enjoyed the personal support of the most powerful man in Spain, the Prince de la Paz—Manuel Godoy, favorite courtier of the king and queen. The Cuban colonial hierarchy took note, and messages began to fly back and forth confirming that the governor of Santiago, the captain-general of Cuba, and the *inten-dente* of the navy would all do their utmost to support the mission. In Havana one person in particular eagerly anticipated the arrival of the sub-inspector—little Mercedes, just eight years old. Obviously, no eight-year-old child would know or particularly care about royal commissions, new settlements, or roads. Her intrigue lay in the arrival of her father, Joaquín, the new sub-inspector general, Brigadier Count de Santa Cruz de Mopox.

Her father had returned home.

Joaquín had left Cuba in the spring of 1789 as a mere captain in the Havana infantry militia, not even a count, just the legal heir to the title and estates of the Count de San Juan de Jaruco. His great-aunt allowed him to use the title of count while in Spain to bolster his prestige and to help promote the family interests, but it was still a steep climb from those beginnings to his current military position and the newly created title of Count de Santa Cruz de Mopox. In February of 1797 Joaquín was still only twenty-seven years old, but in keeping with his restless and driving nature, he had spent eight years in a relentless push to secure ever-growing honors and privileges. While his daughter Mercedes ran freely in her own version of a tropical Eden, basking in the love and protection of her Mamita, Joaquín and his wife, Teresa Montalvo, played the grand game of royal courtiers. Mercedes' parents had planned their European adventure almost from the time of their 1786 marriage. In both 1787 and 1788, the couple applied for a royal license to travel to "the realms of Castilla," describing themselves as young and rich, explaining that they had business to oversee personally and relatives to visit in "those lands." They sent the first petition directly to Madrid, only to have it returned with terse instructions for its submission through the appropriate channels in Havana. With all the delays, the final approval did not arrive until the fall of 1788—while Teresa was pregnant with Mercedes. Since the royal license required Joaquín and Teresa to travel together—there seemed to have been some fear of scandal if this rich young couple separated so early in their married life—the couple had no choice but to wait until after the birth of their second child.

Joaquín always tried to circumvent normal procedure—he seemed to live in a constant race against time, something that Mercedes noted when she described him many years later: "he said that our time here was too short to lose any of it with sleep." Hence, she added, he lived perpetually on coffee—a pot of strong Cuban coffee always at his side—and he sought other distractions to keep him awake. Even before he had left Havana or had even received royal permission to do so, Joaquín had submitted through his Madrid agent the first of countless petitions pleading for promotion to colonel—at a price—in any of the various Havana militias. This, despite having only joined the infantry militia in 1785 as sub-lieutenant and only obtaining his captaincy in 1788. At one point, shortly after arriving in Madrid, he had two simultaneous requests outstanding— including one where he offered to underwrite a regiment of mounted dragoons in the Matanzas region in return for the command of the Jaruco squadron. The minister of Indies, Antonio Valdés, gave his opinion to the first minister: "[Jaruco] is wet behind the ears, without any experience whatsoever, and lacking the military character necessary to entrust him with the command of a regiment, which being newly formed would require particularly vigorous discipline. Nor has he offered enough money for the post considering the salary that he would subsequently receive, without even considering what he would gain in honor and the advancement of his career."

Nothing deterred Joaquín, however. Calling himself the Count de Jaruco, he received, again at a price, the honorary appointment of gentleman of the bedchamber to the king in late 1789. He asked the king for permission to travel to Italy to see more of Europe and to "illuminate the spirit and acquire knowledge useful for the service of Your Majesty," yet within days of receiving permission he sent off a new letter, asking for one thing more—to be inducted into one of the prestigious orders of chivalry—even though he did not yet meet the qualifications. His reasoning, as he stated unashamedly, was that he knew how "decorous such distinctions" were abroad, and he wanted to bask in that glory during his trip. His petition failed.

Even when Joaquín achieved his coveted appointment as sub-inspector general in May 1795, he spent five months quibbling over his exact rank, salary, and expenses. He penned lengthy letters exhaustively citing precedent, articles, and regulations, squeezing every bit of advantage possible—sometimes creatively using information. Frustrated civil servants retaliated with sarcastic comments, noting for example that traveling to Guanabacoa for troop reviews would be a mere stroll rather than a tedious journey.

Joaquín's letters show a man who was always thinking and planning—gossiping for information and maintaining extensive correspondence regarding his Cuban properties as well as his activities in Spain. Particularly enlightening are his surviving letters from 1794 to 1795 to his cousin and adviser Francisco Arango, who at the time was embarked on an eighteenth-century version of industrial espionage with Joaquín's father-in-law, the Count de Casa-Montalvo. Joaquín's letters reflect a constantly changing stream of ideas, plans, and goals. Diplomatic postings, ministerial positions, military rank, and plans for expanding his Cuban holdings—all came rolling from his pen—along with court gossip, reports on efforts to promote mutual friends, and many assurances of friendship and devotion from Joaquín and his wife, Teresa. He followed the court on its annual progressions through royal palaces: December and January in Madrid; spring in the lush gardens of Aranjuez; high summer in the Guadarrama Mountains at La Granja de San Ildefonso, where fountains copied from the Palace of Versailles splashed clear, ice-cold mountain waters; and autumn hunting in El Pardo outside Madrid and in San Lorenzo de El Escorial, the austere royal monastery/palace with its huge Cuban mahogany doors and furniture. While following the king and queen in these endlessly circular court movements, Joaquín longed for more foreign sites and also for a release from his dependence on slaves, bad sugar harvests, and volatile commodity prices.

Such was the tight and insular court life that the slightest gesture was analyzed. In a letter to Arango dated May 2, 1794, from Aranjuez, Joaquín confided that the king had recently taken him and the Duke of Alcudia (as Godoy was then titled) by the arm and walked out of luncheon saying, in full view of others:

> This poor boy cannot continue in the Corps [of Guards]...three days ago I went to his house and was sorry to find him beat up and covered in blood from the results of riding that day; I know he wants to stay in the Corps, but I entreat you," he said to the Duke, "because he is dear to me, give him something else, as he is more than fit for whatever you may want to grant him...." to which the Duke answered: "Fine, let him ask for whatever he wishes.

Joaquín reported that after that small but public exchange, he was nearly overwhelmed by countless fellow courtiers congratulating him on all sorts of wild titles and imaginary honors—none of them real but within the scope of imagination. So he asked for a diplomatic post, and said that the duke received the petition with great pleasure, while Joaquín subsequently joked to Arango, "but I don't know what he has done with [the request]...maybe he had a maid wipe his a...with it." Joaquín clearly knew what was needed to move ahead in the world, but he also expressed frustration with the stagnant and monotonous life of a courtier.

The breakthrough finally began in 1794 when Joaquín was named, in quick succession, the commanding colonel of a battalion of Royal Guards and then Count de Santa Cruz de Mopox in his own right. He also obtained valuable trading licenses and monopolies, all capped off with his nomination as sub-inspector general of Cuba and the rank of brigadier. How had this happened so suddenly?

Shortly after arriving in the Spanish capital, Joaquín and Teresa embarked upon a luxurious lifestyle. Renting various houses in the heart of what is today's Old Madrid, they eventually settled on a home on the Calle de la Luna and offered regular dances and a *tertulia*, a Spanish version of a salon. Their lavish entertainment attracted notice and comments for many decades. They had style and taste, and their musical soirees included the best instrumental and singing artists of the time. Mercedes herself would later say that her father did everything on a magnificent scale. For her part, Teresa became an effective networker and flourished as a popular hostess. Indeed, when Joaquín left for Cuba in late 1796, friends and relatives reported back to Havana that Teresa had become adept at managing business deals. In a letter dated February 1797 to Arango, their mutual cousin and friend José de Jesús Arostegui y Herrera admiringly recounts that "our Teresa is gorgeous and active in supporting Joaquín's interests. It may seem hard to imagine, but she handles his business dealings with the dexterity of a man who is already well-versed in their management, and she has a way of cutting to the chase that allows for her to resolve things in a matter of hours."

Joaquín and Teresa carefully cultivated the friendship of Manuel Godoy, which in turn helped secure the affection of the king himself. Their charm and lavish entertainment were supplemented by a judicious use of monetary contributions to the military costs of the ongoing war with the French Republic, and by well-placed and expensive personal gifts to Godoy. Joaquín's letters reveal him to be fervently patriotic and concerned with the welfare of his country, but he was also aware that aiding the national defense would promote his own cause.

Maintaining the Santa Cruz influence was probably one of the reasons that Teresa stayed behind in Madrid—even though she had not seen either of her Havana-born children, Manuel and Mercedes, since 1789. There were other considerations, too. The Santa Cruz marriage had produced three more children, all born in Spain, but had already experienced the loss of one daughter, María. In 1795, Teresa suffered through a difficult childbirth in her final pregnancy. Joaquín's letters indicate that its aftermath caused her some lingering medical problems. Although she had recovered sufficiently to accompany Joaquín to Paris and London in late 1795, she may not have been robust enough for a long and demanding sea journey.

Joaquín, irrepressible as ever, began working almost from the moment *El Rey* entered Santiago's harbor. He initially focused on organizing his royal commission to explore Guantánamo, and in his first month he wrote no less than ten letters or reports to Spain—outlining his appointments, his plans, and forwarding additional information and ideas for development. The sheer number of letters is overwhelming, reflecting Joaquín's seemingly boundless capacity for weaving dreams and plans. Not only was he looking at the Guantánamo Bay area, he also suggested developing the Bay of Nipe on the northeastern coast—yet another building project. Joaquín soon expanded his Guantánamo venture from a scientific expedition into a review of strategic military and economic development for the island.

These multiple plans and tasks kept Joaquín in the Santiago and Guantánamo area for several months. Since the king had ordered him to commence his military role almost immediately, Joaquín also began the process of reviewing the troops, analyzing their state of readiness, and determining how to incorporate the newly arrived militias from Santo Domingo (today's Dominican Republic), which had been ceded to France. Slowly making his way north and west toward Havana, Joaquín inspected troops in Bayamo and Puerto Príncipe (today's Camagüey) among other cities, finally arriving in Havana sometime toward June or July 1797—almost five months after his arrival on the island.

There in Havana Mercedes and her brother Manuel awaited their first glimpse of their legendary father. Mercedes did not record this first encounter, but one can imagine it was in Mamita's home, or perhaps both children were together with Joaquín's mother, the widowed Countess de Casa-Barreto. Mercedes did describe her mixed emotions upon his arrival: "The delight I felt in meeting my father was muted by the sorrow of leaving Mamita, and I could not be parted from her side without everyone promising that I could see her every day." Barely eight and a half years old, she saw the familiar and loving comfort of Mamita's presence replaced by an unknown albeit dashing father. Nothing is known about nine-and-a-half-year-old Manuel's thoughts, but he was probably intrigued by the charming and affectionate stranger. Manuel might have been ill at this time, as he passed away within a few short months, in December

1797, in the hauntingly beautiful Casa de la Obra Pía, then home to the Cárdenas family. In 1960, renovations of this Old Havana palacio uncovered an inscription in a room in the upper stories, which read: *Murió, Manuel Conde de Jaruco 1797* (Manuel, Count of Jaruco, died 1797). Through some accident, the inscription vanished almost immediately after its discovery. Its strange appearance and disappearance added one more layer of legend to the Obra Pía, a house that has so captured the imagination that even the revolutionary government produced a period miniseries based loosely on its past—*The Orphans of the Obra Pía*. Even more oddly, Mercedes' lengthy memoirs never mentioned this Cuban-born brother even though he was her closest living relative in Havana until her father's return. Besides the church records in the Havana cathedral, there are only a few references to him scattered among the reams and reams of Spanish and Cuban archival records. Poignantly, the last record is a letter from Joaquín, dated December 11, 1797, formally advising Godoy of Manuel's death, since the little boy had been an honorary cadet in the American Company of the Corps of Royal Guards—his father's old regiment.

In addition to the duties of his military position and royal commission, Joaquín also had to oversee his extensive business affairs. When he returned to Cuba, Joaquín had agricultural interests in sugar and coffee, and was beginning to invest in tobacco. He also held various potentially lucrative trading privileges that allowed him to ship cane brandy and molasses/sugar to the United States in return for shipments of flour, which he could then sell in Havana for bread supplies. Royal decrees still controlled the entry of all goods from other countries; therefore, Joaquín and his partners enjoyed near monopolies. All of these business interests kept Joaquín more than occupied, and it may be surprising to learn that Mercedes went to live with him. But Joaquín was always an affectionate man, and as Mercedes explained, "My father loved me with a tenderness bordering on the extreme, and it seemed as though he wanted to compensate for his past neglect by showering me with all the pleasures permitted of someone my age."

Mercedes began her reign as the little queen of Joaquín's new household. She had a carriage at her disposal and could come and go as she pleased with just her personal slave in attendance. The inappropriateness of this conduct could not have been lost on the family, but Joaquín was "young, lively, and cheerful to a fault, and he understood nothing about the upbringing of a young girl." Joaquín's household was in effect a bachelor's house as opposed to Mamita's home for an extended family. Despite Joaquín's wealth and social standing, in 1797 he actually did not own a suitable home in Havana. Many assume that he lived in the *palacio* of the Counts de Jaruco, the stately, columned stone house that takes up almost half of one side of the Plaza Vieja. It has a deep and shady stone portico, a massive wooden door with an intricate Indian-head keyhole, and decorative wall frescos that today help attract tourists to the numerous art exhibitions and other cultural events held in its central patio. Outside the main door there is a large plaque declaring that the building was the family home of the Condesa de Merlin and her father. In reality Joaquín probably never lived there, as it still belonged to his great-aunt. Instead, he most likely rented a house, either one located on San Ignacio and Chacón, in the northern end of the city steps away from the water, or the palace of the Marqués of San Felipe and Santiago on the enormous Plaza de San Francisco, near the Franciscan basilica facing the main arrival point for ships and cargo.

Regardless of the exact location, Joaquín set up his usual sumptuous lifestyle. He had over twenty slaves working as domestics in his household, including several coachmen—called *caleseros* in Cuba. He owned numerous carriages, ranging from grand painted carriages with four crystal carriage lamps to illuminate the dark Havana streets, to the very Cuban *volantes*, perched up high on their two wheels. There were enough carriages and *volantes* for Mercedes to easily have her own particular one. Joaquín's home was his office to a great extent, and he entertained lavishly—friends, family, and colleagues—as Havana was a small social world and Joaquín was now placed close to its epicenter. Joaquín's house was full of carved and inlaid mahogany furniture, including numerous desks and tables in all shapes and sizes, many of them cleverly made to extend as needed and others topped with marble. More than anything, Joaquín had *taburetes*—a sort of rustic chair with leather seat and back popular at this time, which could be easily moved and stowed as guests came and went. He owned over one hundred *taburetes*. Joaquín also had a vast assortment of fine and daily-use china and crystal, totaling over thirteen hundred individual pieces, some of them hand-painted and rimmed in gold, others with his family crest etched on the wine glasses. Juan de Dios ran the kitchen with a younger helper, Antonio, but all sweets and pastries were elaborated by Dorotea, trained as a *dulcera* (sweet maker) and married to another of the domestic slaves, José Dolores. This was a house ready to entertain on a grand scale, with its crystal chandeliers and formal painting of mythical scenes and portraits of famous friends, royalty, and celebrated men of the era. Portraits included Godoy, the Spanish ministers Aranda and Mazarredo, the Austrian emperor Joseph II, and the unfortunate French king, Louis XVI—even, surprisingly, George Washington and Benjamin Franklin.

Mercedes witnessed the dances and other diversions that her father's house regularly hosted. Although she was very young, she already understood the passion that all Habaneros had for dancing—something repeatedly described in other contemporary accounts. The ardor for dancing was particularly notable, Mercedes thought, because the climate, with its oven-hot sun, created a state of "voluptuous apathy" in the general population—the contrast between this state and the energetic feasts and dancing in the evenings was all the more striking. To Mercedes, this constant dichotomy helped render Cuban women irresistibly enchanting; a mix of vivaciousness and languidness. She would deploy these very characteristics herself to charm the Spanish court and the Parisian salons in later years. But Mercedes was still very young, and even if her father thought dances and parties were appropriate for a nine- or ten-year-old girl, Mercedes herself preferred spending more time with Mamita. "Seated at her feet, perched on her knees, I listened with vivid interest to tales from the Old Testament or Roman history and I experienced some unknown sense of conviction that in preferring Mamita's company to a ball, I did well by God. Looking at her, I believed that the happiness that she felt in seeing me was also mine."

As she had with Mamita, Mercedes accompanied her father to his country properties—generally, the Havana landowners went out to their properties on a regular basis but rarely lived on them. Even so, some of the properties boasted impressive houses. Joaquín's Río Blanco estate was especially admired for its luxuries. Given Joaquín's nature, he was likely to make quick trips as he constantly expanded or repositioned his property portfolio. He sought to shift his investments toward tobacco and constantly sought new lands for sugar production. Sugarcane uses the soil intensively, and therefore flourishes best on virgin lands. Also, in the late eighteenth century, wood was the primary fuel for the boiling cauldrons. Every successful sugar plantation needed a nearby woods or forest—something that Cuba had in abundance but which the sugar plantations were stripping rapaciously. Cuba's intricate web of forests containing mahogany, ebony, cedar, and other precious hardwoods, its pride for the first three hundred years of its history as a colony, began to disappear in the Havana area.

In the late 1790s, Joaquín owned two working sugar mills: Santa María de Loreto, alias Seybabo, and San Ignacio de Río Blanco. Río Blanco was a relatively recent acquisition through Teresa's inheritance from her father, but Joaquín had owned Seybabo for some years. Since his time in Spain, Joaquín had been trying to improve its production through the purchase of additional slaves and through more creative efforts like commissioning the first steam engine for a Cuban sugar mill. The Spanish engineer who designed the engine, Agustín de Betancourt, was a colleague of the great Swiss French clock maker Breguet. Betancourt had the engine manufactured in England, the world leader in this new technology. The first experiment with the new machine occurred in January 1797. The steam engine worked successfully for a few weeks but ultimately failed. Still, other planters soon followed suit, finally finding permanent success twenty years later. Joaquín, ever enamored of all that was new, was certainly a pioneer.

Familiar with her father's different rural properties, such as coffee farms and sugar estates, and with the slaves that made up their work-forces, Mercedes obtained a precocious appreciation of the complexity of a slave society. Visiting her father's sugar estates, with their more labor-intensive processes, she saw a much harsher regime than in Havana homes or even on the coffee farms. Indeed, the naturalist Alexander Humboldt, Joaquín's guest on several occasions, noted that Cuban slave owners would scare domestic servants by threatening a transfer to a coffee farm, and would threaten the coffee worker with a transfer to a sugar mill. A world of difference separated a sugar worker from the urban servant of an aristocrat.

Mercedes wrote that she "remember[ed] slavery with horror," and that perhaps surprisingly for a young girl she "felt that the immense distance between the master and the slave was not natural, that there was too much of the violent, forced and monstrous in this domination." Her country visits would have been hateful, she wrote years later, except that her father's doting affection allowed her occasionally to alleviate some of the slaves' suffering. To a certain extent, Mercedes would always associate her father's love with her early attempts at benevolence, and she always considered him the most generous and charitable of persons.

On one of her stays at a sugar plantation, Mercedes was awakened at dawn by screams. Running to her father's room, she went to him in tears, afraid and upset by the sounds that she realized were from a slave being punished. Her father, alarmed, took her in his arms and carried her out to where the punishment was being meted. The screaming had stopped when they arrived, and the man was waiting for the final blow:

My face full of terror and my still tearful eyes contrasted with his air of indifference, almost desensitized. We learned that he had run away for the fifth time. Nevertheless, my father ordered him let go immediately. So it was that my childhood disposition inclined me to exercise charity like a sweet habit. Alleviating the misery of those that surrounded me, I felt a growing need to do good.

Mercedes' benevolent efforts led to another encounter, one that on first reading seems too dramatic to be true, but that finds documentary support. Until the end of the eighteenth century, sugar plantations stopped work once a week to celebrate mass. After all, one of the often-cited justifications for slavery was the conversion of the pagan Africans to Christianity. After the service, if the owners were there, the slaves would be allowed to greet their master. Mercedes recalled that this was the time for petitions and for pardons. One Sunday, Mercedes saw an attractive woman carrying her child rushing up to her father. The other slaves seemed to part respectfully for her, and she had a certain air of majesty and authority. The woman prostrated herself at Joaquín's feet and begged him to change her assigned work from the sugar mill to the relatively easier work overseeing the drying process, to facilitate caring for her young child. However, the rules of a sugar estate were implacable: the most arduous tasks went to the young and strong, while only the weak and frail held the lighter ones. Joaquín denied her plea. At this stage, Mercedes recalls:

> This negress stood up, embraced her son and dissolved in tears crying these words: "my beauty and my youth once were my fortune, why do they now cause my misfortune?" ... Her tears moved me. Clinging to my father's neck I insisted that he agree to her request; his good heart did the rest. The joy of the negress was as vivid as had been her pain ... her tears continued to fall as she gestured in joy.

The whole episode and the rather majestic and mysterious air of this woman caused such a commotion that Joaquín decided to enquire into her history. Mercedes recounted that she was called Cangis and came from the Congo, as was typical of many Cuban slaves. Her beauty had prompted her village to elect Cangis queen, and she in turn chose her own king. Hence she cried that beauty had once been her luck. However, her king soon died fighting a neighboring tribe, and Cangis, already pregnant, fell prisoner and was sold to the captain of a slave ship. Farfetched the story may seem, possibly even romanticized, but the people sold into transatlantic slavery hailed from all classes. There are at least two other known stories of enslaved royalty: one in Río de Janeiro, where "Teresa the Queen" had indeed been a queen in Cabinda until caught in adultery, while the mother of King Gozo of Dahomey was sold into slavery by her stepson. When her son succeeded his half-brother, he searched in Brazil for her in vain.

Exposure to the brutality of slavery may have stirred Mercedes at a tender age, but in the end she was still a very young girl, just ten years old. The countryside could still be her secret Eden, and she was still a mischievous child. Fun could be had and trouble could be found. Her father's military position meant that, even in the countryside, he always needed to remain in communication with Havana. Messengers were always on hand, ready to ride their mounts as soon as needed. Mercedes, never having learned to ride, eyed these horses with longing. Never one to pause for a moment if she wanted something, Mercedes devised a plan. After studying two messengers, she approached the older one, Silva. Mercedes asked to ride his horse, but Silva hesitated, explaining that the horse was too lively and she wouldn't be able to hold on, and then what would the Señor Conde say? Mercedes, knowing that her father always gave in to her, dismissed his worries. Silva still argued; he had children, he could lose his post.... Mercedes gave him no time to argue, jumped up on the horse, and flew off at a gallop. Disaster soon followed the first moments of pure pleasure. Mercedes began to tire and suddenly lost consciousness. When next she opened her eyes, she lay on the grass by a stream, shoeless, with her riderless horse bathing in the water. Silva knelt beside her crying and wringing his hands. Mercedes' first words were "Papá won't know anything," after which Mama Dolores ran out to her and carried her on her shoulders back to the house. Luckily, her father was away for the day and all was well.

After five days, however, Mercedes experienced fever and head-aches and they called for a Havana doctor. Mamita also came from the city, and all were alarmed at the seemingly inexplicable illness. Finally, Silva could contain the secret no more and confessed all to her father. Mercedes was bled and quickly recovered from the ordeal. Silva was forgiven; after all, even good-natured Joaquín was probably now well aware of his daughter's strength of will and stubbornness.

BEHIND THE
CONVENT WALLS

*M*ercedes' relationship with her extravagant and doting father proved sadly to be short-lived. Political factors stepped in to force everyone's hand, as they would throughout much of Mercedes' life.

Joaquín had arrived in Cuba with valuable licenses to trade rum and sugar products for flour, which he would import into Havana on neutral (mainly American) ships. This business was considered incredibly valuable as it infringed on the monopoly then held by merchants from the Spanish port of Cádiz and the Mexican port of Vera Cruz. Joaquín partnered with various influential figures, including his cousin Francisco Arango and the military *intendente* Pablo Valiente. The lucrative deal allowed for the shipment of a certain number of barrels over a period of time, but by late 1797 European politics had shifted, transforming Britain from friend into foe. Fear of a British blockade of Havana drove the decision to import the bulk of the concession as quickly as possible. Valiente, using his control of the Havana fortresses, transformed them into ad hoc warehouses for the flour. Since the Havana market could not absorb the entire stock immediately, most of the flour sat in the improvised warehouses. Slowly, in the Cuban heat and humidity, the flour started to rot. Almost four thousand barrels were eventually dumped into the sea, causing a huge outcry and scandal, aggravated by those citizens who resented the privileged trading and the higher bread prices caused by the restricted supplies.

As though this debacle was not enough, Joaquín saw the value of his special privileges reduced as the threat of war opened the Havana port to all neutral ships. Protesting to the king, Joaquín dramatically also asked for permission to remain in Cuba in order to sell all of his lands, as prelude to a permanent move to Spain. He also sought a waiver of the royal transaction tax. Joaquín had been spending lavishly, as usual, and he had also expended considerable sums of his own capital on the Guantánamo projects, particularly in trying to attract inhabitants to new settlements. He had frequently clashed with local officials. He needed new sources of funds and new privileges from the court. Teresa had already requested various extensions on his privileges in December 1796 and again in December 1797. She had also been obliged to fight off the seizure of the Mopox sugar exports in Cádiz to pay off Joaquín's financial backer, the Marqués de Casa-Enrile. Hence it would have been logical for Joaquín to contemplate a personal plea to Godoy and the king. He requested permission to sail back to Spain in 1799 along with several of his officials, with the official intent of reporting on the progress of the royal commission. An unofficial goal was to address his complex web of dealings.

Joaquín's plans to leave Cuba raised an important family issue: what to do with Mercedes.

For some time, the family's general plan was to marry her off in Cuba, in the type of interrelated marriage that would further bolster the Santa Cruz–Montalvo influence within Havana society. Joaquín and Teresa had another daughter in Spain who could secure their position within the peninsular aristocracy. However, there was no immediate pressing need for Mercedes' marriage; indeed, Joaquín had summarily dismissed Francisco Arango's inquiries in May 1794.

Mercedes secretly hoped that her father's notable fondness for her might translate into a reunion with her distant and idealized mother in Spain. Mercedes imagined that her mother's loving guidance would round out her sketchy education. Europe would provide new thoughts and ideas—something that Mercedes felt ready to absorb. She wrote about this period of her life in her memoirs, stating that "my passionate and precocious imagination strove impetuously to conquer the unknown, and I felt tormented by the desire to learn."

Modern European ideas were all well and good, but were not deemed appropriate for a Cuban lady destined to marry in the colonies. Nor was a passionate imagination combined with a willful nature a sought-after commodity in the marriage market. According to Mercedes, Cuban relatives thought that "the most prudent path therefore was to dampen this tendency [and] leave me in ignorance of as much as possible." One relative in particular looked on in mounting alarm at Mercedes' haphazard education—her grandmother, the Countess de Casa-Barreto. María Josefa de Cárdenas believed that Mamita's extreme tenderness for Mercedes had led to excessive freedom, lack of discipline, and impetuousness, which now posed a danger to all the family plans. Seeking to remove Mercedes from pernicious freedom, María Josefa in her pious mind thought that a convent would be the perfect place to shelter the child in her father's absence and to nourish her soul appropriately. In eighteenth-century Havana there was only one acceptable place for a daughter of the nobility: the Convent of Santa Clara de Asís. Two of María Josefa's own cousins, Joaquín's Santa Cruz aunts, were well established there, and Mercedes could be their protégée, educated under their care and guidance. The Countess de Casa-Barreto wasted no time in convincing her son. Good-natured Joaquín, torn between filial duty and his great affection for his daughter, made the fateful decision.

Along the Calle de Cuba between Sol and Luz, a long, blank-faced, two-story wall dominates one side of the street, with a tall bell tower rising in one corner. The only breaks in the fortresslike facade are three great wooden doors and several windows covered in wooden grilles; the larger ones are placed high on the walls, and the lower ones are paltry given the sheer scale of the structure. The high walls are painted in a pastel shade, like most Havana houses, in part to ward off the reflective glare of the sun. The overall sense is impregnability.

But this is no fortress, although the walls did serve a defensive purpose at one time. This is the Convent of Santa Clara, and its walls formed an enclosure meant to cut off its inhabitants, the holy sisters of the Franciscan order, daughters of the Havana aristocracy. The convent had been founded in 1644 at the request of the leading citizens who needed a place for their daughters who could not marry due to a lack of suitable dowry or suitor. For almost three centuries, until 1922, the convent was sealed off to the average Habanero and was the object of stories and legends. When the sisters sold it to move away from the overcrowded city center, the government opened its doors for a few weeks. The public flocked and was amazed to see the seventeenth-century cloisters and buildings, imagining the life of the early citizens and creating legends about hauntings, cries in the night, and buried bodies—stories that the present-day custodians are still happy to tell tourists.

Santa Clara, as the Countess de Casa-Barreto knew, was no ordinary Havana convent. It would only take novices who could prove their bloodline and who could provide a two- to three-thousand-peso dowry, less than a grand marital dowry, but still expensive relative to the other Havana convents.

The convent took novices preparing to profess and become "sisters of the black veil" as well as *seglares*, usually widows or older spinsters who wished to retire from public life. It also took a select number of young girls to be educated and prepared for their later life, generally ones with family ties. So it was that sometime around 1799, Mercedes prepared to join their number. No more running wild in her beloved Cuban countryside, watching the dancers in her father's house, or sitting at Mamita's knee. Mercedes would be educated and molded into a lady. Mercedes was less than happy—she was appalled.

Joaquín conditioned his agreement on Mercedes herself having no strong aversion to entering the convent. Therefore, María Josefa brought all her powers of persuasion to bear on Mercedes, finally triumphing in the matter. Mercedes, still ambivalent, however, insisted on her father not leaving for Spain until after her entry into the convent. She clearly wanted a way out. Her grandmother tried to pave the way for a happy entry by taking Mercedes to visit her father's aunts and other nuns in the days before her entry. As Mercedes recalled:

> They availed themselves of the most delicate attentions and even to a type of coquetry to seduce me: caresses, flattery, sweet-smelling sachets, pretty scapulars, good quality sweets, they omitted nothing; but all of these measures would be frustrated on the last day upon seeing the fateful grilles, and upon hearing the discordant sound of the locks. It was too late; I had promised it; with an oppressive heart and teary eyes, I embraced Mamita, and for the first time felt the blow of disgrace and the yoke of necessity.

Mercedes, under the tutelage of her great-aunt, Sor María de los Dolores de Santa Teresa,* found herself in a new world. The convent comprised three interconnecting cloisters and an orchard, all surrounded by the high walls. The main cloister was enormous, with a central lush garden surrounded by deep, first-floor arched colonnades, its thick columns supporting the second, more airy galleries. The nuns' cells and the larger common rooms were spread throughout the various cloisters. The second cloister contained a miniature town with little houses and two cobblestoned streets in the middle. Throughout the centuries, wealthy Havana families had endowed particular cells to house their daughters and later relatives, building additional rooms as the convent grew.

Theoretically, the Santa Clara nuns took vows setting them apart from the world as well as vows of poverty and they relinquished their

---

* The nuns added a saint's name to their own and were typically termed Sor or Madre.

inheritance rights, but they lived very different lives to those of other
Havana nuns. The sisters of Santa Clara had personal servants—in
Cuba this meant slaves of course—to tend to their needs. Many, if
not all, had private incomes that they used to provide for particular
needs or wants. Joaquín himself in 1796 had used his property at
Seybabo to guarantee a mortgage that raised fifty-five hundred pesos
in capital for the personal requirements of his aunts. The nuns often
ate or socialized in their cells, and their personal slaves could come
and go from the convent, providing a link to the outside world. In
short, the sisters had never accepted the communal life often associated with convents—the common life. Rather, as in many of the
great Latin American convents in Mexico and Peru, they followed
what was known as private life—*vida particular.*

This way of life was under intense pressure, however, throughout
the Spanish colonies. From the mid-eighteenth century, the Borbón
reformists had been trying to instill greater discipline and a return
to the common life in all convents. Not only did this mean the elimi-
nation of personal incomes and servants, it also called for a more
cloistered existence, a return to the silent discipline that had existed
at their foundation centuries before. In Santa Clara, these enclosure
measures included installing iron grilles with prongs in the *locutorios*
(rooms for meeting visitors), additional wooden grilles in the eight
outward-facing windows, and dense latticework over the grilles in
the choir area where the nuns gathered to hear mass and other services. The choir was particularly important because the nuns were
not permitted to enter the church attached to the convent, which
ran along one side of the main cloister. The choir and the *locutorios*
were their two vital links to the outside world. Little wonder that
Mercedes found the grilles and locks daunting.

The Clarisas fought back with fruitless legal appeals to Madrid,
and by 1783 the existing nuns were asked to choose between their
vida particular or accept the common life. Only nineteen out of
ninety professed nuns accepted the new ways. New nuns were given
no choice in the matter. By 1795, matters were even more complicated, as twenty-five nuns from the nearby Spanish colony of Santo

Domingo sought refuge with their Cuban sisters after Spain ceded Santo Domingo to the French. Overcrowding was an issue, and the religious authorities imposed an embargo on all new novices in 1797. It is a testament to Mercedes' family's influence and prestige that she was even allowed to enter as a protégée.

The crowded conditions within Santa Clara, the dissent and controversy, and the heightened sense of enclosure must have created a claustrophobic atmosphere. For a perceptive and free-spirited child such as Mercedes, it must have been insufferable. The sisters tried their best on the first day. Mercedes noted an almost a festival-like mood pervading the cloisters. Her arrival was an event for all, a break from the unvarying order of their lives. The sisters tried to incorporate Mercedes into their activities—music being one of them. She was invited to join other girls in a choir, rehearsing songs to celebrate their upcoming patron's day on August 11. The nuns were delighted to find that young Mercedes had a lovely voice. But amidst the effusive praise, Mercedes was on her guard. She sensed an underlying motive in their compliments, which seemed to focus on how that angelic voice could best be used to praise the Lord on a more permanent basis. One nun added, "Is it not so, my child, that you would stay with us?"

Mercedes was not to be persuaded. Following her great-aunt's slave, Dominga, through the convent's darkened and hushed corridors, she vowed to leave Santa Clara. Desperately unhappy, she determined to plead her case to her father and ask for a return to Mamita's home. Confident in her powers of persuasion over her indulgent father, Mercedes wrote to him. She was shocked, however, to receive his reply via her grandmother. Joaquín begged her to be calm and patient and reassured her of his affection, but he held firm to his resolution: Mercedes must stay in the convent. Mercedes responded by begging her father to come and see her, hoping that he could never refuse a face-to-face plea. For once, easygoing Joaquín did not waver. Mercedes began to think of other means of regaining her freedom.

Convinced that her grandmother lay behind her father's decision, Mercedes tried a different tack. She discovered that one of the two priests assigned as confessors for Santa Clara was also her grandmother's personal confessor. Declaring that she needed to confess, Mercedes sought out the priest. Her strategy was calculated to alarm the unsuspecting confessor and encourage him to influence her grandmother. In the confessional she cried, "I do not have the courage to stay here any longer; I am desperate.... If I commit a grave sin it will hang on your conscience...do not abandon me!" The surprised priest agreed to help.

Nothing more was heard from the father confessor, and Mercedes continued to fear eventual pressure to take religious vows. She lost her appetite and couldn't sleep. Underlying all was an overwhelming feeling of injustice. For a strong-willed and previously indulged child, the loss of liberty and the forced separation from Mamita and her father contributed to a sense of betrayal. Perhaps it seems exaggerated for a ten-year-old girl to suspect that the nuns and her grandmother were conspiring to seal her within the convent walls rather than merely to educate her. After all, the same reforms that had prodded the nuns to a more austere communal life had also forced a temporary block on new novices, and the only hope for a new recruit lay in petitioning the king. However, if ever a family had the necessary influence, it was Mercedes'. In 1806 Joaquín successfully requested a dispensation to allow his younger half-sister, Conchita, to enter Santa Clara.

The fear of being coerced united with the sense of injustice and abandonment led Mercedes to a new resolution: if no one would help her, then she would have to rely on herself. She felt a sense of empowerment, the freedom to make her own decisions, since all had failed her. Rather unusual for a preadolescent girl, it was absolutely revolutionary for the time and place, when young girls did not make their own decisions. But Mercedes was determined. She thought ceaselessly of how to escape from Santa Clara: "a thousand extravagant projects presented themselves to my imagination." One can only imagine what some may have been.

In the end, help came from a surprising source. While Mercedes generally viewed the sisters with suspicion, there was one young nun that she befriended. According to Mercedes, Sor Santa Inés was twenty years old, a lonely and melancholy nun who had herself been coerced into the convent by her father. In Sor Santa Inés, Mercedes found a sympathetic listener. Her great-aunt did not approve of the friendship; Sor Santa Teresa thought the younger nun was a negative influence on Mercedes. She forbade Mercedes to visit Sor Santa Inés in her cell or spend time with her alone. Mercedes found ways to see her secretly. So taken was Mercedes with Sor Santa Inés that she told her story—probably somewhat tragically romanticized—in a novella attached to the first part of her memoirs. The extent of truth versus fiction is unclear, but Mercedes did receive help and advice from some source.

The convent was undergoing some building work, and the main doors, normally tightly sealed most of the day, were opened regularly to let workers flow in and out. Mercedes' fertile mind thought to use the increased access to escape. She discussed her scheme with Sor Santa Inés, who convinced her of its impracticality but gave her an alternative escape route. There was a small opening in the lower choir, below the upper choir where the nuns gathered to hear mass. The three-foot hatch had two doors, one on the convent side and one on the church side, and was used for communion. Neither door was ever locked. Mercedes only needed to choose the moment.

The morning of her planned escape, Mercedes waited for her great-aunt and Dominga to leave for services in the upper gallery choir with the other nuns. Mercedes entered the lower one, where several servants were praying, and waited for them to leave and for the sacristan to open the great church doors to the public. Knowing that communion was held at 9:00 AM, she could only wait impatiently as the room emptied. Finally, only one old woman, half asleep, remained. Mercedes approached her but unwittingly woke her up. The woman announced that she planned to remain until nine, and Mercedes decided to wait no longer. She felt, she wrote, pulled by a superior force, and almost without thinking she approached the grille next to the doorway. She opened first one door and then the second. "Then...with a movement quicker than a thought I crossed the space and found myself on the church side....I fixed my dress as best I could and calmly crossed the church in front of the choir and the sisters."

Reaching the street, Mercedes was overcome by fear. Wearing her white uniform with a thin muslin veil, she knew that she stood out from other Habaneras. Havana women invariably wore black dresses on the street, and curled and teased their hair. Terrified of being discovered and returned, she quickly dashed through the empty streets to Mamita's house.

Her arrival created uproar, the shock of her escape eliciting both delight and consternation. Salvador, Mamita's old servant, could not contain his stunned happiness and smiled broadly. Mamita, emerging from her devotions in her oratory, could not bring herself to castigate Mercedes, and instead covered her in caresses. Mercedes herself, ecstatic and slightly dazed from her success, cried and laughed simultaneously. But all this joy proved short-lived as Mamita insisted on notifying the convent and her father. Responses came swiftly: Joaquín was on his way, and the abbess and Mercedes' great-aunts replied curtly that the fault lay in her inadequate education. They blamed the person responsible for her upbringing. Mercedes began to see the result of her willful escape in the pain that the critical response brought to her beloved great-grandmother's face.

The scandal that her escape created cannot be overstated. At the dawn of the nineteenth century, Havana was essentially a deeply conservative place. Young girls did not run away from convents, did not race unattended through the city's streets, and did not disobey their fathers. Years later, the story of Mercedes' escapade from Santa Clara would be repeated frequently, and an early biographer called her action "manly."

Joaquín arrived, and told them that his first idea was to return her to Santa Clara. However, the sisters refused to have her, so he decided to punish her intransigence and disobedience in a different manner. He forbade Mercedes from seeing Mamita, and took her to stay indefinitely with a relative, Aunt Paquita. Although saddened, Mercedes decided not to fight this new exile, as she wished through her obedient conduct to minimize criticism of Mamita. Mercedes found her relative to be devout but more indulgent than her grandmother. She had several daughters, and Mercedes soon became friends with these cousins, including the eldest, somewhat older than Mercedes and obsessed with many admirers. Mercedes also found herself living with at least one of the legendary Beatas Cárdenas, her grandmother's spinster sisters. Religion was their passion, yet they dedicated themselves to charitable work instead of taking religious vows. One of these sisters, shocked and appalled by Mercedes' recent actions, devoted her time to augmenting Mercedes' spiritual education.

Still, life was not unpleasant with Aunt Paquita. They soon decamped to San Antonio de los Baños, a town south of Havana founded by the Cárdenas family where various family members had properties, including Joaquín's coffee estate Las Delicias. The surrounding Alquízar region, famed for its dense tropical forests and rich floral plants, was later described by a noted Cuban novelist as brimming with sweet-scented blooms. Mercedes and her cousins frequently swam in the river and stayed in the cool waters until sunset, watching with delight as the fireflies began to emerge. Once again, Mercedes climbed trees in search of fruits, in this case velvety-fleshed *caimitos*. During one such climb, she surprised a snake, fell, and was rescued by the vigilant Mama Dolores.

Later in the year, the family went again to the countryside, offering Mercedes the chance for another illicit escapade. Paquita's property was close to Mamita's and abutted one of Joaquín's sugar mills. Knowing Mercedes' independent character and fearing she would create another scandal, Aunt Paquita only permitted outings under the care of her chaplain, Fray Mateo. Of course, one overweight and lethargic friar could not impede Mercedes from crossing a stream one day, knocking away the wooden plank bridging the water and leaving poor Fray Mateo behind, clutching his breviary and yelling. Reaching her father's cane fields, she came across clusters of *bohíos*, housing some of the slaves. There she found Cangis, the same African woman who had pleaded with her father, now grieving over her son's grave. As Mercedes recalled years later, witnessing the woman's despair made her own escapade seem foolish.

By the time Mercedes returned to Paquita's house, in the carriage that had been searching for her, she regretted creating so much commotion and consternation. She avoided the gathered family in the main entrance and hid in her bed until she heard Dolores cry "*Jesús María!* What has happened to her?" The next day, Mercedes promised not to run away again.

During the stay with Aunt Paquita, the transatlantic mail brought a long-awaited letter. Teresa Montalvo, still in Spain with her other children, sent Mercedes a miniature painting of herself as well as a message that begged Joaquín to bring Mercedes. Mercedes was overjoyed—her longed-for desire seemed now a possibility. She would cherish that miniature portrait until her death.

After the family's return to Havana, Mercedes' father visited more frequently. She sensed that, although unhappy with her conduct, he regretted the whole Santa Clara episode and its aftermath. María Josefa had died March 12, 1800, and with her disappeared the driving force for sending the child to the convent. Perhaps his mother's death had greatly affected him—Joaquín was strongly attached to his family, having lost his father in infancy. The same love of family now brought him closer to Mercedes and led him to finally agree to take Mercedes to her mother in Spain. Mercedes was about to enter a new phase of her life.

5

ADIOS, CUBA

*M*ercedes returned to her father's home as the reigning queen, more secure than ever in his affection. She visited dear Mamita at will, and life resumed as she had known and loved it. Writing years later in her memoirs, she recalled her days passing sweetly in complete idleness. Everyone seemed to have given up imposing any sort of rule or discipline. She "learned nothing and barely knew how to write." While there was little in the way of an academic regime, Mercedes was a curious creature who loved to observe everything and everyone around her.

She spent more time with her father, sitting with him in his study in front of his massive mahogany desk with its silver fittings. He shared with her the enormous genealogy charts he had commissioned to prove his noble descent and his *limpieza de sangre*, which meant his clean lineage. "Clean" at the time referred to the lack of any mixture with the "wrong" families, religions, or races. Joaquín had used this proof of pedigree to support his entry into the chivalric order of Calatrava, for his title of Count de Santa Cruz de Mopox, and he would wield it once more to fulfill his aspiration for a peerage, to be called a *grande* of Spain. While recounting to Mercedes the family legends and explaining her place within its entangled branches, Joaquín would have a large coffeepot at hand, masses of papers scattered about, and small piles of coins ready to hand out as alms to the needy.

Joaquín demonstrated the immense importance that he placed on his family's social position by lingering over his elaborate family tree and ensuring that young Mercedes understood her own position within the closed world of the Cuban oligarchy and the wider Spanish nobility. Social pride was so fundamental to their world that it would influence many critical decisions in their lives. Mercedes herself would carry this lesson into her future life, where it would reappear even as subtly as in her inclusion of the words *née Jaruco* on her visiting cards in Paris. The neat picture she drew of her father in her memoirs seems to mirror all that is known about Joaquín from other sources: his family pride and ambition, his complex and almost messy business dealings, his seemingly endless need to live life at a relentless pace. All were captured in his daughter's memories of family trees, untidy desks, and countless cups of coffee.

Joaquín entertained as usual, and Mercedes recalled the alcohol-fueled toasts, exuberant praises, and flattery of the participants. Beyond seeing the splendor of the feasts and dances, however, she also noted that the next day many of these same so-called friends would be less than flattering about Joaquín. She saw many of these guests as an entourage attracted to the appearance of success. Mercedes sensed the insincerity surrounding her father and had begun to grasp the way business and patronage operated in late-eighteenth-century Havana. If her memoirs impute to her young self a more world-weary tone than warranted for her age, perhaps her later experiences in Spain and France permitted her to appreciate the reality of her father's circle.

Now set on a return to Spain, Joaquín became engrossed in organizing his reports on the results and proposals of the Royal Guantánamo Commission as well as his ideas for the reorganization of the island's defenses. The Guantánamo commission's final reports included representations for the establishment of settlements and fortifications in Guantánamo Bay, the Bay of Nipe on the northern coast, and the Bay of Jagua (today the city of Cienfuegos) on the southern coast. There were suggestions for the further expansion of existing settlements in Mariel and Matanzas, as well as drawings and charts for the Güines Canal to connect the southern coast with Havana, running through the sugar-rich valley of Güines. The final report also included surveys of the lands and ports to the west of Havana and proposals for expanding the network of roads. Joaquín would take with him eighty-six intricately detailed drawings of native birds and fish, ninety-eight illustrations of insects and plants, and boxes of specimens of the island's flora and fauna, which would form the basis for a natural history of Cuba. The impressive submission is stored today in the Naval Museum of Madrid, including the startlingly beautiful drawings of tropical orchids and colorful insects.

Beyond his obligation related to the royal commission, Joaquín also wanted to bring some order to his "complex" business affairs. The naturalist Alexander Humboldt considered Joaquín to be "enterprising," and he certainly always looked for new opportunities to further his fortune. A pecuniary focus sometimes led to awkward situations involving close friends and relatives. While it was perfectly normal in Havana to have business dealings within the small circle of landowners, these exchanges often generated disputes, especially with inheritance and property rights. On top of that, Joaquín's inner restlessness seems to have caused unexpected conflicts in his business life. In April 1801 Joaquín bought another sugar mill, Jesús Nazareno, from his brother-in-law, Rafael Montalvo, for two hundred thousand pesos. Most of the sales price—165,000 pesos—was financed by a loan guaranteed by the sugar production at all three of his mills, plus mortgages on several other ranches, houses, and lands. Before the documents were even finalized, however, Rafael Montalvo heard that Joaquín was in the process of selling a valuable ranch, Aguas Verdes, as well as the sugar mill Seybabo, both part of the guarantee. A bitter dispute over collateral ensued, prompting Rafael to file a lawsuit against Joaquín.

Joaquín also hoped to negotiate yet another exclusive license to import flour to Havana, to recoup some of the lost opportunities from his suspended concessions. New funds were desperately needed. Joaquín had great plans for tobacco at a time when its production was declining in Cuba as sugar took over more and more agricultural land. Moreover, his wish to be made a *grande* of Spain required proof of his ability to finance a decorous lifestyle. The accepted method required placing a portion of his estate, free of debt, in an entail or trust that would be tied to the title and peerage. However, Joaquín had amassed enormous debts over the preceding decade, both to private creditors and to the Royal Treasury. He had used debt in part to make payments for all his various honors, including gentleman of the bedchamber, colonel of the guards regiment, Count de Santa Cruz de Mopox; to finance his contributions to the war effort against France; and to pay the import taxes and the sales tax on transactions. All in all, his debts totaled some several hundred thousand pesos by early 1802.

The journey to Spain presented the opportunity to reorganize his muddled affairs. Joaquín hoped to consolidate his debts to various governmental departments into one massive obligation to the Royal Treasury, and he also had an idea for a favorable repayment scheme tied to his tobacco production. To raise some cash for his plans and to reduce his debt, he had already negotiated the sale of some land in 1799 to the Royal Tobacco Factory, the government department that controlled the royal monopoly on tobacco production.

While Joaquín worried about his business affairs and presentations and Mercedes spent her days in "sweet idleness" under the Havana sun, their actual travel plans depended on the constantly evolving political situation well beyond their insular world. Interminable battles between England, France, and their respective and changing allies exposed transatlantic crossings to more than the usual dangers. This was the age of Nelson, of great sea battles and endless games of cat and mouse on the high seas between the major naval players, including Spain. The safest plan was to wait for a lull in the hostilities—and to insist on an adequate convoy for good measure.

The chance finally appeared in 1802 with the Peace of Amiens and the April arrival in Havana of a squadron under the command of Admiral Gravina. Gravina, a friend of Joaquín's, was happy to offer space on his flagship, the eighty-gun *Neptuno* with a crew of over seven hundred, to her father, Mercedes, and their servants. It was a magnificent escort to Cádiz. Admiral Gravina was one of Spain's finest commanders. His elite squadron was in Havana after supporting France's attempt to wrest back the sugar-rich colony of Saint-Domingue from the liberated slaves. Three months of intense fighting had temporarily placed General Leclerc and his wife, Pauline Bonaparte, in control, freeing Gravina's ships to return to Spain via Cuba.

Now with a fixed date for their departure, Mercedes began her final preparations and farewells. She worried about the impending separation from Mamita and the abandonment of her small world. Her memoirs dedicate a substantial number of pages to conjuring up the feel of the Havana heat, the soft breezes, and the moonlight on the ocean water during these final days. The older Mercedes savored memories of the sights, sounds, and pleasures of Havana life that she would have to leave behind on her journey. It is unclear if she knew how long she would be away from Cuba. Still, as with anyone planning to leave a beloved place, it made sense for Mercedes to soak in the atmosphere of Havana, prior to her departure. She took late-night *paseos*, carriage rides through the Havana streets, drowsing in the breeze. The breeze and the moonlight on the water drew her to the balcony when she should have been asleep, lying on the bed made of stretched canvas, cool linens, and swathed in yards of mosquito netting.

As the final day approached, Mercedes had two personal issues she wanted to resolve. She wished to reconcile with her two great-aunts, the sisters in the convent of Santa Clara, and settle Mama Dolores's future. Her first task was straightforward, if perhaps awkward. She asked to be taken to see her great-aunts to say her farewells. Thus, she entered Santa Clara's doors one last time, meeting with them as well as some younger girls. Mama Dolores presented a more complicated problem.

Mama Dolores had previously been offered her freedom after serving as Mercedes' wet nurse, but she had refused it, not merely because of her attachment to little Mercedes but also because she had children. A Cuban slave owner could easily free a slave, and there were often clauses in wills liberating a longstanding servant, but they did not necessarily free the former slave's family. Likewise, the Spanish colonies were notable for their laws allowing a slave the right to request a new owner as well as the right of *coartación*—the right to buy one's freedom at a set price. Once the price was set, the slave could try to earn the money over time or through a gift from another free family member or friend. The slaves were also allowed to hire themselves out for pay, which was then shared with their owner. It appears a contradictory system—brutal slavery side by side with these seemingly entrepreneurial opportunities. Alexander Humboldt, a committed abolitionist who called slavery "the greatest of all evils to have plagued mankind," was struck by how manumission was more frequent in Cuba than anywhere else in the slave-owning world. He attributed its frequency to Spanish laws, which were "directly the reverse of French and English," although he also thought religious belief and the affections that grew from the close domestic life all contributed.

Offering Mama Dolores her freedom would not have been so unusual in a wealthy and religious family, but the offer of freedom did not extend to her children. Dolores's only hope for reuniting her family would have been to work for years to earn their *coartación* price. So Mama Dolores stayed on as a slave, caring for Mercedes. Now, however, Mercedes would be leaving and Mama Dolores staying behind in Cuba. Mercedes was already thirteen years old. There would be no role for Dolores in the new Spanish life and no mention was made of a return date. Joaquín had even arranged his own attendants so that Mercedes would not need additional personal servants. Their entourage included a French valet as well as two young slaves, Blas and Tomás, to act as footmen for his carriage, another slave, Felipe, and his wife who would see to Mercedes' needs on ship. Mama Dolores's depression upset Mercedes, who many times would sit on the woman's knees, "crying while trying to console her." Mercedes and other family members finally convinced Dolores to accept her freedom, but with her children still enslaved and with no real possessions.

Hearing Dolores sighing and whispering "you are leaving and I am staying," while she carefully, almost tenderly, folded and caressed her mistress's belongings, Mercedes resolved to help this proud woman who had cherished her for so many years. Relying yet again on her father's affections and overall generosity, Mercedes made two requests. She wanted ownership of Dolores's children and a few *caballerías** of land. When Joaquín asked what she would do with these, Mercedes explained her grand plan. She would free the children and gift the land to Mama Dolores so that the newly freed family would have some financial security. Generous Joaquín agreed, and Mercedes began plotting her surprise parting gift for Dolores. The four *caballerías* chosen were already partly planted with tobacco. This was a substantial gift, as good agricultural land could sell for between four hundred and a thousand pesos per *caballería*. Mercedes also had a small *bohío* built, ready for Dolores and her family. Planning her surprise, Mercedes told Dolores that they were going to the countryside for two days, and that Dolores should take her children as well. Joaquín couldn't resist joining them, and they both anticipated the joy that was to come. Mercedes showed them the land and the *bohío* and explained that Dolores was now the owner. Mercedes then added: "Mama Dolores... you are already very happy, but wait, I still have something more to give you!" Dolores then replied, "I [do] not want anything more; I be [am already] too fortunate to stay alone!" all the while crying. Mercedes then took Dolores to where her children were and told her:

> 'Here, take them. They are mine.... I give them to you!' Until that moment, I had been happily laughing at her surprise and exclamations; but in that instant I began to cry uncontrollably and my father had some difficulty in calming me.

While meant as a loving gesture, Mercedes' final memory of her first thirteen years on her island homeland holds the bitter irony

---

* One *caballería* equals thirty-three acres.

inherent in this colonial world, where a teenager could "own" the woman who had raised her. The memory also encapsulates Mercedes' particular experience of the complex relationships between the landowners and their slaves. The story of the gift to Dolores combines all the dispassionate cruelty and personal warmth that could coexist in Cuban slavery in the dawn of the nineteenth century.

Mercedes also cherished the ideal, often repeated in her memoirs, of her father's nobleness, his sincere care for his slaves, and his overwhelming generosity. Surviving letters and documents confirm that Joaquín was a generous man, well-loved by his close friends and relatives. He planned to reward several other close servants with freedom after his death, and he was certainly generous whenever Mercedes called on his charity. Yet Joaquín remained very much a man of his time and position. He may have been moved to ease the workload of the slave Cangis or to donate over one hundred acres to Mama Dolores, but he also was greatly concerned with possible slave revolts. As sub-inspector general, he outlined a plan for rural militias to maintain order.

The slave rebellion of Saint-Domingue and the wars with England had heightened the Cuban landowners' fear of revolts. Cuban landowners feared internal unrest if their slaves and the free black and mixed-race populations became aware of the bloody details of the conflict in Saint-Domingue. Additionally, landowners feared that England might try to undermine Spanish rule by supporting or even inciting rebellion. Cuban landowners may have benefitted from the ravages to Saint-Domingue's agriculture, but they so feared the precedent set by the newly liberated population that they were willing to aid the French with food and supplies in their attempt to retake the colony. These major landowners, including Joaquín's uncle the Marqués de Cárdenas de Monte-Hermoso, fiercely resisted any government constraints on their ability to punish slaves or regulate their working conditions. They felt that any reduction in their "rights" would be perceived as weakness. The landowners vividly recalled the Count de Casa-Bayona, a devout man, who one Easter decided to make a pious act by washing the feet of twelve slaves and then serving them personally at dinner. The chosen slaves, held in awe by the other slaves, then led a particularly violent revolt. To Cuban landowners, the best strategy was to prevent any perception of weakness.

Admiral Gravina's squadron was set to leave Havana on April 22, 1802. Mercedes recounts that on the eve of sailing, she said farewell to Mamita and then spent the night crying. One can only imagine how wrenching the moment must have been, both for Mercedes and for Mamita. Mamita had taken care of her from her first moments, and she must have felt that separation much as she still keenly felt the distance from her son Gonzalo O'Farrill. The next day, Mercedes, her father, the admiral, and their party boarded a launch and rowed out to the *Neptuno*, which was already at sea just outside of Havana harbor. As they sailed out, various ships and forts fired salutes. Mercedes recalled it years later:

> The noise of the cannon, the voices of the sailors, the varied movement of the sails and the rigging would have provided me with an agreeable distraction with their novelty, were it not for the profound sadness that overwhelmed me. Moving away from my country, I was leaving all that I loved, all that I had loved until then.

Mercedes kept her eyes on the city of Havana until it disappeared into the distance as the *Neptuno* sailed away. In the immensity of the open ocean, the *Neptuno* would be her home for the next month. But at the end of the long sea journey, Mercedes would arrive in a new country, to a new home and family.

PART II

Spain

SPAIN

MERCEDES' TRAVELS AND MAJOR BATTLES OF THE PENINSULAR WAR

·❊·

1802–1813

FRANCE

Bay of Biscay

Bayonne
St. Jean de Luz

Bilbao

Vitoria

Urdos

Jaca

Burgos

Valladolid

Ebro River

Zaragoza

Barcelona

Salamanca
Ciudad Rodrigo

PORTUGAL

Sierra *Guadarrama*

MADRID

Teruel

Talavera Aranjuez Ocaña

Almonacid

Valencia

Badajoz

S P A I N

Albacete

Mediterranean Sea

Sevilla

Bailén

Cádiz

100 miles

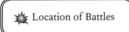 Location of Battles

MERCEDES' JOURNEYS

- •••• Arrival (May 1802) – Cádiz to Madrid
- – – Joseph's retreat (August 1808) – Madrid to Vitoria
- ═══ Evacuation of Madrid (August 1812) – Madrid to Valencia
- ─── Escape to France (September 1812) – Valencia to Urdos (France)

6

MADRID

GRANDEUR AND DECAY

he *Neptuno* took almost five weeks to cross the Atlantic on its journey to Spain. The initial excitement of the adventure soon settled into the regular rhythms of a long sea journey, but Mercedes quickly encountered sufficient distractions. Suffering initially from seasickness, she was spoiled with care and attention by the admiral and his staff. One young captain discovered her interest in French, and spent time reading Racine's plays with her. The hint of romance floated in the sea air, but worldly Joaquín quickly dashed it. Perceiving the dangers from the young officer's attentions, he soon had Felipe blocking Mercedes' doorway at night.

Any lingering tedium transformed into terror when a vicious storm hit the squadron off the Azores. The storm pitched the ship violently throughout the night and Mercedes, who had been seasick at the beginning of the voyage, suffered again. The ordeal prompted a lifelong aversion to long sea journeys, keeping her away from her beloved Cuba for years. The *Neptuno* arrived in the Spanish port of Cádiz on May 25, 1802, almost exactly one month after leaving Havana.

Mercedes welcomed the arrival into ancient Cádiz, a trading city founded by the Phoenicians. It seemed as though they "had built it expressly, rising from the middle of the waters, to offer the pleasures of life to the poor travelers…who reach its hospitable shores." The city, then the principal port to the West Indies and home to the Spanish navy, sits on a spit of land surrounded by water in the southwest corner of Spain, facing the rougher Atlantic Ocean rather than the softer Mediterranean Sea. Cádiz lies just beyond the Strait of Gibraltar with the Cape of Trafalgar to its south. The city, with its charming white merchants' houses, many with tall *miradores*— elegant little towers built so that their owners could look for their ships sailing into the harbor—was Mercedes' first sight of Spain, the mother country.

Joaquín agreed to stay a few days to acclimatize her to the land and the new country. He made good use of their arrival, wasting no time in composing the first of countless official messages. Hosted by family friends, Joaquín could also deal with business in this city dedicated to the transatlantic trade. Joaquín's sugar crops generally arrived in Cádiz, and he had his agent there. Cádiz shared some similarities with Havana: it was a port city and boasted one of the Spanish Empire's largest shipyards. The great ship *Santísima Trinidad*, originally built in Havana, received its fourth deck in the Cádiz shipyards, officially becoming the largest naval ship of its time.

After Cádiz, Mercedes and her father traveled northeast through Andalucía toward Madrid, stopping for a few more days in Sevilla, famed even then as one of the most beautiful cities of Spain. Even in the early nineteenth century, Andalucía in general was renowned for its architectural and natural beauty. The Moors had lavished effort and money on creating their exquisite palaces and gardens, while the great churches and convents in Sevilla had been the focus of pious donations originating from the wealth of the Americas. Mercedes should have been both delighted at the new sights and happily comforted as the typical Andalusian house, with its hidden flower-filled courtyards, balconies, and brightly patterned tiles, would have reminded her of Havana. But she was not. The "sad olive trees" appeared small in comparison with the gigantic trees of the Cuban forests, and she had nothing good to say about the famous orange and lemon trees. Remembering the rich profusion of the Cuban landscape, Mercedes found the Spanish citrus groves like specimens from a greenhouse.

From Sevilla they continued northward toward Aranjuez, thirty miles south of Madrid. Aranjuez was one of the royal establishments where the court spent the spring months. Mercedes may have found the road conditions somewhat poor, as did other foreign travelers, such as the Duchess d'Abrantès, a childhood friend of Napoleon. However, arriving from Cuba, Mercedes probably felt no surprise at the extensive use of mules to pull all types of vehicles, even carriages. The Duchess d'Abrantès expressed amazement at the seven mules under the charge of a driver known as the *mayoral*, helped by a younger boy who would run alongside the lead mule. Both Mercedes and the duchess recalled how the mules all had feminine, military-sounding names—Generala, Capitana, or Coronela—and all of them followed their master's voice. The duchess and another traveler, Lady Holland, a London political hostess and wife of the influential Lord Holland, also highlighted the wary attitudes shown toward foreign women who flouted local customs by not wearing the obligatory black skirts of a *basquiña*. Lady Holland was shocked by the "scorn with which a woman is treated who does not conform to the Spanish mode of dressing." Travelers recognized Spain's charm but noted the stark differences from much of Western Europe.

Mercedes and her father arrived in Aranjuez at its busiest time of the year. If Cádiz appeared as a safe harbor after the arduous sea journey and Andalucía was somewhat wanting, Aranjuez must have come as a shock to the thirteen-year-old colonial girl. The town rises from the dry plateau south of Madrid, a fertile oasis located between the rivers Tajo and Jarama. The enormous royal palace, surrounded by elegant gardens, ornamental lakes, and subtly landscaped natural walks, presented a scale and sumptuousness previously unknown to the young girl.

Spain's royal family had been spending the spring months from Easter until late June in Aranjuez since the reign of Felipe V, the first Borbón ruler and grandson of France's Louis XIV. As the royal family made their move to Aranjuez, the whole court and machinery of government transferred to this lovely town, continuing to rule the empire from there. So many people had business to transact in Aranjuez or came in hopes of currying royal favor that during these spring months a regular coach service ran twice a day from Madrid. A special mail courier also ran between Madrid and whichever royal palace was in use.

Joaquín, as one of the fortunate with official business to report, had access to the center of power. While the royal palace represented a focal point for the town and all the courtiers and office-seekers, its labyrinthine corridors and rooms delineated various layers of hierarchy. Following the sweeping principal staircase, one entered a series of opulent rooms, each with a different decorative motif. Vividly colored porcelain filled one entire room, while another bore ceilings covered in mythological deities and walls hung with silks. Each room denoted a particular level of access, from the rooms for the Spanish Guards to the gentlemen in waiting, and further in, the various private rooms of the king and queen: their offices, dining rooms, dressing rooms, and bedchambers. Stepping further into each one constituted a step closer to the royal presence and therefore a step closer to power and influence. Joaquín's access allowed a private audience with the king, queen, and first minister, Manuel Godoy: the pinnacle of access in this absolutist kingdom.

While Joaquín fulfilled his official duties, Mercedes would have seen what travelers often praised as "a ravishing spot in the universe." One part of the palace held a familial memory: the royal chapel, located in one of the wings and facing the main plaza, had been the site of her younger brother's baptism. She would have also seen the famous gardens and fountains—the Jardín del Rey, the French-style Parterre, and the gardens on the island on the other side of the Tajo. Carlos IV also built the Jardín del Príncipe—a garden project still incomplete at the time. These gardens, set further from the palace grounds, offered enchanting walks, following the more "natural" English style with the river running along its back. Pleasure boats sailed on the lakes decorated with elegant landings. In the Jardín del Príncipe the king and queen had begun to build the Casa del Labrador, their version of Marie Antoinette's Petit Trianon—a "workman's cottage" on a lavish scale. Far from being a rustic getaway, in reality it constituted a series of jewellike rooms, intricately decorated. The billiards room, for example, featured inlaid marble floors, a magnificent gilded billiards table, and walls hung with embroidered silks depicting scenes from Valencia, where they were created, as well as motifs inspired by the Raphael loggias at the Vatican.

All the courtiers focused their movements on the king and queen of Spain: Carlos IV and his wife, María Luisa de Parma, a cousin from the Spanish/Italian branch. Unfortunately for Mercedes, she did not witness the height of Spanish grandeur or political might; rather, she encountered a weakened and decayed monarchy. Carlos IV succeeded his strong and rather austere father, Carlos III, who had at least temporarily stopped some of the political and economic decline. His son Carlos IV was, lamentably, a "good but slow-witted boy" with a sense of duty but no real passion except for hunting and was clearly dominated by his strong-willed wife.

One only has to look at Francisco de Goya's many portraits of the queen to comprehend that she was no great beauty. Many of the portraits reveal an almost fascinating ugliness. Yet contemporary accounts, while generally agreeing about her lack of looks, also comment on her good figure, graceful movement, and incredibly vivacious eyes. The court and foreign diplomats also recount her passion for handsome young guardsmen and her highly inappropriate coquetry. The French ambassador thought that she sacrificed the interests of the monarchy for her scandalous pleasures. Her son Fernando's mentor deemed her heart naturally depraved. Still, her husband seemed oblivious to her behavior. A celebrated anecdote tells how Carlos III, always despairing of his son's naiveté and dullness, would laugh when he heard his son say that a prince did not need to worry about his wife's infidelity because, unlike commoners,

a royal wife was more strictly educated and if so inclined "could sel-
dom find any royal personages with whom they could indulge such
evil propensities." Carlos III would then be heard muttering to his
son, "Carlos, Carlos, you are so silly. All of them, yes all of them
are whores."

María Luisa's passion for young guardsmen and illicit affairs has
never been fully verified, but it was common talk, believed throughout Spain. Her particular closeness with Manuel Godoy, fifteen years
her junior, became an obsession with her and led to a bizarre, almost
familial relationship between the king, queen, and their anointed
favorite that the queen called "the earthly trinity." The guardsmen,
generally from noble or well-born families, stood sentry on the corridors of the royal palaces, providing ample opportunity to see and
be seen, yet Godoy's rise appears remarkable even by the standards
of the time. Soon after the ascension of Carlos IV and María Luisa
to the throne, in December 1788, Godoy became cadet major of the
Royal Bodyguards, and by February of 1791 a field marshal. Four
years into the new reign, Godoy, now Duke de Alcudia, served as
first secretary of state —the equivalent of prime minister—following in the footsteps of much more experienced statesmen such as the
Count de Floridablanca and the Count de Aranda. Godoy was the
man that Joaquín courted so assiduously, whose favor he had boasted
about in his letters to Arango. Godoy, as the supreme favorite, could
provide direct access to the royal largesse—at a price.

Reading María Luisa's letters to Godoy provides a sense of their
intimacy, as well as her superficiality and pettiness. She wrote to him
almost daily from wherever the court sat, and addressed him always
as "Friend Manuel." She seemed to have three primary topics in all
her letters: her countless ailments, horses, and her cutting observations on all those around her. She detailed her every headache,
stomach problem, or cough, and constantly commented on prized
horses. She sniped about politicians, courtiers, and even her own son
and heir, Fernando, the Prince of Asturias ("a sly coward"), and his
wife, María Antonia, her own niece ("a venomous viper"). She com-
municated her fears of intrigues against her and the king by many

of their courtiers—to the point of saying that "Judas didn't have anything on the Duke [and Duchess] of Osuna" upon learning that the ducal couple had paid an early visit to the new French ambassador. She also expressed tender concern for Godoy's welfare and happiness, and assured him of her affection and the king's, signing off letters with words such as "believe that we are and always shall be your true friends."

This seemingly contradictory world, full of grandeur and decay, was ruled by a rigid hierarchy but dominated by corruption. Dramatic events would turn it all on its head within the next six years.

Absorbing the new milieu and her magnificent royal surrounding was probably more than enough for Mercedes to manage. Mercedes confronted the need for adjustment while she nursed a much greater concern: the anticipated and now imminent reunion with her mother. For unknown reasons, Teresa had chosen to stay in Madrid rather than joining Joaquín and Mercedes in Aranjuez. Mercedes was further alarmed by her mother's many acquaintances who came to greet her—and to Mercedes' suspicious mind, inspect her. She resolved that whatever news they might send on to Madrid would be complimentary. She felt for the first time the desire to please, even aspiring to a certain flirtatiousness in order to enchant these visitors.

After several days in Aranjuez they departed for the final journey to Madrid. As they neared the house on Calle de la Luna, Joaquín, with his fun-loving nature, conceived the idea to present Mercedes to Teresa within a group of other young girls. The joke would be whether Teresa's maternal instinct would lead her to the correct young lady. Luckily for Mercedes, and for domestic tranquility, Joaquín did not actually put this idea into practice. But merely entertaining the thought underscores the bizarreness of the situation: a mother and daughter who had been apart almost since birth—thirteen years in fact.

Mercedes always remembered vividly her first sight of her mother. At that very moment began a passionate maternal adoration, almost beyond normal bounds. She often repeated she would do almost anything to please her mother. In Mercedes' eyes she beheld a vision:

> How beautiful she seemed to me. Who would have been able to see her for the first time without being moved? Who could have known her without worshipping her? Her majestic bearing, her perfect features, her black hair and beautiful black eyes were gracefully drawn upon an alabaster skin; her admirable arms, hands and shoulders; and what even surpassed these perfections, the tranquil and moving expression of her appearance, that mixture of pride and sweetness....I can still see her in that dark blue silk gown that highlighted the whiteness of her arms and that delicate veil, whose pleats I can still count, which half covered her beautifully braided hair.

Other accounts of the young and beautiful Countess de Jaruco, still only thirty years old, support Mercedes' rather extravagant praise of her mother's beauty. The French memoirist the Duchess d'Abrantès recalled that "there was in Madrid in that era [1805], one particularly beautiful woman....She was tall for a Spaniard and proportioned like all the women of that nation, especially those born in the colonies. They have a perfection in their figures that even the Andalusians don't possess." D'Abrantès thought Teresa so dazzling that when writing to Paris about an evening at the Dutch ambassador's residence, she dwelled more on Teresa than the party.

Likewise, Lady Holland thought her beautiful, but also discerned another aspect of Teresa Montalvo's personality, describing her as "extremely voluptuous and entirely devoted to the passion of love." This description has stayed with the Countess de Jaruco, often repeated, the source of much speculation as to her private life. Joaquín had been gone for most of the prior five and a half years, and Teresa had been living in Madrid for almost half her life. During that time she had grown and changed from the young bride arriving from colonial Havana, ready to explore the Old World and absorb its famous sights and fashions. Within little over a year of arriving at court, Teresa gave birth to another daughter, and by 1795 the couple had three Spanish-born children. Two little girls, María Josefa (Pepita) and another María, had been born in rapid succession in 1791 and 1792, in Madrid. Francisco Javier (Quico) was born a few years later, in 1795, in Aranjuez. Tragedy struck the family in those whirlwind years; the younger María died sometime between summer of 1794 and the autumn of 1796, possibly of the measles, which she and Pepita had in June 1794.

Beyond her private family life, Teresa had learned her way around the court and elite Madrid society, helping to maintain the family interests in Joaquín's absence. By the time Mercedes met her, Teresa Montalvo had become an established hostess with a fashionable home. Her *tertulia*—or Spanish salon—was well attended, especially by the literary and art world. According to her daughter, Teresa had a passion for the arts and seemed to shine within this milieu, holding her own in discussions with the stars of Spanish literature. Her accomplishments were particularly impressive given the sketchiness of her education in Cuba. In effect, Teresa had educated herself. Drawn to these talented intellectuals, Teresa had absorbed their knowledge and enthusiastically followed their lead.

She had a natural inclination toward French style and taste, a proclivity encouraged by her uncle, Gonzalo O'Farrill, and his Cádiz-born wife, Ana Rodríguez de Carassa. General O'Farrill had been educated at the French military academy of Sorèze from the age of ten, and Ana was a known admirer of French politics and philosophy. Teresa formed a close friendship with Ana in 1792 when the O'Farrills stayed with the Jarucos in Madrid. Their intimacy would help sway Teresa's later decisions and have lasting effects on the lives of her children.

While Teresa's salon revolved primarily around the arts, most gatherings crossed into political spheres. Although generally hosted by women, Spanish salons were well known for attracting men. Husbands rarely attended, so the wives were surrounded by their gallants, known as *cortejos*. Besides readings and musical performances, the guests enjoyed food, games, and some gambling. Teresa's salon was not overtly political, like others. Perhaps she made a calculated decision to avoid the fate of the New Orleans–born Countess de Gálvez. The latter's exile from Madrid to Valladolid reflected the culmination of political intrigues fomented by her own salon, well known for its Francophile tendencies and French-speaking guests. Even her late husband's impeccable reputation as the hero of the siege of Pensacola and his positions as former governor of Louisiana, Cuba, and viceroy of Mexico, could not help the unfortunate Countess de Gálvez.

Even a purely literary or artistic salon could be hazardous in an absolutist kingdom. Queen María Luisa detested what she viewed as the intellectual pretensions of women. She berated her daughter-in-law, the Princess of Asturias, for reading French novels and books with "diabolical engravings." She specifically named the Countess de Jaruco in an 1804 letter to Godoy complaining about these despised women who "presume to be intelligent, holding themselves equal to men, which I believe is improper of our sex; nevertheless, I know that there are those who have read a great deal, and having learned some current phrases now believe themselves superior in talent over all others, such as *la Jaruco* and others, not to mention the French. But since I am a Spaniard, by the grace of God, I do not sin there."

In the house on Calle de la Luna, Mercedes greeted her two surviving younger siblings, Pepita, aged eleven, and seven-year-old Quico. Acquiring a mother, sister, and brother all at once bred a pivotal occasion. Her memoirs would recall strong but contradictory emotions: happiness at discovering a new family but awareness too of the challenge to establish her place in this household. She could no longer rely on the automatic affection engendered by long-established familiarity, as she had in Havana at the heart of Mamita's family. Conscious also of the picture she presented to her new immediate family, she feared being too different. Mercedes candidly described herself:

> At eleven years* old I was fully grown, and while very slim, I was
> as fully developed as an eighteen year old. My creole coloring,
> my black and lively eyes and my hair—so long that I could barely

support it—gave me a certain wild or primitive aspect that well matched my moral disposition. I barely knew how to read or write, and I reasoned with self-assurance... over all topics. Lively and passionate in the extreme, I didn't understand the need to rein in my emotions and even less the need to hide them. Frank, naturally self-confident, and never having been constrained, I didn't know how to dissimulate, and I had as much an aversion to a lie as for any evil. I was indomitably independent with strangers, and pliable with those I loved. Extremely sensitive to the pleasure of being loved—I would have cried all day long if the merest shadow of discontent had clouded my father's face. These tendencies... which had never been modified by education... resulted in highly changeable moods, one moment of lively happiness another of sadness.... This composition, at eleven years old,* must have appeared surprising to Europe.

Confronted with this wild-looking teenager, Teresa took her time examining her daughter. She asked about her lessons and accomplishments, and Mercedes answered in her usual honest manner. Teresa was delighted to learn that Mercedes was musical, possessing a lovely voice, although as yet untutored. At least there, mother and daughter shared a common passion. However, Teresa found Mercedes somewhat lacking in most other areas. Teresa spoke with frankness, telling her eldest daughter that her education was quite deficient and that she would need to work hard if she wished to reach the standards of her brother and sister. Her mother presented this situation as a challenge that could, if met, provide her with many advantages, but Mercedes would need to make a conscious decision.

While Mercedes settled into her new life and family, her father left Madrid for Havana. Joaquín sailed from Spain in the autumn of 1802 and arrived in Havana by December. He spent the intervening months obtaining as many favors as possible. As a final gesture to ingratiate himself with Godoy, Joaquín presented him with the two

---

* Mercedes was really thirteen years old—in her *Mémoires*, she started taking years off her age beginning with her arrival in Spain.

young slaves, Blas and Tomás, whom he had brought from Havana. Godoy had admired them and happily accepted this exceptional gift, but as Joaquín was about to depart, Godoy asked the pair if they wished to stay or return to Cuba. Blas and Tomás chose to return, and Godoy freed them—requesting that Joaquín settle them into a new life. Joaquín did so, and after arriving in Havana he found them good apprenticeships in the free black community.

Writing to Francisco Arango in July prior to his return to Havana, Joaquín expressed optimism about his future, believing he had secured many of the goals that he had formulated when planning his journey. The king had granted him a new trading concession for flour imports to Havana and agreed to let Joaquín consolidate all of his existing debt to the Royal Treasury and repay it in tobacco. Joaquín also seemed on track for appointment to field marshal, and he had achieved the coup of a private audience with the king, queen, and Godoy for well over an hour, reviewing the plans, maps, and overall work of the Royal Guantánamo Commission. The royal couple approved of his conduct, and Godoy requested Joaquín to accept responsibility for the development of the province of Matanzas as well as of the formation of Mariel. But Joaquín begged off—not wishing to be caught up in more expensive obligations. As he said to Arango: "Independence and away with responsibilities, as without them I will always achieve what I desire."

Joaquín considered his grandest achievements to be the trading and tobacco concessions. The flour contracts were considered incredibly valuable, and even before he arrived in Havana, word had spread about them. The American consul in Havana wrote to James Madison, then secretary of state, that he thought the Count de Jaruco would earn some five hundred thousand dollars over the term of the contract and that he would immediately be advanced one hundred thousand dollars in cash and sugar as well as one hundred slaves by the merchants acting as agents. Joaquín certainly needed the advance, as in 1803 he anticipated sending to Cádiz in sugar or in trading profits a minimum of sixty thousand pesos to pay various creditors and to cover Teresa's living expenses. Joaquín thought that with this privilege he would finally emerge from his perceived poverty and successfully reestablish his fortune. He expressed this sentiment over and over again in his letter to Arango, saying bluntly that "this could be the final chance and if it slips away..."

The opportunity to aggregate all his outstanding government debt and repay it by developing his tobacco production and then selling the produce to the state represented another incredible coup. The terms were so favorable that Joaquín eagerly asked Arango to chase down every last item of debt; the more the merrier, in order to give himself greater flexibility. However, he would also have to use part of his trading profits to start the transformation of his lands into tobacco fields, finding tobacco farmers and paying to clear the land for planting.

So Joaquín would leave Spain, and his family, for an undetermined length of time. His final letter to Arango reveals some discussion of Teresa returning with him, but he had proposed that she stay. In a rather cryptic statement Joaquín confesses that "it is convenient to our domestic happiness and the decision was taken with all the due care required and we are in complete accord, never has more peace and tranquility reigned." Major considerations seemed to have prevailed, yet Joaquín also makes it clear he truly wanted to return to Havana.

It is difficult to understand fully the condition of Joaquín and Teresa's marriage after more than five years spent apart. Perhaps it had subtly changed from a rapturous affair to a more pragmatic enterprise. The couple seemed to have been quite in love at the start of their Spanish adventure. Their joint will, executed in March 1789, had a clause where each bequeathed to the other the fifth of the estate capable of free gifting under the law. While that was not unusual, the wording seems out of place with all the dry legal language: the bequest was "a demonstration, even though small, of the great love which we have for one another." Joaquín's subsequent letters also portray a warm and affectionate father and husband—always mentioning his wife and children yet in a lovingly careless way. By the time Joaquín sailed for Havana in late 1796, his new will stated more simply that he bequeathed his fifth to his wife "attesting to the great affection that I have always professed...to her good companionship and the care and effort with which she has raised and educated our children."

Whatever the state of the marriage, his departure would have had a profound effect on Mercedes. Once Joaquín returned to Havana, she would have lost the one person who doted on her unquestioningly, and who served as a link to her old life and homeland. She briefly stated that "my father was my oldest ally in the house and my heart still had no other refuge than his."

A SENSE OF LOSS

*H*er father gone, Mercedes began to adjust to life with her new siblings. She instinctively liked her younger sister, Pepita, who was a sweet, good-natured girl. It did not take long, however, for Mercedes to perceive that her mother had a marked preference for Pepita.

Mercedes rationalized her mother's preference as a natural consequence of circumstances but still felt wounded, and her once robust self-confidence suffered in innumerable and subtle ways. She noticed that her siblings naturally used the more informal *tú* with their mother while Mercedes was relegated to the more distant *usted*. This simple distinction came to symbolize Mercedes' view of her place within the family. The word *tú*, "so sweet, so tender that approaches and inspires confidence was the province of the other two and was forbidden to me." Mercedes' siblings quickly comprehended the family dynamics, and all three children realized that special requests met a better reception from their mother if made by Pepita or Quico. As time passed, Mercedes came to believe that her mother's love was not spontaneous and maternal but based on Mercedes' good and caring behavior, while "the tender abandon and weakness of a mother was reserved for my sister." Now Mercedes worked to earn the love that her brother and sister inherited naturally.

A difficult family situation, exacerbated by her father's departure and even the new, colder climate, led to a depression that affected Mercedes' health. Moodiness, tears, and languidness alarmed her mother, and their doctor ordered a change of venue. In late November, Mercedes went to the countryside in Moncloa to recover her energy. Melancholy, as she termed it, amounted to a very typical nineteenth-century diagnosis, a catchword for doctors who could not pinpoint the cause of an ailment. Yet Mercedes had a compelling case. Sensitive and probably a bit high-strung, Mercedes must have felt overwhelmed.

Today Moncloa forms part of Madrid, but in 1802 the capital was much smaller. With an approximate population of only 160,000, Madrid was limited to the present-day center—bounded by the royal palace, the Paseo del Prado, and the Buen Retiro park. Even the present day's grand Paseo de la Castellana and the fashionable Serrano shopping district would have been outside the walls. Just a few miles away, Moncloa was already countryside.

After three weeks or so recovering her strength, Mercedes returned to Madrid. The center of her world consisted of the streets and plazas emanating from the Royal Palace of Oriente, crowded with convents, churches, and the palaces of the nobility. The streets in this area, still narrow and cramped, once served as home to many prominent inhabitants like Mercedes' family.

Mercedes and her sister continued their studies together, including music, history, and literature. Mercedes excelled at music, where she felt that "learning was actually remembering." She certainly loved to sing typical Spanish songs, but felt the lack of truly excellent teachers in Madrid. Nevertheless, Mercedes and Pepita sang and played the piano and Spanish castanets. They also delighted in dancing the fandango and the seguidillas, both typical dances of Castilla.

Mercedes made extensive use of her mother's library, full of more serious literature but also containing numerous novels that the sisters could read to their hearts' content. Mercedes enjoyed the typical novels of the age, such as Samuel Richardson's *Pamela* and *Clarissa* and the books of Madame de Genlis. The year 1802 also saw the publication of Madame de Staël's *Delphine*, influenced by the works of Jean-Jacques Rousseau. Mercedes later admired Madame de Staël's *Corinne* and enthusiastically absorbed its romantic sensibility. She yearned to read Rousseau himself—his *Nouvelle Heloïse* and *Confessions*, especially, but they were deemed too controversial for a proper young lady and were strictly forbidden. Mercedes looked forward to marriage in part to acquire the freedom to read these proscribed volumes.

Teresa kept her children to a very strict routine and generally limited their presence in social gatherings. They dined with their mother and her guests but worked the rest of the afternoon and evening. Only occasionally did their mother allow them to stay until 11:00 PM in the salon, and almost never to stay for the late Spanish suppers. They had few friends their own age; Mercedes thought that her mother wanted to insulate them from all alien influences.

Teresa maintained an open table. Once invited to the house, an acquaintance never again required a specific invitation. Lavish hospitality was the norm for the *tertulias* but could be expensive to sustain as one never quite knew how many guests to expect. The popularity of the salon moreover provided another form of education for Mercedes and her siblings—even if they were not regularly permitted to socialize with the guests. As Mercedes noted, all kinds of characters attended the salons, offering her the chance to observe multiple idiosyncrasies. Occasionally, the sisters seized the chance to have some fun at the expense of the more superficial guests. In their more intimate evenings, Teresa would sometimes show off her children's work—their art or music, for example. Most of Teresa's circle knew about her perceived preference for her younger daughter, so Mercedes and Pepita decided to cause mischief by secretly switching their paintings, which were about to be shown to the grand master Francisco de Goya. A friend confided the secret to Goya, who went along with the joke and lavished praise on a Mary Magdalene supposedly painted by Pepita. One of the more sycophantic of Teresa's coterie immediately followed suit—only for Teresa to come along and indicate that he was in reality praising Mercedes' painting at the expense of Pepita's—much to his chagrin and the sisters' delight.

Mercedes barely had time to enjoy her newfound family when in the spring of 1805 Teresa decided to send Quico to Paris for his education. Her uncle O'Farrill was in Paris on his way back to Madrid from an ambassadorial posting in Berlin, the perfect opportunity for this decisive move. General O'Farrill committed to finding the best placement for Quico, whom Teresa would accompany to Paris before returning with the O'Farrills to Madrid. Mercedes and Pepita would stay behind in the capital with their great-aunt Manuela de Cárdenas, their grandmother's sister and the wife of General Pedro Mendinueta, former viceroy of Nueva Granada (Colombia). Quico was just ten years old then. He and Mercedes had but three brief years of shared family life. Mercedes retained her memories of a sweet young boy. Except for a brief time in 1812, they never again lived in the same country, let alone the same home.

Aunt Manuela was an eccentric lady who had married later in life and never had children. Suffering from debilitating migraines, she often could not move from her bed or her couch. Still, she loved to play cards, entertain friends, and gossip. She hated everything related to the French, and favored Mercedes for having been born in Manuela's adored city of Havana. Manuela surrounded herself with tropical souvenirs including various brightly plumed birds. She also had several servants from Cuba in her household, including her black chef, Francisco, and a young girl whom she doted upon. She and General Mendinueta adored Mercedes and Pepita as they enlivened the atmosphere with laughter and music. Their time in the house on the Calle de Hortaleza was enjoyable, briefly animated by a mild flirtation with the Marqués de Cerrano, their neighbor across the garden. He tried to lure the girls to the balcony each night by bribing a band of gypsies to stop by Mendinueta's gate. Flashing their smiles and dancing with tambourines and castanets, the gypsies entertained Mercedes and Pepita. At this point, any flirtation was lighthearted, and no real plans for marriages had yet been broached.

As Mercedes recorded, her mother often told friends that the greatest benefit of their wealth was the ability to allow her daughters to marry as they pleased.

Teresa returned home in June 1805, and the girls went back to live in the Calle de la Luna. Their mother had thoroughly enjoyed her Parisian stay; her letters had told a tale of a frenzied social life, and the fine French luxuries in her baggage reinforced her reputation for extravagant tastes. Her reputation lingered in the communal memory of Madrileños for many decades. Even in 1857, a popular novelist would weave into her stories a young and beautiful Cuban countess who lived so lavishly that she would send her linen back to Cuba to be laundered in the soft waters of the island, returning them to Madrid redolent of tropical scents. Teresa's spendthrift ways may not have reached those extremes, but she brought back enormous quantities of perfumes—some five thousand francs worth—from the most renowned Parisian perfumer, Monsieur Gervais-Chardin of the Cloche d'Argent on the Rue St. Martin. Mercedes recalled that her mother adored fragrances and filled her home with rare and exquisite scents like a temple. Along with the perfumes came all sorts of fashionable items as well as a special offering for the queen, María Luisa. In keeping with the queen's passion for fine French fashions as well as her childlike love of gifts, every courtier who traveled to Paris was expected to bring back something for her. One could only imagine her rage should a courtier return empty-handed, suffering a consequent blow to prestige and influence.

Teresa returned in the company of her uncle, General Gonzalo O'Farrill, and his adored wife, Ana, whom he called Anita. Mercedes finally met the legendary great-uncle, one of Mamita's many children, and the two families briefly shared a home until Ana left for the south to stay with her family. O'Farrill followed in October, continuing on with his wife to a new posting in Florence.

As Gonzalo O'Farrill arrived in Florence on February 10, 1806, an event occurred in Havana that would unite him and Mercedes in shared grief. The next mail from Havana brought word that Mamita had died on the eighth of February— "the best of mothers" in

O'Farrill's words. Mercedes' fevered imagination conjured up the scene: Mamita lying on her deathbed surrounded by most of her extended family, candles burning around the room, priests devoutly praying for her soul and the numerous household slaves lining up the stairs leading to the second floor gallery, crowding into the chamber's entrance.

Only one thing was missing in Mercedes' re-creation: her own presence, that last link in the familial chain. Mamita's death severed that link, the connection to Havana and to a free and loving childhood. Only one remaining bond connected her physically to her birthplace—her father.

Since his departure in the fall of 1802, Joaquín had not left Cuba nor made any known attempt to visit Spain. He continued to busy himself with his trading privileges, repeatedly renegotiated his debt to the Royal Treasury, and continued to cultivate his tobacco interests. Not all went his way, as the trading privileges were once more suspended with the outbreak of hostilities with Britain in 1805. By 1806 Joaquín had only repaid some sixty-eight thousand pesos of his government debt in tobacco powder. The debt had increased from nearly 550,000 pesos in 1802 to some 714,000 pesos. At that repayment rate, the treasury bureaucrats decried the number of years it would take to extinguish the liability. Still, with his court influence he was able to renegotiate his contracts three times between 1802 and 1806. He promised to put even more lands under cultivation and to provide the final houses and buildings for the new town of Nueva Paz in return for a more favorable repayment rate and the right to receive all of the Matanzas tobacco production for resale to the crown.

True to his nature, Joaquín had even grander plans in place. His new goal was to be made a Grande de España—a peer of the realm. A *grandeza* would place him above most noblemen—it was an honor added to a title, the supreme prize in the Spanish Empire. As usual, these honors came at a price. Joaquín offered to donate two hundred *caballerías* of land worth two hundred thousand pesos to the crown. He also promised to entail an additional four hundred thousand pesos for the benefit of his successors to the *grandeza*—two hundred thousand pesos in his lifetime and the final portion upon his death. In support of his claim, Joaquín provided an accounting of his properties and income showing over three million pesos of unentailed assets generating approximately 185,000 pesos annually. He also noted income from the entailed Jaruco estate—some 300,000 pesos in lands producing 19,350 pesos of income annually.

All seemed in hand, but proved to be an illusion when another letter arrived in Madrid in late May 1807 with shocking news: Joaquín was dead.

Mamita's passing had been emotional but perhaps not unexpected given her age. Joaquín was only thirty-seven years old, and as Mercedes wrote:

> we lost him in the flower of life, in the midst of a brilliantly fortunate career and bright future. Spoiled by his good star and by nature, he wished to live much in a short time and because of it he neither feared fate nor illness; he had always been happy, and nature had endowed him with a prodigious strength.

Mercedes felt that his restless nature and agitated lifestyle directly contributed to his death. His sudden illness, possibly a fever, had arisen shortly after a lightning trip into the interior—to an area Mercedes called a land of fire. Joaquín died of the unknown malady within days. Having so loved her father, Mercedes regretted the fate that had prevented her from caring for him in his final moments.

Mercedes and her family were not the only ones shocked by the news. The whole court was dumbfounded, from the king on down. In a royal order dated June 1807, the king expressed his surprise; he had not even known his valued official had been ill, let alone dying. As the news spread through Madrid, in Cuba the Spanish legal machinery had already begun its course, meaning the start of the *testamentaría*.

The *testamentaría* was the legal process of executing the deceased's will. In Cuba, it sometimes took years to resolve. Disagreements among the beneficiaries could occur, and warring heirs or creditors might take to the courts with their petitions. However, colonial Cuba had never seen anything like the *testamentaría* of Joaquín de Santa Cruz, Count de Jaruco y Mopox. It would go on for almost fourteen years, and its ramifications and ancillary litigation would still be running well into the 1840s, outlasting not only some of the heirs and executors but also entangling numerous members of the Santa Cruz, Cárdenas, Montalvo, O'Farrill, and Barreto families in confrontational positions. It would involve the Royal Treasury and two successive Spanish kings and would reflect the consequences of the Peninsular War. As with everything involving Joaquín, his *testamentaría* was anything but ordinary.

It began with the utmost confusion due to the unexpected nature of Joaquín's death. As the captain-general of Cuba was personally informed, no one could find a will. Joaquín died on April 5, 1807, and was buried the next day in the new Espada cemetery. His death certificate states that he died intestate. Within days, the 1789 will that Joaquín and Teresa had signed shortly before sailing for Spain emerged and was presented to the court. The multitude of interests involving Joaquín led to a bitter jurisdictional dispute between the military tribunal, the office of the captain-general, and the Royal Treasury. The Royal Treasury in particular—panicking at the thought of the 714,000-peso debt that Joaquín had recently renegotiated—began a campaign to wrest control of the process from the captain-general, namely the Marqués de Someruelos, and the military tribunal. The royal mail from Madrid to Havana brought seemingly daily missives filled with bombarding demands, petitions, and pleas. The newly appointed executor—the Marqués de Cárdenas de Monte-Hermoso (Joaquín's uncle Gabriel de Cárdenas)—fought to retain jurisdiction, urging that the tribunal appoint a representative or "protector" for the widow. He nominated Teresa's brother José Montalvo, Count de Casa-Montalvo. Perhaps Casa-Montalvo had a premonition of the nightmare to come. While accepting the appointment, he stressed the magnitude of his own business affairs and offered to serve only until Teresa could appoint another. Guardians were also appointed for the three surviving children—Mercedes, Pepita, and Quico—all under legal age. Eventually, in late summer, Teresa sent an updated will—one executed in the days before Joaquín sailed back to Cuba in 1796. In the middle of these political clashes, however, the tribunal heard rumors of a possible third will—one that Joaquín had desperately tried to sign at the time of his death, and that possibly contained several new clauses and "secret sealed letters."

Joaquín's uncle Monte-Hermoso, a highly respected Habanero known for his integrity, felt compelled to present to the court information about this unsigned will and the accompanying secret missives "so that at all times it could be known his final wishes especially those that related to the fifth [of his assets] for the unburdening of his [Joaquín's] conscience...." Monte-Hermoso later clarified that one of the clauses discussed two sealed letters to be delivered to two close friends, Joaquín's cousins the Count de Santa María de Loreto and Nicolás Peñalver y Cárdenas. The clause ordered Loreto to act in the strictest secrecy and to withhold opening the document until the conclusion of the estate valuation. Joaquín forbade his heirs and the tribunal to question the disposition of his fifth, and if anyone did dispute it, he then revoked the clause and gave the fifth outright to Loreto (who presumably knew what to do with the assets). Monte-Hermoso felt some obligation to explain these matters but absolutely refused to discuss publicly what so burdened Joaquín's conscience in his final moments.

Not only was this unsigned will a tantalizing mystery, but Joaquín's actual final moments seem to be taken from one of Mercedes' favorite romances. A related judicial petition contains startling witness statements recounting the events of his death and his frantic efforts to sign the will. The notary had been summoned urgently to write a new will that Joaquín dictated from his sickbed. Also summoned were eight friends and relatives to act as witnesses—as Joaquín seemed desperate to ensure the acceptance of his will by all as legally binding. The scene was dramatic: Joaquín propped up on his bed with the attending slaves, the close friends hovering in the next room, and the notary Dr. Ayala seated at a small writing desk by the bed as Joaquín dictated the final clause and waited for Ayala to read it back in order to confirm the bequests. After the additional clauses were written and approved, Joaquín intended to sign it, but at that moment his doctors arrived to administer treatments. Worried that Joaquín would become distressed, the doctors urged him to rest, and assured him that he could sign later that day.

Ten minutes later, at two in the afternoon, Joaquín was dead. The astonished Ayala was left with the unsigned sheaves of paper still in his hands. Knowing how desperately Joaquín had wanted to authorize this final will, his friends agreed to sign and seal it themselves, hoping that this action would give it some validity.

What lay hidden within the sealed letters that required such secrecy and caused Joaquín to preempt anyone questioning his instructions? It was a most intimate matter and it is in some ways a tribute to Joaquín that the matter weighed on his conscience. The sealed letters referred to two illegitimate daughters: Matilde María de los Dolores (Matilde) Valdés, born March 1804, and María de la Merced Sofía (Merced) Valdés, born March 1805. In the sealed missives, Joaquín tried to bequeath to them a coffee farm in order to ensure their future.

These two little girls, three and two years old at their father's death, had been passed through the foundling home, the Real Casa Cuna, as soon as they had been born—giving them a judicial if rather illusory legitimacy and a legal last name, Valdés, as all Casa Cuna children were named. There is so little known about Matilde and Merced, it is not even clear if they shared the same mother. They seem to have been fostered or cared for by different people, although their birth almost exactly a year apart is oddly coincidental. Matilde was placed in the care of Doña María de Jesús Montalvo, while Merced was placed by the Count de Santa María de Loreto in the newly established Convent of the Ursulines before her father's death. Because of Loreto's interest in little Merced, some information remains about her mother. With the estate entangled in litigation and pressed for cash, payments for boarding fees to the Ursulines stopped arriving in early 1808, and the mother superior personally pleaded to Loreto and to Captain-General Someruelos to intercede since the nuns could not afford to keep the girl. All three parties worried about Merced's future if she were returned to her mother, described by Loreto as "a prostituted woman, well known in your honor's tribunals for her excesses." Loreto pleaded movingly for this "defenseless" and "innocent" victim, adding that she had no one under the sun to plead for her, and that he felt compelled to act in memory of her father. Needless to say, he added that this plea could not move through the regular channels.

Joaquín had not expected to die. He left his affairs in such disorder that his estate was financially compromised, despite containing well-organized, diversified, and productive farms and plantations. Creditors feared they wouldn't be paid and demanded immediate repayment of all loans or the lands themselves that served as guaranties. The 2.1 million-peso value of the estate vastly exceeded the bulk of the estimated 1.3 million debt; yet the creditors pressed for liquidation. So enormous were the debts and so relentless the demands from creditors, including close family, that the executors took the difficult decision to close down Joaquín's household in order to reduce administrative costs. A detailed inventory was taken and for several days in August 1807, all the accoutrements of Joaquín's renowned hospitality were auctioned off—including his twenty-four personal slaves. The auctions were a citywide event that offered Havana residents the opportunity to glimpse the private life of one of its elite residents. The account of the auctions eventually made its way into Cuba's greatest antislavery novel, *Cecilia Valdés*, where the principal slave protagonists are former slaves of the Count de Jaruco, sold to pay the costs of the *testamentaría*.

The debacle clearly threatened the lifestyle and future prospects of Joaquín's family in Madrid. What was less apparent to most was the impact that Joaquín's entangled affairs would have on at least five persons whose very life and liberty now depended on the interpretation of Joaquín's intentions—and on the goodwill of his friends and family. Among the endless legal petitions were three poignant ones from slaves demanding their liberty: Luis Francés and Domingo Polo, two personal servants; African-born Genoveva *lucumí*,* whose freedom even Monte-Hermoso agreed was repayment for her "good and extraordinary services"; and Blas Montalvo and Tomás Santa Cruz, the two young men freed by Godoy and brought back to Havana, but without papers to prove it. All five relied on the right under Spanish law for slaves to be represented in court in matters dealing with their demands for freedom. Genoveva, Blas, and Tomás were fortunate in that they found high-ranking witnesses who testified publicly regarding their cases and faced little opposition from the executors. Blas and Tomás received their letters of freedom in 1812 while Genoveva, represented by Loreto and Ignacio Peñalver, received hers in 1813.

Luis and Domingo had worse luck, possibly due to an unfortunate set of circumstances. Their case hinged on the validation of Joaquín's unexecuted will and whether his expressed intentions sufficed for legal purposes. Two witnesses provided sworn statements supporting the two men, but the executors and Casa-Montalvo argued vigorously against the possibility that any part of the will could be valid. Luis and Domingo's public counsel argued eloquently that Joaquín's expressed wishes should be honored as a pious legacy since nothing was more detestable in law than the enslavement of men, and therefore there was no more worthy act than the gift of freedom. The executors, however, were unmoved by these sentiments. The value of two slaves, about one thousand pesos, would not resolve the estate's tangled finances, and it would have been easy enough to liberate these two faithful servants, but unstated was the underlying fear that acknowledging one clause in the third will could give validity to others. Implicit validity could then strengthen the argument for honoring Joaquín's last wishes regarding the fifth of his estate, possibly ending in the acknowledgment of Matilde and Merced Valdés as his daughters; reprehensible to the honor and finances

---

* African-born slaves were often identified by tribal affiliations—*lucumí, congo, arará*, etc. Once freed, they took their former owner's last name.

of the legal heirs. So Luis Francés and Domingo Polo returned under force to Casa-Montalvo, and nothing further was noted on their case.

Throughout the remainder of 1807 and the winter of 1808, creditors and claimants attacked the estate from every angle. While Monte-Hermoso and Casa-Montalvo held them off in Havana, Teresa used all her influence at court to stabilize the situation. She had some success at first. In June 1807, the king ordered that all of Joaquín's privileges and contractual obligations be passed on to his widow and heirs. The decree was crucial because the Royal Treasury had argued that the debt and tobacco agreement had terminated upon Joaquín's death; all the debt should be immediately payable. Carlos IV specifically expressed his royal wish that "neither the widow nor the heirs should be bothered nor any proceedings be made against the assets... things should continue in the same fashion as though the *Conde* still existed."

After this royal decree, the Royal Treasury accepted the existing contract and in 1808 accepted a lien on the majority of Joaquín's assets as a guaranty. To stop the financial drain from battling private creditors, Teresa managed to receive a further decree dated March 19, 1808, prohibiting any judicial recourse against the estate for six years. Teresa also managed to obtain the longed-for peerage for her son as well as for herself during her lifetime.

Joaquín's embattled family had seemingly obtained some breathing space. But the very date of this final decree is crucial, as it coincides with the Mutiny of Aranjuez, the fall of Godoy, and the abdication of Carlos IV in favor of his son, Fernando VII. Within two months, Napoleon managed one of the most audacious coups in history, held the Spanish royal family hostage in France, and bestowed the throne of Spain on his brother Joseph. The ensuing civil war, involving the Spanish army, the French army, and anti-French allied troops led by Arthur Wellesley, future Duke of Wellington, would last for five years.

8

TREASON, HATRED,
VENGEANCE

*D*uring the five years preceding Joaquín's death, Mercedes had left her childhood behind. By 1807, at the age of eighteen, Mercedes was no longer the self-described savage child newly arrived from Havana; she had transformed into a ravishing creature. Her natural beauty complemented careful nurturing under Teresa's watchful eye, and she now presented an exquisite figure in Madrid society. Even as early as 1804, Lady Holland called Mercedes "the most magnificent glowing beauty I ever beheld; the offspring of the sun." The Duchess d'Abrantès, who later knew Mercedes in Paris, remembered the image of the incomparable Teresa surrounded by her beautiful daughters, but significantly added that the graceful Mercedes was more charming than Pepita. Not surprising, then, that this glowing beauty should begin to attract attention as she and sixteen-year-old Pepita entered society. Casual admiration soon yielded more serious pursuit.

One man in particular, called only Quesada in Mercedes' memoirs, caused her great consternation. He was one of her mother's inner circle of admirers; he aspired to Teresa's hand after her widowhood.

The drama unfolded in Teresa's *tertulia*, where Quesada presented a cool detachment in public while secretly and obsessively pursuing Mercedes. Appalled, Mercedes was terrified that her mother would discover his duplicity and would then blame her daughter rather than her admirer. Finally her mother's longtime lady's maid, Isabel, guessing the truth, advised Mercedes to seek out Father Anselmo, their confessor. Father Anselmo showed a welcome worldliness for a priest, advising Mercedes to procure—by trickery if necessary—a note or letter from Quesada as incontrovertible proof of the duplicity. The ruse worked, and Mercedes finally dared to approach her mother. Teresa was shocked but expressed a reassuring trust in Mercedes' account. Subsequently, Teresa confronted Quesada in a private and emotional meeting.

Quesada continued attending Teresa's salon, but he never bothered Mercedes again. Teresa later explained that she had tolerated his presence to avoid any gossip. The crisis itself was resolved, although the lingering emotional impact must have been great. Overhearing the final scene so overwhelmed and drained Mercedes that she became hysterical and had to be sedated. It seems that while outwardly blossoming since her arrival in Spain, inwardly Mercedes remained an emotionally fragile creature, unsure of her place in this world or even the depth of her own mother's affection.

Mercedes' second romantic experience began around her nineteenth birthday, in February 1808. The young Count de Gálvez, a regular *tertulia* attendee, introduced Mercedes to the Marqués de Cerrano, a reputed libertine, who masterfully preyed on her naiveté. Gálvez told Mercedes that Cerrano had loved her for some time but feared rejection due to "perfidious influences" and his mediocre fortune. Mercedes was immediately sympathetic: "Cerrano's delicacy touched me; his timid tenderness inspired my gratitude and flattered me at the same time because I had difficulty believing that I was pretty." His fear of refusal for financial reasons further stirred all Mercedes' intuitive anger at perceived injustices, "the humiliating calculation of money where affections count—it is the shameful part of life. It destroys all that there is generous and elevated in the heart of man."

Cerrano finally asked Teresa for permission to marry Mercedes. Wary, Teresa told her daughter that while Cerrano's birth was honorable, he was not wealthy, his conduct was careless, and their characters were poorly matched. Despite these reservations, Teresa let Mercedes decide. Led by her passions, Mercedes ignored all arguments, suspecting the resentful Quesada of prejudicing her mother. Mercedes thought that any financial concerns could easily be overcome. Her self-described ardent nature, the will that she had always confused with the voice of destiny, the desire to right an injustice—all led to an instantaneous decision and an engagement.

But no sooner were they engaged than Cerrano's true character emerged: cold, jealous, and casually cruel. He sometimes ignored Mercedes for days. He arbitrarily forbade her to attend the Duchess de Osuna's ball (the duchess was the premier hostess in Madrid), not wishing her to be seen by the world. A disappointed Mercedes agreed, only to endure Cerrano's later visit, dressed in elegant evening attire, having himself just come from the Osuna ball. Despite her growing unhappiness, Mercedes seemed helpless to stop events, feeling a sense of resignation and fearful of disappointing her family. Teresa saw Mercedes helplessly crying one day, however, and addressed her daughter's despondency by breaking the engagement.

Around this time, the family happily learned that Gonzalo O'Farrill, his wife Ana, and her son Pedro were returning to Spain. The two families remained close, bound by the dual ties of kinship and affinity. The strong affection between Teresa and Ana also endured. Seeing Teresa in Paris in 1805, Ana had written that embracing her was so different from embracing other friends, for the others did not touch the heart.

General O'Farrill had gone to Florence in late 1805 to command the Spanish troops serving the young king of Etruria and his mother, the Spanish Infanta María Luisa.* The Treaty of Fontainebleau, signed in October 1807, eliminated the kingdom of Etruria, itself a Napoleonic invention of 1801, to placate the Italian Borbóns for the

---

* *Infanta/Infante* is the title used for the children of the Spanish king.

loss of the Grand Duchy of Parma. Napoleon casually played musical chairs with various European kingdoms and rulers; deciding to place Tuscany directly under France, he promised the young king a new kingdom in Portugal. That kingdom, approximately half of Portugal, unfortunately did not yet exist—a combined French and Spanish army had to conquer it first—so in the meantime the ex-king of Etruria and his mother would return to her homeland in Spain.

Escorting the ex-rulers, the O'Farrills arrived back in Madrid in February 1808 and once more accepted Teresa's hospitality. Teresa, far from her immediate family in Cuba, welcomed the thought of having her uncle nearby for advice. Sharing a home would also reduce some financial pressures from the uncertainty of her late husband's estate. Teresa was particularly accommodating, offering them the first floor, where the Santa Cruz family lived during the winter months. Teresa, Mercedes, and Pepita moved to the ground floor, where they normally spent the hotter summer months. The families could socialize easily together without stepping outside their own home, and their respective salons often overlapped.

By the time that the O'Farrills finally returned to Madrid that winter of 1808, the general and his wife had been away from Spain almost continuously since 1799, including his five years as the Spanish minister to Berlin. The cold climate of Berlin gravely affected Ana's health, but they had enjoyed an intimate relationship with the Prussian royal family, especially the Queen Mother. Ana's delicate health had also offered them the opportunity to take long sojourns away from icy Berlin to other parts of Europe. In their travels they made extensive and long-lasting friendships throughout the diplomatic communities in various countries. Foreign travel offered the opportunity for O'Farrill to satisfy his passion for military science and new technologies and allowed Ana all the cultural stimulation she craved.

Despite enjoying their time abroad, O'Farrill and his wife keenly felt the pain of separation from their respective loved ones. Additionally, they shared a concern that their foreign postings were in truth a quasi-exile from Madrid. When O'Farrill was secretly sent abroad in 1799, Anita immediately requested an audience with the Spanish queen, fearing that political intrigue drove the posting. Although the king and queen reassured her, the O'Farrills always suspected that malicious gossip and conspiracies lay behind various appointments. O'Farrill even speculated whether his Tuscan command arose from a "favorable election or because there was no motive to distance me [from Madrid] again without an honorable commission." They may not have been far from the truth. The king and queen had actually considered O'Farrill for the prestigious role of ambassador to France in 1799 but rejected him because, as María Luisa told Godoy, O'Farrill "is not a realist and has little affection for us, and even less for me, for I have information that if we put this person there...he could harm us....It would be better if he went to Prussia."

Lady Holland recalled that in 1804 O'Farrill was widely considered one of the best officers in the Spanish army, yet his perceived opposition to Godoy and his wife's "indiscretion and violent speeches in favor of Jacobism" caused him to be "out of favor at present."

Most commentators esteemed Gonzalo O'Farrill and considered him an honorable man; however, the same cannot be said for his adored wife. Even his bitterest enemies saved some of their most vicious vitriol for Ana, blaming her for almost all his later political choices. The public accusations and attacks were so well known that after her death, he published an extraordinarily moving seventy-five-page letter to his stepson, defending his beloved Anita and emphasizing the goodness of her heart. Ana's virtues were probably real, as her husband provides numerous examples of her public and private benevolence and devotion. Nevertheless, she was also described as a "very fat, very chattering person, who could not even remain silent whilst the Queen [of Etruria] was speaking to her husband [O'Farrill], but would keep interrupting the conversation, frequently causing the General to exclaim 'Be quiet! Be quiet! You shall talk afterwards.'" Based on her diary extracts, Ana admired the French Revolution at its beginning, believing that it would "lead mankind to a greater happiness." But she was certainly not a fan of the Terror and became disillusioned with Napoleon's rise as "ambition and deep scorn for men led him down the opposite path that sane reason and a love for humanity would have [led]."

The O'Farrills had been concerned for some time with the political situation in Spain due to "the clouds that covered the political horizon." They were not the only ones to worry. Since the Peace of Basel in 1795 had ended the Spanish war against the French Republic, the two countries had been locked in a series of alliances. The various treaties generally required Spain to support France in some fashion: troops, access through territory, naval assistance, or even cash compensation. Even worse, allying with France meant direct confrontation with England, hence the various outbreaks of hostilities from 1796 to 1807. By early 1808, Spain had lost its once great navy at Trafalgar as well as its territories of Trinidad and Louisiana. Its American income was significantly reduced due to English blockades, and approximately eighty-two thousand "friendly" French troops had invaded. Napoleon's brother-in-law Joachim Murat strategically placed the troops in some of Spain's most important military bases, including Barcelona and Valladolid.

Aggravating the political situation was the ongoing internal battle between the king and queen and their son and heir, Fernando, Prince of Asturias. Fernando loathed the royal favorite Godoy, the most powerful figure in Spain. Even today, controversy swirls around Godoy. Was he a competent albeit greedy individual dealing as best he could with an impossible political situation, or a complete fool who couldn't even distinguish between Prussia and Russia and slowly but surely led Spain into Napoleon's hands?

Court opposition to Godoy naturally drifted toward the young heir, Fernando. The bitter internal Borbón feud contained some bizarre psychological aspects, as Fernando truly believed that Godoy had usurped his rightful place in the family, while the queen displayed an almost rabid disaffection for her eldest son. Oddly, given that Napoleon was no friend of the Borbóns (he slowly threw them out of their Italian realms), both the royal couple and Fernando looked toward him for support.

Passion finally overtook reason in November 1807, when the king and queen accused Fernando publicly of plotting their downfall. Confined to his rooms and threatened with a trial, Fernando broke down and begged for pardon—implicitly admitting his guilt. His closest allies were tried and exiled. The public felt Fernando's humiliation, and their sympathy toward the young man fed their hatred of Godoy. Voicing their feelings at the first subsequent royal public appearance, the people greeted the king and queen with icy silence in contrast to their wild cheers for Fernando.

November 1807 also saw the main French army, led by General Junot (the Duchess d'Abrantès' husband), finally enter Lisbon after a horrendous march through difficult terrain (a prelude of things to come in the Peninsula). They found an abandoned capital. The previous day, the entire Portuguese royal family and a thousand courtiers and wealthy citizens had sailed under British escort to Brazil—along with the entire treasury, the national archives, and a third of the available currency.

Napoleon, worried about instability on his border, threatened to take Spain's eastern provinces, exchanging them for Portugal. His threat sparked alarm at court, galvanizing Godoy to recall Spanish troops in Portugal for a possible conflict. Lord Holland later wrote that "the palace was a scene of cabal, enmity, and conspiracy, and the two allied governments in a state of ill-disguised distrust and hostility."

Rumors flew around Madrid by early March, 1808. Was the royal family secretly planning to retreat toward Sevilla and then possibly onward to the Americas, following the example of the Portuguese rulers? The majority of the Madrid garrison was ordered to Aranjuez in a preparatory move. Courtiers and counselors alike begged Carlos IV not to abandon his kingdom. The people of Madrid felt restless, as did the guards units in Aranjuez. Fernando's supporters secretly agitated the people further—the Count de Montijo was seen in disguise arousing passions on the streets of Aranjuez.

Finally, an incident outside of Godoy's home on the evening of March 17 set off the crowd, which overpowered his guard and ransacked his luxurious residence. The crowd—by now a raging mob—searched in vain for the favorite. The next day, the king, greatly alarmed, exiled Godoy and stripped him of his highest posts. The measures failed to calm the mob, and the following day the commanders of the royal guards told Carlos IV that an even larger uprising was planned for the evening, and that their men would listen only to Fernando. But even as Fernando agreed to calm the troops, events slipped from any control as Godoy was discovered in his own ruined palace, having hidden in his attic. Desperate, he came out of hiding and was seized. The crowd would have torn him apart except for the guards, who managed to get him to their barracks. Hearing of Godoy's predicament, Carlos IV commanded Fernando to intervene. Upon their encounter, Godoy asked whether Fernando was now king. Fernando responded, "Not yet but later I shall be." That evening, March 19, Carlos IV abdicated in favor of his son, who became Fernando VII.

Meanwhile, in Madrid, word had started drifting back of the violent events in Aranjuez. The Madrid mob took to the streets on the same day and attacked the home of Godoy's brother Diego near the Paseo del Prado. Unable to find Diego Godoy, the infuriated mob—using paving stones to smash the windows, doors, and roof of the house—ran inside. They threw out everything they could find, burning it all in a bonfire. Everywhere the mob went, they cried "Long live the King!" and "Death to Godoy!" All through Madrid, the crowds attacked the homes of Godoy's family and cronies.

One of Teresa's military friends had come earlier to warn her of the royal family's plan to flee. However, he found the family facing its own crisis: General O'Farrill was gravely ill with pneumonia. Ana and Teresa took turns nursing O'Farrill night and day while the fever continued unabated. He finally started to recover around the time of the uprising. Late at night, Teresa asked Mercedes to look out the window to see what the commotion below was. Mercedes recounted seeing "[a] frenzied crowd, torches in hand heading for [their neighbor] General Branciforte's house...their faces, white with rage." Men and women mixed together to form this "horrible band." Another witness said the rioters looked like devils covered in soot and sweat from all the sacking and burning. The crowd still had some civility, however, because as this "infernal cortege" passed underneath, a voice was heard saying, "General O'Farrill is very ill, see here his house; silence, comrades!"

Prior to the events at Aranjuez, Napoleon had ordered Murat to march to Madrid, and he arrived with some twenty thousand troops on March 23. Fernando entered the next day and was received rapturously by the Madrileños, yet, ominously, Murat did not pay his respects at the palace that day. Fernando quickly formed a new government, naming the still convalescent O'Farrill as his minister of war on April 5, 1808.

Fernando still lacked the emperor's recognition, but Napoleon's envoy, General Savary, assured him that Napoleon was traveling to Madrid in order to resolve Franco-Spanish relations. He also encouraged the new king to make a gesture of friendship by traveling north to Burgos to greet the emperor. Fernando's counselors expressed unease over the king leaving Madrid, but Fernando agreed to make the journey. He rode out on April 10, leaving his uncle, the Infante Antonio, at the head of a Junta Suprema de Gobierno (Supreme Governing Council) that included Gonzalo O'Farrill.

No sooner had Fernando left than Murat imperiously demanded Godoy's transfer into French custody, even threatening to send troops and kill anyone in the way. The Junta refused repeatedly, until word came that Fernando had offered to send Godoy to Napoleon. Then, on April 16 Murat called General O'Farrill to a meeting and delivered a shocking blow: the emperor recognized only Carlos IV as king of Spain. The old monarch apparently decried his own abdication as illegally coerced, and Murat threatened to publish a proclamation to this effect. A stunned O'Farrill responded that no one would obey the proclamation. Murat replied that "the cannon and bayonets would make them obey." O'Farrill told Murat that neither option would work, adding that "if the Emperor wished to base his glory on seeing Spain reduced to ashes, then he could indifferently decide on either option."

Relations between Murat and the Junta remained tense for the remainder of the month as first the former Carlos IV and María Luisa traveled to Bayonne in France, and then word came that Fernando had also entered France to meet Napoleon. Finally, on April 30, 1808, the ex-queen of Etruria and the youngest *infante*, Francisco de Paula, were ordered to travel to Bayonne and join their parents. The Junta agreed that the ex-queen could do as she pleased but refused to send the prince. Madrid was now full of rumors that the final members of their royal family would be forcibly taken to France. The Madrileños, who had originally greeted the French as supporters of their new king, were by now seething with injured pride at Murat's arrogance. They gathered by the palace on the morning of May 2, ready to protect their last remaining prince.

The sight of Murat's aide arriving was enough to start the violence, and a passing French patrol responded. From there, the city appeared to explode, with shots ringing out and fighting flashing up in different quarters. French troops started pouring in from the outskirts, both cavalry and infantry. In the middle of the mayhem, Gonzalo O'Farrill and his ministerial colleague, Miguel de Azanza, tried to calm Madrileños in the surrounding streets. Eventually they returned to the palace, mounted horses from the Spanish Guards, and raced up to Murat's position to try to explain that this was no planned insurrection but rather a misunderstanding that could be quelled without creating a bloodbath. Murat agreed to let one of his generals ride with them to calm both sides. Along with some other Spanish and French officers and government officials, they distributed proclamations exhorting calm.

Mercedes recorded the sight of her great-uncle, still in his silk stockings and gold-buckled court shoes, riding through the street trying to calm passions. Where he could, he tried to save innocent victims. He managed to save one group of Catalan traders found with firearms. However, very little could be done. By the end of the day, some two hundred Spaniards were dead, several hundred wounded, and three hundred more executed during the night. This fateful day is forever remembered as the Dos de Mayo and commemorated in two Goya masterpieces, one of the fighting on May 2 and the other showing the executions in the early hours of May 3, 1808.

In the aftermath of the Dos de Mayo uprising, the Junta and all Madrid received the disheartening news that in Bayonne both Fernando and his father had abdicated the Spanish throne in favor of Napoleon. The events at Bayonne played out like a surreal drama. Once he had gathered the main players, Napoleon, far from recognizing Fernando, briskly informed him that the crown belonged to his father and that he must return it. Fernando resisted, and there followed demeaning scenes with parents screaming at their son and a nearly silent and besieged Fernando stubbornly holding out as long as he could. Finally, on May 6, the day after his father ceded the crown to Napoleon, Fernando signed the abdication decree. Another treaty, dated the tenth of May, established financial compensations for the various members of the ex-royal family.

Napoleon now had to decide on a new monarch, but in reality he had been considering one brother after another as a possible king since March 27, soon after he heard about Aranjuez. He had tried his brother Louis, king of Holland, in March, but Louis replied that he still felt some loyalty to his existing subjects. Jérôme Bonaparte also refused. Finally, Napoleon turned to his elder brother, Joseph, then king of Naples, and on the tenth of May ordered him to Bayonne. He noted that Spain was a much wealthier state than Naples and that it was critical to France given its common border. Napoleon also added that being in Madrid, Joseph would in effect be in France. Despite any discussion of independent kingdoms, in Napoleon's mind, all were subservient to the empire.

O'Farrill and the Junta, along with all Spanish government institutions and the *Grandes*, had to decide what to do with this fait accompli. They calculated that it would take a month to call up, at best, twenty thousand men. The French also held the major garrisons and fortresses in the North and in Cataluña. So not surprisingly, most complied with an imperial decree calling a Council of Notables in Bayonne on June 6, where Napoleon proclaimed Joseph king of Spain. The underlying hope was to avoid war and anarchy by salvaging from this debacle an independent kingdom, albeit allied to France. Ana recorded in her diary: "My O'Farrill was convinced that the country had insufficient means to resist, especially since with the disappearance of all royal persons, the country had lacked a center...without this unity, anarchy would follow due to the efforts of a misdirected patriotism."

But even as the news spread throughout the realm, uprisings began in various provinces. One by one, Valencia, Sevilla, Cádiz, Zaragoza, and other cities cut off communications with Madrid. Violent mobs killed any military governor, commander, or other official who even hesitated to declare against the French, in some cases dragging them through the streets. Across Spain, the French troops were forced to fight, laying siege to Zaragoza, deploying troops to subdue Andalucía, and defeating Spanish forces near Valladolid.

This was the kingdom that Joseph encountered when he entered his new capital on July 20, 1808. He was greeted by a subdued population and shuttered windows—a greater contrast to the jubilation that greeted Fernando two months prior could not be found. Joseph had appointed his ministers and confirmed most of Fernando's choices, including General O'Farrill.

Joseph's stay in Madrid did not last long, as disturbing news arrived around July 27 of the shocking capitulation of the French commander General Dupont's forces at the Battle of Bailén and the subsequent loss of twenty-four thousand men. Consequently, Joseph decided that the French forces should retreat northeast toward the city of Vitoria, just beyond the Ebro River and closer to the French border. By August 1, the French had abandoned Madrid.

The decision to evacuate created a stark choice for Joseph's new Spanish adherents: follow the new monarch and abandon their families and properties, or stay and face possible retribution. Joseph left them free to choose. The majority decided to stay, including most of the nobility, which had just sworn fealty to the new monarch and constitution at Bayonne. Gonzalo O'Farrill and the majority of the ministers followed Joseph. O'Farrill explained that the Spaniards took different paths based on their views of Bailén. Some considered it an isolated victory and still feared ultimate defeat and anarchy from war with France. Others, however, saw in the unexpected victory the patriotic wrath of a nation ready to expel an invader. O'Farrill chose appeasement, believing in Napoleon's invincibility as well as fearing the mindless anarchy experienced in other cities. Ana's diary records their fears "that the mob would remain in control of the city, and that this class, the most fearsome as well as the most unjust would judge the conduct of good men, [so] it was necessary to undertake a painful decision…the 30th of July 1808 will remain in my thoughts as one of the most ill-fated of my life."

Teresa and her daughters joined the O'Farrills on the road to Vitoria. Mercedes remembered her mother's fear of possible retaliations against any suspected adherents of the French, as it was widely known throughout Madrid that she shared a home with her uncle. As one of Teresa's servants later testified, everyone remembered the events of the evening of the nineteenth and morning of the twentieth of March and the attack on the neighboring Branciforte home.

The early hours of July 30, 1808, were scenes of upheaval at the Calle de la Luna, with trunks hurriedly packed, furniture secretly stored in other houses, and fine china, crystal, and other valuables locked in a garret. In the general confusion, Mercedes worried about her old spaniel, Jasmín, brought from Cuba and unable to accompany them. Mercedes finally left him with an old family pensioner.

Their coaches fled north through the city, where the coachmen reported that they met the French army and took on hired carriages, followed by a cartful of additional trunks and bedding. All sorts of other vehicles joined them, their occupants unsure of the duration of the exile. As Mercedes noted in the aftermath of Bayonne:

> So finished the first act of this horrible drama: treason, hatred, vengeance, nothing was missing…; no, I am wrong, there is missing… a foreign war, civil war, bloody, terrible war! There is missing…the ruin of the world's most beautiful country!

THE GOOD DEVILS

ercedes' temporary exile lasted four months, until Napoleon, furious with his brother, his generals, and the entire Spanish nation, swept in from France and overwhelmed the opposition. In the first days, traveling north from Madrid, Joseph's entourage stayed in whatever lodging they could find. Arriving at empty, abandoned houses, they would set up their camp beds, the young officers of General O'Farrill's staff sometimes sleeping on makeshift beds in one room. Other times they boarded with local families. It was a world away from anything Mercedes, her mother, and her sister had ever experienced. Only her uncle O'Farrill and Ana might have felt familiarity, for he had fought in hard campaigns from North Africa to the eastern Pyrenees, and she had accompanied him at times.

Arriving finally in Vitoria, they stayed on the main plaza. While normality was impossible, the family tried to maintain some aspects of their old life. Their little group consisted of the Santa Cruz and O'Farrill families, their cousins the Marqués de Casa-Calvo and his son, Ignacito Calvo, and O'Farrill's aides-de-camp. Mercedes and Pepita were young enough to be able to view the lighter side— giggling at the sight of one of the aides pitched from his horse into the Ebro River and still enjoying their love of dancing the fandango and seguidillas. A romance even blossomed between Pepita and Ana's son, Pedro. "The young people," wrote Ana, "maintain their gaiety even in these most painful circumstances and we all shared in it, at least they distracted us many times from our sorrows."

Mercedes recalled the lightheartedness of youth, unaware of their uncertain future, unlike their elders who felt the unrelenting tension. In the months of September and October they were placed on constant alert—under orders to evacuate the city at the first sound of battle. Nevertheless, Mercedes' insouciance was such that she would fall into a trouble-free sleep, trusting that her mother would hear any alarm and wake her up.

All around them in the northern provinces of Spain, fighting proceeded between the various French troops and Spanish forces in the region surrounding Bilbao. Both forces repeatedly took and relieved the city. Meanwhile, Napoleon organized over one hundred thousand reinforcements, personally arriving in Vitoria on November 6, 1808. His arrival proved electrifying for the French forces. Mercedes described the sense felt by everyone:

> The Emperor Napoleon arrived at Bayonne and, superb like an infuriated tiger, charged onto Spain. Immediately, the French armies were on the move and spilled out in all directions.

General O'Farrill later noted that it took Napoleon approximately three weeks to defeat the various Spanish armies and open a clear path to Madrid. "The sensation which he caused in the nation is impossible to depict to those who did not witness it." By early December, Napoleon and the French armies were at the gates of Madrid.

Once in Spain, Napoleon acted as both conqueror and ruler, shunting aside his brother Joseph and his concerns for the Spanish people. From Napoleon's perspective, Spain had rebelled, and he would now take the country by right of conquest, impose his rule, and show no regard for Spanish sensibilities. A frustrated Joseph told Ana that the fatal blindness of those that believed that Spain could shake off the yoke of France has condemned her, and they have made me a poor wretch: far from achieving their goal, they make the chains that they would have broken even more oppressive: they did not want a King dependent on the Emperor, now they will have him not only a slave to the Emperor but also to the marshals: they did not want a 100,000 person army for some time, now they will have one of 250,000 as a conquered land for much time.

As Napoleon advanced through Burgos, he issued proclamations condemning as traitors to "both Crowns" the various Spanish nobles who had rejected Joseph. The nobles faced arrest, execution, and forfeiture of their estates. Forfeited assets along with some church lands would become the basis for the so-called "national assets" sold to repay the expenses of the French treasury and fund Joseph's kingdom. Napoleon finally ordered his brother to leave Vitoria, and the entire convoy arrived in Burgos two days after the French victory on November 10. An appalling sight met them: deeply rutted roads showing the marks of the artillery trains led them through a plain still strewn with fallen soldiers, the accompanying stench of decomposition in the air.

Mercedes could only shut her eyes, hide her face on her knees, and cry. In particular, the sight of the sacked monastery of Las Huelgas, the graves ripped open, valuables stolen, and the remaining bones scattered about, and the despoiled Charterhouse of Miraflores shocked not only Mercedes but even seasoned officers. Once in the shattered city, the group had difficulty obtaining lodgings and food. General O'Farrill finally found them a house, and his young aides managed to buy some looted mutton, beef, and chickpeas from the French soldiers.

After defeating the Spaniards at Somosierra, Napoleon reached the outskirts of Madrid on December 2. Joseph, wishing to be part of any negotiations, joined his brother but was quickly sent off by Napoleon to the nearby royal palace of El Pardo. Napoleon wasted no time in demanding a general surrender. The remaining Spanish

military representatives (the ruling Junta Central had fled to Aranjuez initially and eventually continued to Sevilla) were stupefied—
equally terrified of Napoleon's wrath and the Madrileños' vengeance.
Napoleon threatened to destroy Madrid if it did not capitulate. By
December 5, the new French commander of the city, General Belliard, had entered with his troops.

Mercedes and her family returned to Madrid as soon as it capitu-
lated. On their arrival, they found empty streets and shuttered windows. Madrileños ignored even the great Napoleon as he entered the
city on his only visit, to see the famed palace. The Santa Cruz family
also found that, prior to Napoleon's victory, the Junta Central and
the Council of Castilla had moved against those Spaniards viewed
as traitors for supporting *el Rey Intruso* (the intruder king), especially his ministers. All had been declared traitors, their property and
assets subject to seizure. The local officials had acted against General
O'Farrill on August 20, going to the house he shared with Teresa on
the Calle de la Luna. His steward, Florencio González, an old servant of Teresa, had refused to say that his master had gone with the
French, repeating many times that Don Gonzalo had only left in fear
of reprisals against his family and property. González added that the
Countess de Jaruco and her daughters had also left at the same time
as the general, similarly fearing the mob but also planning to visit
the Countess de Torre Alta in the Basque border town of Fuenterra-
bía, to try to bring Quico home from Paris. Once the officials heard
this information, however, they quickly secured an order to seize
the Jaruco property both in Spain and in Cuba. Teresa had officially
joined the ranks of the Afrancesados, the followers of the French.

The officials had initially found a home stripped of most valuables, with sad remnants of the family scattered throughout—a silk-
and-lace-trimmed parasol in the girls' room, cooking utensils in the
kitchen. The officials finally found a hidden cache locked in a garret,
but in the spirit of the times, a useful informant quickly provided
details of mysterious furnishings stacked in the rented lodgings of
a young guards officer, a member of General O'Farrill's staff. Similar
events occurred in the home of their cousin, the Marqués de Casa-

Calvo, where an anonymous Cuban informer let the authorities know that Casa-Calvo's son, Ignacito Calvo de la Puerta, had his own two-hundred-thousand-peso inheritance in Cuba. The same informant told them that General O'Farrill co-owned a sugar mill with his brother, Ignacio O'Farrill. The Madrid authorities had moved to seize everything they could find and had started valuing the goods immediately. Joaquín's old secretary, Don Manuel Díaz Moreno, had argued that all the properties effectively belonged to Joaquín's estate, which was still not resolved. Don Manuel had even added that after Teresa retrieved her son, she intended either to return to Madrid or sail back to Cuba. To corroborate Teresa's defense he offered various witnesses, including Aunt Manuela and three servants. One final witness also staunchly stood by his longtime friend: Manuel Quintana, the celebrated poet, playwright, and civil servant. Quintana, a regular attendee at Teresa's *tertulia*, had stayed in Madrid and begun a patriotic newspaper, *El Semanario Patriótico* (the Patriotic Weekly). He would eventually make his way to Sevilla and later to Cádiz to continue his anti-French work. But in November 1808 he gallantly supported his old friend Teresa, agreeing that she had often stated her desire to bring back her son and return to Havana. He also swore that no French nationals had ever entered her salon.

Given the virulent attacks that would be published in newspapers like *El Semanario Patriótico* for the next five years against any Afrancesado, it is startling to read Quintana's sworn testimony. He would also later write how in the early days of the uprisings O'Farrill had asked him to work with the new regime to consolidate public opinion. Quintana's disillusionment was more profound since he had known and admired O'Farrill for over ten years, calling him a man who easily combined urbanity with the austere customs of a philosopher. Yet Quintana was still willing to support Teresa Montalvo, even though her story was flimsy at best. All over Spain, the political upheaval tested familial bonds and long-standing friendships, but old loyalties and compassion still lingered.

Mercedes and her family also found that the turmoil had affected the course of the litigation in Cuba. The Junta Central had issued a decree revoking the special grace halting all claims by creditors for six years. Attempts were made to seize Teresa's dower portions. Now representatives of the Royal Treasury as well as creditors, including Teresa's brother-in-law's father, the Marqués de San Felipe y Santiago, moved against the estate. Fortunately, Monte-Hermoso and Casa-Montalvo thwarted these attacks, explaining that the heirs were minors who could not be responsible for alliances with the French, and that the estate had not yet been divided. A final blow was the disruption in communication with Havana, as the mail had to cross the Atlantic, which the British heavily patrolled. Eventually, Madrid lost control of its colonies that remained loyal to Fernando. Any income from the embattled estates was effectively gone.

The family now found Madrid society dramatically changed, as many of the nobles and intellectuals had accompanied the Spanish forces or fled to the non-French-controlled areas, primarily Sevilla. The majority of Teresa's salon had dispersed, and Mercedes described the despair felt at losing the familiar routine. Even Manuela de Cárdenas suffered through the arrest of her husband, who had refused to swear loyalty to the new regime. Poor Aunt Manuela, with her lifelong hatred of the French, had a French officer billeted at her home. She found herself torn between her displeasure with the situation and her natural hospitality, calling the officer a good devil and wanting to ensure his comfort.

Slowly, some of their normal routine reemerged. Music and dance lessons recommenced, the sisters sometimes dressing up as *majas* (the typical Madrileñas depicted in Goya paintings) to dance the bolero. General O'Farrill's position ensured that they met and socialized with the generals based in Madrid and the other French officers who comprised much of Joseph's staff. French officers regularly attended evenings at General O'Farrill's home or Teresa's salon. General Bigarré, one of Joseph's aides-de-camp, recalled the social whirl, with Madame O'Farrill receiving several times a week and receptions by the French ladies. Not surprisingly, Mercedes was very popular with the officers, who were enchanted by her radiant beauty and her charming voice. Aunt Manuela's lodger, Monsieur

Lebarbier de Tinan, an amateur musician, begged his reluctant hostess to introduce him to Teresa so he could hear this voice others praised so much. A devotee of Handel and Mozart, he encouraged Mercedes to sing these composers' works for hours on end. Mercedes soon had a virtual coterie of passionate music lovers, including General Dessolles, who would come running as soon as she approached the piano. The future French foreign minister had an almost fatherly interest in her, but others seemingly combined the pleasures of music with romance. One officer in particular attracted the twenty-year-old Mercedes, holding her spellbound with his tales of the court of Constantinople and other far-off lands. He was General Horace Sébastiani, a Corsican like the Bonapartes, commander of the IV Corps fighting in Spain. Sébastiani, his troops garrisoning Madrid, attended the O'Farrill and Jaruco salons nightly, paying particular attention to Mercedes, even declaring his love. She in turn found him handsome, endowed with natural nobility, but still something unnerved her. Her friend General Dessolles confirmed her doubts, telling Mercedes that he would be unhappy to see Sébastiani win her affections, explaining that "Sébastiani is very much in love with you, but carried away by his feelings, he fails to appreciate the consequences. All his interests are in France; he is ambitious; the Emperor's will is all to him. A marriage on his part with a foreigner might not be approved by his master." Teresa, also concerned, told Mercedes to avoid Sébastiani, who she thought should have sought Napoleon's permission as well as hers before making his declarations. Mercedes, for once, heeded the advice, avoiding Sébastiani as best she could. Sébastiani must have understood, or perhaps Dessolles spoke with him, because nothing more occurred—and in any case, his troops would soon be fighting in the battles that dominated the summer of 1809.

Mercedes and her family were also becoming acquainted with the king and his new household. Joseph Bonaparte was a handsome, cultured man with appealing, almost seductive manners, who loved art, literature, poetry, and science. He genuinely wanted to improve the welfare of his subjects, and he hoped to introduce more liberal and efficient laws to his new country. His desire to rule an independent kingdom, albeit closely tied to his native France, soon proved difficult to achieve, with the majority of Spaniards rejecting his rule and his brother's increasingly aggressive policy. The Spaniards who worked closely with him, however, found him someone they could respect and esteem. The feelings were reciprocated as Joseph came to appreciate greatly the honorable and loyal O'Farrill, his favorite minister. Joseph told Mercedes many years later, after reading her description of her great-uncle in her memoirs: "General O'Farrill was just as you depicted him, the best of men…he was more than a Spanish patriot, more than a *chevalier* bound to his word, more than a friend. He was a sage wishing to obey all his duties."

General O'Farrill and some of the other ministers, such as Miguel de Azanza and his close military aides, regularly dined with Joseph, often joined by ladies including Ana and Teresa. The Spanish patriots attacked Joseph in their press, depicting him as an inept drunkard, but they overlooked what his courtiers well knew: Joseph, who loved all beautiful things, could not resist beautiful women. His aide-de-camp, General Bigarré, who followed him from Naples, as did most of his staff, admitted Joseph's "particular predilection" for women and his flirtations. Joseph revered his wife, Julie Clary, who stayed at their French estate, Mortefontaine, with their daughters, Charlotte and Zénaide, but reverence did not stop him from having numerous liaisons. He had children by one Italian mistress, and in Spain had a well-known relationship with the Marquesa de Montehermoso, the wife of one of his chamberlains. He had more passing affairs too, including a singer in a visiting Italian theater company. There have also been persistent, if unproven, rumors that he had a romantic attachment with Mercedes' mother, the youthful and alluring Dowager Countess de Jaruco.

As one would expect, Mercedes makes no mention of any liaison between her mother and Joseph. Nor is there mention of Teresa in any period documents, unlike la Montehermoso, who occasionally appears in the official correspondence of the French ambassador, the Count de La Forest. But beginning around 1853, in an article on old Madrid, the distinguished Spanish writer Ramón de Mesonero

Romanos, who himself met Mercedes, suggests a possible connection. By the time the same author wrote his often-quoted memoirs in 1880, the romance is clearly stated, no longer a vague allusion. Proving a liaison is impossible, but serious historians of the period, both French and Spanish, have regularly cited it as fact. The patriotic press also attacked Teresa as "dissolute, scandalous in the extreme." The story would resurrect time and again over the next 150 years in newspaper and magazine articles, some speculating on possible liaisons with Godoy in exchange for privileges (Godoy was known to favor petitions presented by pretty women). As late as 1956, in Havana, Teresa's descendants threatened litigation for the perceived insult to her good name. One can confirm only Joseph's intimacy with and affection for the entire Santa Cruz family. He wrote movingly to Mercedes in 1836 that he concurred with her loving portrayal of her beautiful mother, and that Teresa had left a lingering impression.

The newly established court life did not last long without interruption. That April of 1809, Wellington and additional British troops arrived in Portugal. The French army's progress stalled, and Joseph seemed unable to finish the conquest begun by his brother. Opposing forces finally fought at Talavera de la Reina, a town southwest of Madrid, on July 27 and 28. The battle, involving nearly one hundred thousand soldiers, ended in somewhat of a draw, with Wellington winning the field but in the end being forced to withdraw toward Portugal. Both sides claimed victory, and Wellington received the title Viscount Wellington of Talavera.

The population panicked over the lack of clear information from Talavera. Rumors spread that a Spanish force was marching on a defenseless Madrid. Fearing an uprising within the city, General Belliard herded all French and Afrancesado families into El Buen Retiro palace complex on July 30. Joseph's supervisor of the royal household, Miot de Melito, recalled the scene: "From early dawn, a long file of carts, wagons, men, women, and children, on foot and on horseback...crowded the road....In a short time, the limited space which served as shelter was full. Men, women and children, huddled together on all sides, vehicles and horses in hideous confusion, presented a terrible spectacle." Mercedes compared it to a herd of sheep trapped in a narrow pen.

The ghastly situation continued through the first of August, when the imminent threat disappeared. However, with the English still at Talavera and Joseph awaiting Marshal Soult's reinforcements, the king thought it safer for all those in his service to retreat to San Ildefonso, the royal palace in the Guadarrama Mountains outside Madrid. The convoy left at dawn on the fifth and stayed until after the French victory at Almonacid, returning to Madrid on August 13. Although uprooted for the third time in one year, Mercedes at least found the palace a true delight, offering some relief from the hot Madrid summer. It was full of gardens, fountains, and shady forested walks in the fresh mountain air.

The new regime obtained some respite from the retreat of the English and through Sébastiani's solid victory over the Spanish at Almonacid. Joseph and his generals returned to Madrid on August 15, a *Te Deum* was sung, and celebrations were held for the emperor's feast day. Court life resumed. Joseph decided that it was time to compensate those Spanish supporters who had lost properties following the flight to Vitoria. Using the funds established for these purposes, he gave generously to his ministers and officials. He offered Gonzalo O'Farrill four million reales, one of the largest grants, although the general only accepted two hundred thousand reales, instead asking that the grant be given to his niece, Teresa. So, in early September, Teresa received two million reales, and Mercedes and Pepita each received one million. Although Teresa had not lost any property, Joseph knew that both families were worried about the lack of funds from Cuba—especially after Napoleon had issued an edict in late 1808 that confiscated colonial produce arriving in Europe to avoid aiding the Junta. Joseph wrote to his brother on January 21 specifically asking for the edict's repeal, noting its effect on O'Farrill and his nieces. This concern became a moot point as O'Farrill's share in the Cuban sugar mill was sold in November 1809 and the Jaruco estate continued in disarray.

Mercedes recalled the strain felt by her mother who, accustomed to an opulent lifestyle, was ill-prepared to face the loss of her wealth. In contrast to Teresa's apprehension toward the future, Mercedes was blithely unconcerned. Her mother's habitual calm facade continued, but to Mercedes her mother seemed to view their reality as though it were a dream. Joseph's monetary gifts could not completely resolve their situation, since it was in the form of state bonds backed by the value of nationalized assets rather than cash. These bonds had a very low liquid value as they could only be used to purchase nationalized assets, commanding steep discounts if cashed.

At this time Mercedes' life took another unexpected yet decisive turn. Her mother approached her one day, telling her: "Mercedes, the king wishes you to marry." Mercedes was incredulous, more so when her mother went on to explain that the marriage would be with Joseph's newly appointed captain-general of the Royal Guard, Christophe-Antoine Merlin. Mercedes could only protest that she had never even met the man. After the Sébastiani interlude, Mercedes had thought that her mother did not wish her to marry a foreigner. Her mother quickly waived away these concerns, telling her daughter that she would meet the general that night at her uncle O'Farrill's home, and that as to his being a foreigner, General Merlin meant to stay in Spain. Teresa, however, did concede that Mercedes would not be forced into the marriage; she could meet him, and then they would discuss the matter.

While this marriage would appear to be completely unforeseen, in reality it or some other similar arrangement had been under consideration at least since January 1809. It appears to have been a favored plan of both Joseph and General O'Farrill. When Joseph had pleaded with his brother regarding colonial produce, he had added that one of the Jaruco girls would be marrying a French general. The French ambassador, Count de La Forest, also believed that this was the reason that Joseph had given the four million reales to Teresa and her daughters, in order to facilitate the marriage to General Merlin by compensating for the lack of an accessible dowry. Whether Teresa had been part of these discussions or whether she had just been convinced toward the end of the summer is not clear. Joseph at least had a known history for encouraging marital alliances or close ties within his inner circle—creating a familial air to his Spanish court. Thus, several aides were married to Clary relatives, General Jamin was the son-in-law of Miot de Melito, and General Franceschi was the son-in-law of Joseph's marshal of the palace.

O'Farrill's motives are less obvious. La Forest thought the reason was to help strengthen O'Farrill's influence with Joseph by having a close ally within the palace. La Forest commented in his reports that in addition to the marriage, O'Farrill maneuvered his cousin, Casa-Calvo, into the position of counselor of state. General O'Farrill's reasons for wishing to strengthen his influence over Joseph most likely stemmed from the desire to maintain Joseph's resolution to keep Spain an independent kingdom, undivided. From the perspectives of O'Farrill and his fellow ministers, this stance was critical if there was any hope of convincing the rest of Spain to accept the new regime.

The proposed bridegroom, Christophe-Antoine Merlin, was a thirty-eight-year-old cavalry officer at the height of his military career. Merlin was now a *général de division*—the highest rank in the French army (the title of marshal being a personal honor) as well as captain-general of the Royal Guard. Beginning his career as a mere twenty-year-old volunteer in 1791, he had benefitted from the enormous social changes arising from the French Revolution, which opened the higher echelons of the military to a meritocracy. Indeed, looking at the Merlin family—four brothers and one sister from a bourgeoise background in Thionville (Lorraine)—one could say that the Merlins had had a good revolution.

Three of the Merlin brothers achieved the rank of general, and the eldest, Antoine Merlin, known as Merlin de Thionville, was a celebrated member of all three revolutionary assemblies, instrumental in many phases of the Revolution. Merlin de Thionville was considered extremely radical, a Montagnard and an aggressive proponent of the execution of Louis XVI. In some circles he was considered a regicide, although he had actually been away on a government mission during the fatal vote. He also helped bring about the fall of

Robespierre in July 1794, served as commissioner to the armies, and was postmaster general. As he hated autocracies of all kinds, Merlin de Thionville retired from public life upon the rise of Napoleon.

Christophe-Antoine Merlin enjoyed a rapid rise, becoming a major within two years and enjoying praise as a "frank republican *sans culotte*," a radical revolutionary capable of following in his brother's footsteps. Moving between various army units, Merlin had even fought against the Spanish before the Peace of Basel in 1795—the same battles that Joaquín had financially supported and where O'Farrill had played a major role. By 1805 he was in Naples as a *général de brigade* in the army of Italy, and then as Joseph's aide-de-camp, commanding various divisions. A light cavalryman, he led his troops into several headlong charges against the enemy at Talavera and Almonacid, destroying an English brigade in the former and driving the Spanish troops into disarray at the latter. Brave but somewhat impetuous, he had made at least one questionable decision while in Spain, allowing his troops to pillage and sack Bilbao, an event criticized even by the French consul, although Joseph expressed private pleasure.

This scion of an ardent republican family was now an intimate part of the royal Spanish court. Joseph had recently conferred on him the Grand Band of the Royal Order of Spain, adding to Merlin's honors as commander of the Legion of Honor, and grand dignitary of the Royal Order of the Two Sicilies. In September 1809, Joseph also rewarded Merlin with two million reales, increasing his attractiveness as a marital catch. Little is really known about the man himself, although it is noteworthy that both the highly cultured Joseph and General O'Farrill esteemed him. In his 1836 letter, Joseph praised him, saying that he retained tender memories of Merlin, who was "always perfect" to him.

As expected, Mercedes spent the fateful day preoccupied. Although secretly fearful, she was willing to place her trust in her mother and meet this foreign stranger who could decide her entire future.

10

ADIOS, ESPAÑA

*M*ercedes met her future husband in the brilliance of an evening salon. She left a vivid description of the moment and her thoughts on Merlin, nearly twice her age:

> His exterior appeared to me cold and severe; he seemed more of a man of the North than the other Frenchmen...with their white skin and blue eyes; all of which, without displeasing me, overwhelmed me at first. As for the rest, Merlin was a handsome military man; he wore his favored hussar's uniform marvelously; he seemed to me simple and natural in his manners, even a little timid, doubtlessly due to his desire to please.

Merlin, by contrast, seems to have fallen immediately in love with Mercedes. He later admitted having been entranced upon first seeing her from afar in the ravaged garden of the monastery at Burgos. Whether it was his dashing uniform or his being passionately in love that convinced her, the arrangements went forward at a rapid pace as the groom pushed for a quick wedding. By October 21, 1809, the marriage contract was signed, noting that Joaquín's estate was still unsettled and promising to assign Mercedes' share as her dowry as soon as possible. Teresa gave Mercedes a trousseau worth 141,398 reales comprised of linens, dresses, and diamond and gold jewels. The contract further stipulated a "special contribution" of one million reales in state bonds. The couple obtained a dispensation waiving the normal banns, and the enthusiastic Merlin effectively pleaded on behalf of Pepita and Pedro, who also begged to be married. General O'Farrill and his wife approved the organization of a double marriage for the thirty-first of October, at the house on the Calle de la Luna. Joseph added a final gift to the sisters—each received a parure of diamonds, possibly the ones mentioned in the contract.

On the eve of their wedding day, Mercedes and Pepita went to church at San Ginés. Despite her dislike of cloistered life, Mercedes always found a sense of calmness in Catholic rituals. On the way back home they learned of the planned execution, the next day, of two young Spaniards who had deserted from the army. The contrast between her own joyful plans and her countrymen's dire fate weighed on Mercedes' conscience—much in the way that the slave's cries had moved her to beg leniency from her father so many years before. Sensitive to any bad omens, Mercedes spent a restless night. The next day, while Mercedes and Pepita were at their toilette, they heard commotions outside—the cries of *"Viva el Rey!"* rang out from street to street. The reason for the tumult was soon clear as a group of women arrived at the house to thank Mercedes. Friends and relatives of the condemned thronged the entrance, offering boundless gratitude— General Merlin and General O'Farrill had procured a reprieve for the two young Spaniards just minutes before they faced the firing squad. Joseph had given the Jaruco girls one final wedding gift.

At 3:00 PM that afternoon, Mercedes and Pepita, both wearing their gold and diamond diadems, were married in their home under the auspices of the king, with Merlin also receiving approval from the emperor. The respective witnesses reflect the Santa Cruz family's position at the heart of the new regime: Mercedes' witnesses were two of Joseph's aides-de-camp—Général de Division Lucotte and the Count de San Anastasio—while Pepita's were two government ministers, José Mazarredo and Miguel José de Azanza.

Mercedes offered no additional details regarding her marriage, not particularly unusual for the era. Her memoirs already included more personal sentiments than most. Any honeymoon period proved short lived, as Merlin left his bride to go fight at the Battle of Ocaña on November 17. Luckily for the newlyweds, the French won a decisive victory and Ocaña granted the new regime two months of relative tranquility. During that time the quasi-arranged marriage turned into a veritable love match. Mercedes and her ardent heart seemed more than ready to be swept away; the combination of spirited military style, dangerous times, and the chance to please all those close to her proved to be a powerful combination. Above all, having someone like Merlin so in love with her, so willing to surround her with care and comfort, must have influenced Mercedes' feelings. Possibly Merlin's age in some ways too was an advantage. The twenty-year-old bride, who had so adored and abruptly lost her doting father, might have secretly been happy with the stability that Merlin provided. Indeed, Joaquín at his death had been one year younger than Merlin.

The proof of the love match lies in Mercedes' letters to her husband written during Joseph's 1810 Andalusian campaign. The king and his army, including Merlin, General O'Farrill, and Pedro, set off on January 8 to conquer the southern part of Spain. For once, Joseph succeeded in his military endeavors, sweeping through the cities of Córdoba, Granada, and Sevilla—forcing the Junta to flee to Cádiz, which stubbornly resisted his armies. Joseph and his troops only returned to Madrid in May 14, 1810, and during those four months Mercedes wrote to her husband nearly every day. Her passionate nature fairly flies off the pages as she bombarded her new husband from the moment he rode away—acknowledging ruefully that six letters at once might be too much even for a young wife. Longing for her love, she described the sadness tingeing her eyes in the portrait she sent him painted by Guillermo Ducker, the fashionable miniaturist recommended by Goya. Her heart envisaged rivals in the legendary Andalusian women surrounding Merlin, while he could not tolerate any man suspected of gallantry toward his bride.

She laughed these thoughts off but then confessed that she would like him to maintain a reputation for jealousy.

In the first letters she hinted at a possible pregnancy, but then lamented she was not with child. Mercedes feared disappointing Merlin, and assured him of her conviction that she would conceive soon upon his return. The naive girl even ventured into slightly piquant comments as she expressed her ardor, sending her beloved violets that had been pressed to her breast and urging him to kiss the red wax seal so that he could feel her lips. Merlin showered her in Parisian luxuries—six dozen pairs of gloves, five dozen pairs of shoes, court gowns, plumes, lace, and even negligées. Still Mercedes, while adoring these gifts coquettishly, insisted they could not distract from her sorrows. She constantly pleaded for permission to join him as her aunt O'Farrill and her sister Pepita went out to join their respective husbands and to visit her aunt's family in Sevilla. Mercedes could not bear to write to them, so envious was she of their proximity.

Her first letter set the tone for the remainder:

> I repeat, my dear Merlin, all the opportunities are not sufficient to demonstrate how ardent my love—how vivid and profound are my sentiments.... Towards you are all my thoughts directed. Without you, Mercedes conceives neither happiness nor even existence itself.... Adieu, my dear Merlin, only enchantment of my life. Receive a thousand kisses from your Mercedes.

While Joseph enjoyed the popular acclamation of the Andalusian people, an unexpected political blow arrived from Paris. Through a proclamation dated February 8, 1810, Napoleon ordered the Spanish provinces under French army control to be governed directly by the French commanders reporting to Paris. Not only would Joseph lose politically, he would also lose desperately needed tax revenues, leaving him ruling a nearly bankrupt rump state. This de facto dismemberment of Spain represented a betrayal to all the Spaniards who had supported the new regime as the only way to save the country. A disconcerted Mercedes wrote to Merlin, "What will happen if the people sense that Joseph's authority is relative, fictitious, that it is not dependent on him to maintain promises, that a single caprice of Napoleon's can destroy in one moment the admirable work that Joseph has been developing!"

Joseph resisted the measure. Using the excuse of his brother's recent marriage to Marie Louise of Austria, he sent Miguel de Azanza as his personal emissary to Paris. After two more cities were also taken away, Joseph sent yet another emissary, carrying a strongly worded letter threatening abdication unless Napoleon withdrew the measures. He also accused the French generals of abusing their positions for financial gain. In turn, Napoleon complained about the heavy costs of maintaining the French troops in Spain, insisting that Joseph's government had to cover costs, and chastising Joseph for his largesse to his courtiers given the state of his finances. La Forest continually lamented the infernal influence of the men surrounding Joseph—especially O'Farrill—who continued to argue for the independence of Spain regardless of the emperor's needs.

These demoralizing developments led to government paralysis. Joseph spent more time at Casa de Campo, a sprawling retreat just outside Madrid. La Forest complained of long afternoons and evenings spent only in the company of his close allies—O'Farrill, Melito, Merlin, and their respective wives and other guests. And even among this intimate circle, disputes and jealousies arose, as Monsieur Melito and General Merlin detested each other.

What was a difficult time for the government was, conversely, a happy time for Mercedes. She called this the most beautiful period of her life. While Merlin was away, they had bought two properties from the nationalized estates using some of their bonds: the sumptuous town palace of the Dukes de Osuna for ninety-nine thousand reales, and the Villaviciosa estate with its handsome income. Merlin already owned the nearby Boadilla estate, which, like Villaviciosa, had belonged to Manuel Godoy's wife.

Mercedes now lived in her new home—the Osuna palace—with her husband safely back from the campaign. Completely in love, she wished to please her husband in all things. Although she said they led a retired life, Mercedes followed in her mother's footsteps and started hosting musical evenings much appreciated by aficionados. Despite her sociability, General Merlin maintained his reputation as a jealous and suspicious husband—perhaps too much in love with his young wife and capable of losing his head. Merlin's vigilance doubled whenever they visited the palace. Mercedes wrote, "It used to be said that the king was very flirtatious, and when we spoke I gaily told my husband: don't worry, if I were ever so unfortunate as to forget my duty, it is not those merits of the king that you should fear." Still, one day in Casa de Campo, Mercedes lost patience with her husband's excessive care. Having fallen behind with Joseph while strolling through the grounds after an outing, Mercedes suddenly heard her husband fiercely telling her "you would do well to walk faster and rejoin the ladies." Joseph delicately smoothed over the embarrassing situation by assuring Mercedes to "walk at your own pace—I am in no hurry." Once home, Mercedes complained bitterly, but Merlin merely told her that the words were meant for the king, because protocol prevented him speaking more directly.

Perhaps Merlin knew Joseph better than Mercedes. Several days later, Joseph lightly asked General Merlin what he would do if a king courted his wife. Merlin answered simply: I would kill him. Joseph laughed it off, saying, "That Merlin is inflexible—he doesn't understand a joke." Years later, Joseph claimed no memory of this conversation, but he did acknowledge admiring Mercedes, as had "all who had ever seen you even for one instant."

When the emissaries returned from Paris in early December of 1810, they offered only the vague hope that France would honor Spain's integrity if Joseph could obtain recognition for himself and the 1808 Bayonne constitution from the opposition. In return, Joseph could acknowledge the *Cortes* as a legitimate assembly, but otherwise, the emperor would do as he wished. Once again, Joseph was undecided. The various active French campaigns achieved varying success throughout the remainder of 1810 and early 1811. Marshal Masséna's Portuguese campaign foundered, while Marshal Suchet met with success in Cataluña. Neither directly involved Joseph, who, frustrated, determined to travel to France, possibly to renounce the crown. Plans changed when word reached him in April 1811 of the birth of Napoleon's son, along with an invitation for Joseph to be one of the godparents. Joseph left for Paris in late April, taking along several ministers including General O'Farrill. He was ever hopeful of a rapprochement with Napoleon.

Unfortunately, Joseph returned to Madrid in July 1811 having achieved very little. By this point, Marshal Marmont had replaced the defeated Masséna, and the army of Portugal was now based around Salamanca. Nearly two hundred thousand French troops still remained in Spain, although Joseph controlled only about fifteen thousand, mainly his Royal Guard, a combination of French officers and soldiers as well as some Spanish regiments. With almost the entire government owed months of wages and Joseph's troops barely paid, morale remained very low. It dropped further still in response to an imperial decree dated August 26, 1811, outlining the loss of French citizenship and rights to those soldiers and officers serving "foreign powers" as well as those receiving titles. Panic gripped the Royal Guard as everyone, including General Merlin and Joseph, sought clarification. Joseph feared that he would lose the two thousand Frenchmen in his guard, and told Marshal Berthier, Napoleon's chief of staff, that Spain should be exempt from the decree. General Merlin's actions did not help tensions in the guard: On September 20, La Forest reported that an officer of the Royal Guard had deserted, taking with him some ammunition. Rumors at the time characterized the desertion as revenge for perceived unfair treatment by his commanding officer—General Merlin had displayed hostility toward the young man because he suspected him of excessive gallantry toward Mercedes.

In addition to these grave political and financial concerns, Madrid faced another crisis as an earlier shortage of bread turned into outright famine in the city. Between French troops absorbing resources and the opposition guerrilla bands stopping food convoys arriving from Andalucía, Madrid had very little wheat for bread. Costs soared. The situation was so dire that even the French soldiers were moved to provide charity. Ana Rodríguez de Carassa, long a member of the Junta de Honor y Mérito de Damas, a prestigious women's charitable commission, dedicated herself particularly to the task of ensuring the survival of the children in Madrid's orphanage La Inclusa. She interceded with Joseph for financial help, and convinced her husband to divert some army rations for the orphans. She also recruited new patrons as many had fled from Madrid. Mercedes joined in 1811, experiencing for the first time charitable work on a public scale—and in dire circumstances.

In addition to these profound national problems, Mercedes' family faced more personal worries. Word reached Teresa that Joaquín's half-brother, José Francisco Barreto y Cárdenas, Count de Casa-Barreto, had petitioned the *Cortes* in Cádiz to grant him the title of Count de Santa Cruz de Mopox—claiming that Joaquín's son and heir was either a traitor to Spain or dead. Acting aggressively, Casa-Barreto sent his son to present the petition in person. By September 1811, Casa-Barreto had possession of the title and also claimed the lands that Joaquín had sought to entail. Back in Cuba, the loyal Monte-Hermoso fought the usurpation as best he could, although he was in a delicate situation, as Casa-Barreto was also his nephew. While Casa-Barreto questioned his uncle's administration of the lands, Monte-Hermoso told the courts that as Joaquín had never actually created the entail, the disputed lands were still part of the estate—and Casa-Barreto had no right to them. But there seemed little that anyone could do from Cuba, especially with Teresa unable to present any form of defense given the political circumstances.

Teresa had for some time been trying to organize Quico's return from Paris to Madrid. At last, in early 1812—much to his mother's joy—the seventeen-year-old arrived. Despite the problems with the estate, Teresa and General O'Farrill still had some hopes that Quico would finish his education in Madrid or join either the army or council of state. However, as Joseph would later explain to Mercedes, it was he who actually decided Quico's fate: "Monsieur O'Farrill brought him to the palace; I judged it in his interest to return to Havana via Cádiz, to take possession of his great estates." Joseph even argued with Quico, Teresa, and O'Farrill until all regretfully agreed to the plan.

Quico made the dangerous journey from Madrid to patriot-controlled Cádiz, facing the constant threat of being mistaken for a Frenchman by the guerrillas. Arriving in Cádiz, he found that many of Teresa's old friends remembered him and offered assistance. The complexities and inconsistencies of war-torn Spain were endless: a young man, speaking Spanish with a French accent, sent on his way with the blessing of the hated *Rey Intruso*, could find a warm reception in the heart of the anti-French resistance because of long-standing ties.

The emotional impact of separating again from her youngest child was too much for Teresa. Her health collapsed. Mercedes, at last pregnant with her first child, found herself nursing her mother. Teresa now lived in the rented lower floor of the O'Farrill's new home on the Calle de la Cruzada, near the palace, but Mercedes judged it an unhealthy, damp place. In her own home, she had a room redecorated for Teresa, containing images of her long-ago Cuban childhood. There were majestic palm trees, fruit-laden papaya trees, and brilliantly plumed hummingbirds—a world that Teresa had not seen for some twenty-three years. The doctor ordered fresh air, but as Teresa was too weak to walk, General Merlin carried her daily in his arms to a waiting carriage. Mercedes barely left her side, but all was in vain. Teresa never recovered, dying April 17, 1812, aged only forty.

Teresa's requiem mass was held at the partially rebuilt church of Santiago, one of the many churches Joseph had razed, rebuilt, or relocated in his quest to transform the cityscape of Madrid. She was buried in the newly opened cemetery to the north of the city beyond the Fuencarral gate—another innovation to stop burials in convents and churches. But a strange story developed over time regarding her final resting place. According to the Spanish chronicler Mesonero Romanos, shortly after burial, her coffin was disinterred and taken to the garden of her house, then buried under a particular tree. The reburial was ordered by Joseph himself since he had often met Teresa under that very tree—at least according to the legend. Mesonero Romanos gives his source as a friend of Teresa's, although he also identifies her house as Calle del Clavel, an address never associated with Teresa, neither in documents nor in Mercedes' memoirs. The romantic story has persisted nevertheless, with the ghostly anecdote still found in numerous books describing the streets and houses of Old Madrid.

Exactly two months after the Countess de Jaruco's death, Mercedes gave birth to a daughter, María de las Mercedes Josefa Teresa Ana Manuela Merlin, known always as Teresa. On July 20, 1812, they baptized her at Santa María la Real de la Almudena, the court's parish church, with Gonzalo O'Farrill as her godfather. Mercedes experienced a difficult birth that threatened the life of both mother and child for several days. In the aftermath, weakened by the delivery and fraught with nervousness, Mercedes found that she could not feed her child. The family employed a wet nurse, not an unusual arrangement at the time, yet one that caused Mercedes further anguish.

While Mercedes and her family experienced their personal grief, French forces suffered various serious reverses. In January 1812, the English took Ciudad Rodrigo in a particularly brutal siege that placed them at the edge of Castilla. Then in April, they took Badajoz in one of the bloodiest fights of the peninsula. Wellington now had the chance to attack the army of Portugal. From June onward, both armies spent several weeks shadowing each other near Salamanca, but Marmont needed reinforcements to ensure a decisive victory against Wellington.

Joseph, now technically in command of all the French troops in the peninsula since Napoleon's departure for Russia, twice sent an emissary to Marshal Soult and the army of the Midi for assistance. Soult categorically refused, as did Suchet in Valencia. Ultimately, on July 21, Joseph decided to go himself with his small Army of the Center and his guard. Communication between all the forces was difficult, as couriers were routinely stopped. General Merlin and General O'Farrill accompanied the king, leaving Mercedes to worry in Madrid with her newborn daughter. By chance, guerrillas captured one of her letters along with official missives and turned them over to British intelligence. In the note, Mercedes expressed all the fears of a military wife whose husband was fighting: "I fear so many things which perhaps pass beyond common sense but which torment me. I don't sleep any more and my only pleasure is to watch my daughter....If only she could understand and console me!"

Joseph never reached Marmont. On July 24, a local man told them of a battle at Arapiles (near Salamanca) where the Allies had defeated the French—two days earlier. Joseph was shocked, unable to understand why Marmont had not waited. After confirming the fact, Joseph decided to return to Madrid, concerned that Wellington could now reach the capital. Joseph arrived on August 1, maintaining an appearance of calm. But on August 8, news reached him that Wellington's advance guard had passed the Guadarrama. The next day, Joseph ordered the evacuation of Madrid.

Confusion reigned as everyone had just a single day to organize their affairs. The resulting convoy encompassed nearly twenty thousand civilians. According to General Hugo, father of the writer Victor Hugo, the evacuation resembled an enormous migration: men, women, and children "on foot, on horseback, on donkeys, on mules, all ages, all ranks." The king and his army and guard of eighteen thousand would also leave, in a parallel march to protect the evacuees. They would retreat toward Valencia, over two hundred miles away on the Mediterranean coast, crossing the arid plateau of La Mancha in the intense heat of the summer.

Mercedes found out about the evacuation while driving along the fashionable Paseo del Prado. She rushed back home and began trying to organize their belongings amid the chaos dominating her household. Few of the servants wished to follow the French, but Mercedes' main concern was for her maid and her baby's wet nurse. Her personal maid, Casimira, was devoted to Mercedes, having served in Teresa's household since Mercedes' arrival. But Casimira's mother begged her not to leave, thinking she would be killed. Another, older, maid, Juliana, eventually volunteered. The wet nurse, an Asturian girl called Ama Pepa,* belatedly agreed to accompany them after Mercedes offered to hire the nurse's wastrel husband.

---

* Wet nurses were called *Ama*—followed by their first name.

The civilian convoy met Joseph and the army near Ocaña. From then on they marched in parallel. Although fairly safe from Wellington's troops, which took Madrid, they remained at the mercy of the severe daytime heat and dust, as well as acute shortages of food and water. Mercedes obsessed about Ama Pepa's needs so she could properly nurse little Teresa. General Merlin would ride nightly from the king's encampment, often bringing whatever food or water he obtained. At Villatobas they found the wells spoiled, either by guerrillas or the locals. Sometimes the water they bought was bad. As the evacuees passed near the fortress of Chinchilla, its Spanish garrison fired on them, forcing the caravan to take a more circuitous route. At Corral de Almaguer, the young Duchess de Cotadilla gave birth in her carriage.

Both the civilian convoy and the army arrived in Valencia on August 31, after twenty-one days on the road. All known accounts would later recall the relief they felt when they entered the fertile region of Valencia, bordering the Mediterranean Sea. From the high, arid terrain of interior Spain they passed into a flowering garden. In the city of Valencia, the archbishop, other clergy, and civic officials, in addition to Marshal Suchet himself, greeted them with full honors. Nevertheless, Joseph quickly realized he and his court were mere refugees. Given the trying circumstances, a decision was made that after a short rest, all the wives and families of the French officers and officials would be sent to France, across the Pyrenees. There would be no exceptions—Mercedes and her baby Teresa would leave Spain. Her sister Pepita and her aunt O´Farrill would stay, along with their husbands and General Merlin.

Difficult as the separation from all her family would be, Mercedes had to face yet another crisis. Ama Pepa, the baby's nurse, refused to travel to France without her husband. The thought of how to feed her daughter consumed her. It was an enormous relief when Ama Pepa inexplicably relented. A happier surprise occurred before they left Valencia, when Casimira unexpectedly arrived from Madrid, along with several chests of Mercedes' belongings. Defying her family, some of whom were ardent patriots, Casimira had made the dangerous journey and now agreed to go to France.

The convoy of French families left Valencia on September 10, escorted by numerous troops. General Merlin chose twenty-five guardsmen under the command of one of his aides, Captain Depuis, and commissioned them specially to guard his wife and child. Additional protection was not an exaggerated gesture. For some time, numerous guerrilla bands had been attacking heavily defended French transports—almost with impunity. The fate of one particular convoy lingered on everyone's mind. On April 9, a large and strongly protected convoy traveling to France via Vitoria fell under attack. Among the dead was Jean Deslandes, Joseph's personal secretary, killed protecting his pregnant wife, who was captured and kept hostage for some time. General Thiébault recalled seeing Madame Deslandes, the daughter of Miguel de Azanza, about to give birth, lacking all essentials, and alone in Vitoria. He managed to loan her some money when she was at long last allowed to travel on to France. Merlin did not want his own young Spanish bride to share a similar fate.

Mercedes traveled in her coach as the caravan moved north along the sea and then turned inland toward Aragón. When they reached the rugged Pyrenees, they were forced to use mules. Mercedes, upset at the thought of exile and still somewhat weak from the aftermath of childbirth and the flight from Madrid, became ill with fever. Because she refused to get on a mule, the increasingly desperate Captain Depuis searched incessantly for a sedan chair. Even after he found one, accidents continued to arise, including the loss of three of Mercedes' baggage mules during the crossing. At length, the group arrived at Urdos, the first village on the French side.

Mercedes had left behind Spain, Cuba, and everything she had ever known. Ahead lay her new, "beautiful adopted homeland." Bravely she would embrace it, ultimately feeling the warmth of its hospitality, flourishing to the point that she would "believe myself under the Havana sun."

PART III

France

Family portrait of Teresa, Joaquín, Manuel, and Manuel's slave nurse, Agueda.

Havana's Plaza de la Catedral. All day long the different people of the city would pass by—merchants, artisans, soldiers, slave traders, aristocrats, and slaves.

Manuel Godoy, Prince de la Paz, as depicted by Goya.

☞ Manuel Godoy (1767–1851) Duke of Alcudia, "Prince of Peace," 1801 (oil on canvas) (detail), Goya y Lucientes, Francisco José de (1746–1828)/ Real Academia de Bellas Artes de San Fernando, Madrid, Spain/The Bridgeman Art Library

Teresa Montalvo and her daughter, Mercedes.

☞ Detail from Carteles/Courtesy of the Cuban Heritage Collection, University of Miami Libraries, Coral Gables, Florida

Gonzalo O'Farrill. Joseph Bonaparte considered him the best of men.

☞ Detail from Nobiliario Cubano/Courtesy of the Cuban Heritage Collection, University of Miami Libraries, Coral Gables, Florida

LEFT: Joseph Bonaparte, the "intruder king" of Napoleonic Spain.

☞ Portrait of Joseph Bonaparte (1768–1844) King of Spain, 1808 (oil on canvas), Wicar, Jean Baptiste Joseph (1762–1834)/Château de Versailles, France/Giraudon/The Bridgeman Art Library

RIGHT: Christophe-Antoine Merlin.

☞ Domingo Figarola Caneda, *La Condesa de Merlin*

Battle of Bailén as depicted in a patriotic 1808 edition of *Diario de Madrid*. The shocking French defeat led to Mercedes' first exile. ☞ Courtesy of The London Library

Mercedes, La Belle Créole.

☞ Courtesy of Jacques Mercier du Paty de Clam

Mercedes as Bellini's *Norma*, wearing the
costume belonging to her friend the diva
Giulia Grisi. ☞ Courtesy Jacques Mercier du Paty de Clam

Salons were at the heart of elegant Parisian society during the July Monarchy—
and Mercedes organized them beautifully.

☞ *A Family in an Interior*, 1842 (color litho), Lami, Eugene-Louis (1800–90) (after)/Private Collection/Archives Charmet/The Bridgeman Art Library

Programme.

1re Partie.   2me Partie.

LEFT: Concert program from one of Mercedes' celebrated musical evenings—April 17, 1845.

☞ Courtesy of the Museum of Music History (London)

BELOW: On her return to Havana, Mercedes delighted in *paseos* through the city. Behind the carriages is the Teatro Tacón, where Mercedes sang in a grand benefit concert. ☞ Teatro Tacón, Frédéric Mialhe (lithograph)/Courtesy of the Cuban Heritage Collection, University of Miami Libraries, Coral Gables, Florida

During Mercedes' 1840 voyage to Havana, her cousin the Count de Peñalver hosted a concert for her. People flocked to the Alameda de Paula in the moonlight to catch a bit of Mercedes' performance.

☞ Alameda de Paula, Frédéric Mialhe (lithograph)/Courtesy of the Cuban Heritage Collection, University of Miami Libraries, Coral Gables, Florida

Mercedes'daughter Teresa Merlin.

☞ Courtesy of Jacques Mercier du Paty de Clam

Teresa Merlin offered her mother a cherished retreat at the Chateau de Dissay near Poitiers, France.

☞ Courtesy of the author

Gonzalo O'Farrill's double monument to his "Anita" in Père Lachaise cemetery and officially Mercedes' final resting place too, though no one can be sure where Mercedes lies today.

☞ Courtesy of the author

STARTING OVER

*I*f Mercedes had thought that reaching France would provide a respite from the threat of battle, she quickly learned otherwise. News arrived of an attack by guerrilla bands upon her brave escort; several members had either died or been captured—a reminder of her immediate family's continued exposure to danger. Mercedes and her infant daughter Teresita now made their way to Pau, the nearest large city in the French Atlantic Pyrenees, to wait for Merlin. Even though France was her husband's native land and the heart of the Napoleonic Empire, Mercedes had no guarantee of security or stability given the unfurling events.

General Merlin arrived before year's end, having reached some agreement with Joseph to leave Spain. Tensions within his immediate staff were wearying Joseph. Perhaps, too, Merlin had finally lost faith in Joseph's rule, and with fewer than two thousand men left in the Royal Guard, no longer viewed his future prospects optimistically. Whatever the case, when Merlin entered France in 1812 he was no longer a member of Joseph's army in Spain or a member of the main French army.

Once reunited in Pau, the family traveled to Paris, and Mercedes had her first glimpse of the city she had so often read and heard about—the city that her mother had so adored and where her brother had spent so many years. Mercedes' memoirs stop at this point, so one can only imagine what thoughts rushed through her mind, heightening the feelings of loss and separation, and intermingling with the wonderment of the new. During the course of that first year in France, the Merlins attempted to forge some stability by purchasing a country property in Brunehamel, in northern France by the Ardennes forest, near the border with present-day Belgium. The location was close to Commenchon, the country estate of General Merlin's older brother.

Although nine years separated the brothers, Antoine Merlin de Thionville had always held strong family feelings and had helped his youngest brother—also his godson—in the early days of his military career. A complex man, Merlin de Thionville had gone through various transformations in his life—seminarian, lawyer, deputy to the first National Assembly at the beginning of the Revolution, radical republican and Montagnard in the Convention, and member of the Council of Five Hundred. He was particularly remembered for his heroic military defense of Mayence (Mainz) against the Prussians in 1793, yet many aristocrats and clerics gratefully acknowledged him as their savior from the guillotine. With a seemingly rough exterior, but intelligent and charismatic, Merlin de Thionville was sometimes called "terrible" for his fierceness. Still, his son Paul recalled that "if Merlin had in his nature an intensity, he had in his heart a profound sensitivity and, if carried away at times, no one was easier to calm and to move." He displayed a tender heart publicly when moved to tears before Louis XVI, Marie Antoinette, and their children in June 1792 after the mob had stormed the Tuileries. Representing the assembly, Merlin de Thionville admitted tears for the misfortunes of a father and mother—but not for a king and a queen who had called a foreign power against France.

It was probably at the wedding of Merlin de Thionville's daughter, Rose, on December 21, 1812, that Mercedes first met her husband's family: his brothers Merlin de Thionville, Gabriel, sister Anne-Marie, Merlin de Thionville's second wife Amélie-Charlotte, assorted nieces and nephews, and Merlin's elderly mother, Elisabeth Augustine. Commenchon, her brother-in-law's charming home, comprised some 222 acres, including the former abbey of St-Éloy-Fontaine, agricultural lands, two ponds, fountains, a park, and a house with a long nine-windowed facade and a pavilion at each end. Mercedes would have been at ease in this graceful milieu, especially as her new sister-in-law—Amélie-Charlotte, the daughter of a German baron—was her contemporary in age as well as background. Both Antoine and Christophe-Antoine, despite their early republican leanings, were easily charmed by the daughters of the nobility. Not surprisingly, Merlin de Thionville got on well with Mercedes, so much so that at the birth of his second daughter in August 1814 he named her Marie-della-Mercédès Augusta Merlin.

By September 1813, Mercedes was expecting her second child. Given how much she had longed to become a mother from the earliest days of her marriage, she should have been blissful. But as in her first pregnancy, wider world events provided substantial and incessant worries.

The year 1813 brought news of Napoleon's catastrophic defeat in Russia and the destruction of the Grande Armée, which emboldened Prussia to reengage against France. The news from Spain was equally disheartening: Joseph was defeated for the last time, by Wellington, in early summer. The aftermath of the battle of Vitoria became legendary for the chaos and spectacular looting of the French baggage train by the British. As Miot de Melito vividly described it, "The treasure chest of the army containing over twenty-five million, that of the King, the fortunes amassed by generals, officers and civilians during five years of warfare, plunder and extortion, were all abandoned, and became the prize of the conqueror."

Joseph, his senior generals, and General O'Farrill barely escaped— a retreating Joseph literally going out one side of his royal carriage with the British entering through the other door. In the carriage, Wellington discovered drawings, prints, and paintings, which he sent to London, having any damaged ones repaired. Realizing later that some may have been from the royal collection, he asked his brother

Sir Henry Wellesley to contact the Spanish representative to identify them. Fernando VII eventually gave them to Wellington in gratitude, and they can still be seen in Apsley House, Wellington's London home.

By June 28, Joseph and General O'Farrill were in France, at St. Jean de Luz. From there, Joseph wrote to Napoleon to intercede for his Spanish supporters and officers who were now stateless—and penniless. He particularly noted that the French army had great need of good generals and officers, and he could recommend several: Merlin, Bigarré, Tascher, Hugo, and others. Napoleon initially forbade Joseph's followers from crossing the Garonne River, wishing the news of the defeat to be kept silent as long as possible.

When Mercedes received the news of the defeat, she would have at least been reassured that her uncle O'Farrill, as well as Pepita and her husband, were safely in France. Pepita and Pedro had followed Joseph from Valencia to Madrid, on to Valladolid and Vitoria, although they had left in a convoy ahead of the battle. One person, however, remained trapped in Spain: O'Farrill's wife Ana Rodríguez de Carassa. She had fallen gravely ill May 13 in Valladolid and did not regain consciousness until June 5—the day Joseph and the army evacuated the city. General O'Farrill faced one of his most trying moments as he told his beloved Anita that she was too weak to follow. Slowly realizing the situation, she cried, "I can't stay here nor survive any humiliation." Her husband tried to calm her fears, even bringing in the bishop of Valladolid for reassurance. Still, it was a heart-wrenching farewell. Later, they would discover that Ana was indeed protected: the city council set up a citizen guard to surround the house, and Wellington confirmed her safety. Even the crown prince of Holland, serving on Wellington's staff, sent affectionate greetings from his parents, a poignant reminder of those bygone days of diplomatic missions. Despite Wellington himself forwarding her letters and petitions, and Joseph asking the emperor to swap her for a high-ranking Spanish officer, Ana did not reach Paris until April 27, 1814.

Beyond the suffering and displacement of her family, the loss of Spain had other consequences for Mercedes and her husband. Since the evacuation of Madrid, the Dowager Duchess de Osuna's steward had moved to take back her house and protect it from reprisals. Don José Galiano immediately confronted Mercedes' maid and ordered her not to remove any more valuables, posting a sign that indicated the house belonged to the "legitimate Spanish Government." The Merlins' losses were compounded when Napoleon signed the Treaty of Valençay, restoring Fernando to the throne with no protection for those who had bought nationalized assets. Given that Mercedes and General Merlin had invested a substantial part of Joseph's gifts in such assets, and that Joaquín's estate remained far from settled, the financial blow was substantial.

By late 1813, Wellington's army was in France marching toward Paris from the west, while allies including Prussia, Austria, and Russia drove in from the northeastern frontier. France confronted war within its own territory for the first time since the Revolution. General Merlin decided to offer his services to defend France, while his brother Merlin de Thionville, still not completely trusting the emperor, raised his own Corps Franc. Confirmed as a général de division in the French army in January 1814, and initially assigned to the cavalry depot at Versailles, by February Merlin headed a cavalry division in the northeast, fighting off Cossacks and other allied troops. By the end of March the battle reached Paris, with the city's defense under the charge of King Joseph, along with Marshals Marmont and Mortier. General Merlin commanded a cavalry division in Marmont's VI Corps, which saw fighting all through March 30 on the outskirts of Paris. The French faced an impossible position against superior numbers. Nevertheless, the events of the day proved controversial, as Marmont agreed to the capitulation of Paris on March 31 despite the emperor sending word that he was within a day's march from Paris.

After the capitulation, the VI Corps went to Essonne, where on April 4 and 5 Marmont reached a secret agreement with the Austrian prince Schwarzenberg to surrender the French troops. The VI Corps marched under cover of darkness to Versailles, the uneasy soldiers believing they were going to Napoleon at Fontainebleau while secretly flanked by enemy troops. Only one general refused to leave his post: Lucotte, Merlin's comrade from Naples and Spain— one of the witnesses to his marriage. Once at Versailles, they were completely encircled and eventually sent on to Normandy. Marmont later claimed his reason was to save France from a needlessly prolonged battle, and historians have debated how much his generals knew in advance. However, for Napoleon it was a betrayal and the final blow: he abdicated unconditionally on April 11, 1814.

The triumphant allies marched into Paris led by Tsar Alexander I of Russia and the king of Prussia. Cossacks set up camp on the Champs Elysees, and arguments ensued as to whom to put on the throne: Napoleon's son or the Bourbons. The Bourbons triumphed, and Louis XVIII, brother of the last king, was proclaimed monarch. Along with changes to the government, France lost its empire and the need for the enormous army that had comprised Napoleon's war machine. While many senior officers, including Merlin, were quickly awarded the royalist Order of Saint-Louis, many were placed on nonactivity and half-pay as there were not nearly enough positions for all serving officers. General Merlin was relatively fortunate; while not given an active command, he was employed as an inspector general of cavalry for the 5th Division in May 1814.

Mercedes and her husband used the early days of the Restoration, as the era was called, to establish their lives in France more firmly. Bureaucracy presented numerous requirements, including the need for legal recognition of their marriage. Under the rules for the imperial army, officers needed formal approval before marrying foreign wives. Although General Merlin had received approval from Napoleon before his 1809 marriage, he still had to go through formalities in January 1814 when he reentered the French army. Even more ludicrous, at the height of the fighting in France, they had to record their marriage in the Parisian civil registry and had to finalize the purchase of various properties from Merlin de Thionville. The properties included two woodlands totaling some three hundred acres in the Aisne and Ardennes departments in northeastern France, as well as a house in nearby Dizi-le-Gros, at a price of one hundred forty thousand francs. Still, they were fortunate to have capital to invest, in contrast to General Lucotte. He had lost millions of reales worth of Spanish properties, and in Vitoria lost everything he had managed to bring from Madrid. He complained bitterly of three years of overdue wages from Spain, which the Restoration government refused to honor. Without any resolution for the Cuban estates, there was a real sense that the Merlins had to be financially prudent. In early January 1814, while awaiting his first posting in the army, General Merlin pleaded with the minister of war for any temporary position outside Paris to avoid the ruinous costs of stabling for his horses and equipage in the city.

Mercedes certainly did not lead the opulent life experienced by her parents in the early days of their marriage. Moreover, the countryside offered little haven during the intense fighting of early 1814 as the Prussians pillaged Merlin de Thionville's estate—helpfully directed by a royalist neighbor. The soldiers terrified the heavily pregnant Rose Merlin, who gave birth to a stillborn child. Nevertheless, with the arrival of her aunt O'Farrill in April and the birth of her son, François, on June 9, 1814, Mercedes experienced some happy moments. She always enjoyed the intimacy of family life, especially surrounded by her extended relatives.

General Merlin focused on rebuilding his career under the new regime, although one piece of unfinished business consumed significant time and energy through the beginning of 1815. In the early days of the Restoration, much confusion existed regarding ranks, honors, and titles of the old imperial regime. The ministry of war had started with the recognition of honors such as the Legion of Honor, but also addressed numerous concerns over the status of imperial titles: the barons and counts of empire that Napoleon often awarded to officers, as well as titles given by his sibling kings in their own nations. Holding a title was a matter close to General Merlin's heart. As he explained in various letters to the Ministry of War between September 1814 and January 1815, Napoleon had created him a baron in July, 1808, in Bayonne as Merlin entered Joseph's Spanish service. For inexplicable reasons, however, Merlin never received the letters patent that would have confirmed the title. Merlin emphasized that while he had been offered other titles in Spain, he had never accepted any, and he now asked to be made a count in recognition of his long years of service or, at the very least, to be confirmed as a baron. He wrote to the minister and also specifically to the Marquis de Beaufort, who was charged with reviewing numerous similar demands, and to General Durrieu, division chief at the ministry—appealing to their longstanding acquaintance.

Why was a title so important? An obvious answer would be pride; Merlin specifically mentioned other comrades with similar service and status who held titles, and he felt it appropriate recognition. Moreover, he happened to be correct. Napoleon did indeed name Merlin a baron, an act the emperor had confirmed to Joseph on July 7, 1808. Furthermore, there was Mercedes to consider. Merlin would later stress, on another matter to the ministry, that he had married the daughter of a count and *grande* of Spain. One only has to remember Joaquín's machinations in search of higher ranks to understand the importance that the Santa Cruz family (and other Cuban elites) placed on rank and lineage.

Was there perhaps pressure from Mercedes for Merlin to obtain this honor? There has long been a claim that Joseph made Merlin a count in 1810—if so, Merlin makes no reference to it, perhaps motivated by caution in a turbulent time. Certainly neither the Spanish nor French governments ever recognized any such title. Yet in Paris, Mercedes was always known as the Comtesse Merlin, and in Cuba most believed that it was her husband's title. In Paris, the title seemed based on some misconception that Spanish custom made her a countess as the daughter of a count, although in Spanish law there is only ever one title holder. Quico was the actual Count de Jaruco y Mopox, and in Cuba, Mercedes never called herself Countess de Jaruco. Yet that title appears in numerous French legal documents and on her own calling cards: *née Comtesse de Jaruco et Mopox* or just *née Jaruco*. One Cuban friend did notice this oddity, but he simply attributed it to some unknown French custom. It did not matter; Mercedes would go down in history as the Comtesse Merlin. In 1884, her son François corrected the oversight and obtained a papal title, Count Merlin.

General Merlin's request appeared to progress positively if somewhat slowly through the military bureaucracy. Unfortunately for him, a rather unbelievable event occurred on March 1, 1815, which quickly made all a moot point: Napoleon landed near Antibes, set to retake his old throne.

Napoleon's surprise return caused fear, jubilation, and overall pandemonium. Louis XVIII and his government sent Marshal Ney to confront him, and Ney famously promised to bring him back in an iron cage. However, Napoleon's magic enthralled his old troops, who rather than fight him soon joined his cause. Instead of caging his old leader, Marshal Ney also embraced the cause. By March 20, Louis XVIII and the rest of the Bourbons had fled the country, and Napoleon entered Paris. All over France, officers faced difficult decisions from the first days of his landing. For those on half-pay and with few prospects, the choice was relatively easy. But for those who were actively employed and had sworn fealty to their king, it was a matter of picking the right side—whatever their personal beliefs.

General Merlin was based in Strasbourg at the time, carrying out a cavalry review nearby. His precise actions in those early days are disputed. Both he and Marshal Suchet, who commanded the 5th Military Division, insisted that they did nothing but maintain the troops in order while the king remained in Paris. Merlin claimed to have focused solely on his work, and only realized what was happening from the excitement running through the town. Far from rushing to join Napoleon, he feared retribution from his role in the Marmont affair and believed himself marked by other senior and junior officers as being Louis's staunch supporter.

Whatever his thoughts and actions before Louis XVIII fled France, by April 1 Napoleon had appointed Merlin commander of a cavalry division under General Rapp's V Corps (the army of the Rhine) based in Strasbourg. At this juncture General Merlin somewhat impetuously undertook a step that would yield unexpected career ramifications. The still unresolved matter of his title seems to have festered, provoking him to write an incredibly blunt letter directly to the emperor dated May 14, 1815:

> Sire, If a long-serving soldier with more than twenty-five years of service, ten as a colonel of hussars and as a senior officer, who has fought in all the campaigns without interruption, Dares for the first time to seek a boon from Your Imperial Majesty, It is for him to give a new pledge of his loyalty and his boundless devotion at the moment of beginning a new campaign. I beg Your Majesty confer on me the title of Count if he thinks me worthy. I will redouble my efforts and zeal to merit Your Majesty's benevolence. I am with the most profound respect, Sire, Your Imperial Majesty's most loyal subject, Lieutenant General Merlin.*

Not surprisingly, there is no record of a response. It is difficult to understand why General Merlin thought that this time of turmoil was an appropriate moment to make his case. He sent the letter to the Ministry of War in Paris, where it was filed in General Merlin's military dossier—inconveniently at hand upon Napoleon's final defeat at Waterloo on June 18, 1815.

When word came that Louis XVIII and the allied commanders had entered Paris in July, General Merlin returned to Strasbourg to await further orders. He then found himself in a difficult position, along with many other officers who had supported Napoleon during the Hundred Days. This time around, Louis XVIII and his most ardent royalists were in no mood for clemency. Napoleon's earliest supporters faced threats of arrest, and some, like Marshal Soult, were temporarily banished from Paris. The resurgent royalists seethed with animosity and a desire for vengeance. Colonel the Count de La Bédoyère, about to flee France, was betrayed visiting his young wife in Paris in August, brought before a court martial on the fourteenth, and executed on the nineteenth. All pleas by his wife, the daughter of a well-known royalist family, were coldly rebuffed.

---

* From the Restoration, Merlin was called Lieutenant General.

Marshal Ney's arrest in August and execution in November also sent a chill throughout the ranks.

Ordered back to Paris September 1, Merlin was placed on the inactive list, as were all the officers who had followed Napoleon. His first interview with the war minister was inauspiciously cancelled as Merlin suffered a "violent attack" of gout. By letter he protested his loyalty to the king, but four days later a royal ordinance dated October 12, 1815, established a commission to "examine the conduct of officers who have served during the usurpation." The commission would review and place each officer into one of fourteen main categories—determined by their perceived culpability. Each officer awaited judgment. Higher rankings implied worse prospects, with those in the fourteenth category deemed unemployable.

In General Merlin's case, the commission focused primarily on one factor: did he join the "usurper" before or after Louis had left France and Napoleon arrived in Paris on March 20? Suchet was accused of agitating in the northeast, and Merlin was suspected of aiding him in those early days. In contrast to Merlin's statements, the commission received testimony that he was close to Suchet and had coordinated his efforts to "assure on all points the execution of their orders during the events of March, " including undertaking trips throughout the region to "direct opinion in a way favorable to Suchet's projects." The commission also heard that upon receipt of a newspaper reporting on Napoleon's progress, Merlin told other officers: "It is finished…we served the King in 1814, we will again serve Bonaparte in 1815, and perhaps another the following year." The owner of his lodging testified to his sarcasm toward the celebrations of King's Day (August 24) as evidence of his disloyalty. She reported that Merlin declared, "There is no more army, they can organize all they like, as for me I don't wish to serve anymore." But by far the most incriminating piece against Merlin was the letter to Napoleon requesting a title and swearing his "boundless devotion."

Balancing these contradictory declarations, the commission concluded "General Merlin is at least in the 10th class for having demanded the title of count from the usurper in protesting his fidelity—if he does not merit paragraph 1 of [the] 14th [class] for aiding the progress of the usurpation before the 20th of March by the... manner that he supported Suchet's revolt." Merlin had avoided permanent dismissal but was unemployed for the time being. A further consequence of his suspected disloyalty was nearly constant surveillance by the police through at least 1825, whether in Paris or the countryside. Even his requests for permission to travel would indicate his classification by the commission. Nevertheless, the police surveillance, which also covered Merlin de Thionville and colleagues such as the liberal politician General Foy, at times seemed incredibly inept. The police informers could not seem to distinguish between the various suspect Merlins, often confusing General Merlin with his brother Gabriel or even with Eugène Merlin, also a general but the son of the exiled attorney general Merlin de Douai.

One can only imagine the strain Mercedes must have felt during the course of the commission's investigation and deliberation. Their entire future depended on the outcome. She had already lived through expulsion from Spain, the commotion and disruption of the Hundred Days far from her husband, and then experienced the pain of occupation by the allies. Escaping to Brunehamel from the turmoil of Paris in November 1815, the Merlins found Prussian soldiers. Mercedes fled with Teresita to picnic by the pond at the Merlin de Thionville estate, as a family member wrote to Paul Merlin that "it was a full inn at the old *castel* of Brunhamel [*sic*]." Faced with the coarse lodgers, Mercedes' Spanish maid, Casimira, proved her worth; she slept with a kitchen knife to protect her mistress' door. Finally one jubilant family event occurred. On October 6, 1816, Mercedes gave birth to her third child, Gonzalve-Christophe-Constant (Gonzalo). At times in those first tumultuous years in France, Mercedes must have wondered if her family would ever enjoy stability and peace.

12

THE RISE OF
LA BELLE CRÉOLE

There was a tremendous crush in the ballroom; during a momentary pause, the Comtesse M took me by the arm and to escape the stifling heat, carried me to the card room; there was also a curious inspection to be made as all the artistic, literary and political celebrities of the day were there.... Madame M identified them each with a charming complacency, accompanying each name with a comment such as was often envied by the wittiest society chronicler.... The ball was interrupted. Liszt sat down at the piano.... The effect was magical; the sounds floated in the air like vapor.

The scene reflects a typical evening in the brilliant salon of the Comtesse M, as described in Alexandre Dumas' early novel, *Pauline*. But who is the Comtesse M? Any contemporary reader who followed the light and fashionable sections in the newspapers would have immediately identified her as Mercedes. A world of change had once again swept through her life, but this time Mercedes had initiated the transformation.

From his impoverished Parisian exile on March 24, 1824, General O'Farrill wrote to his former monarch, Joseph, who was then enjoying his own comfortable—if somewhat surprising—refuge on his American estate in New Jersey. The aftermath of empire had separated the ex-king and former minister by an ocean, yet the two men maintained an affectionate bond and corresponded regularly. O'Farrill, widowed since 1816, saw little of the world except his "compatriots and companions in misfortune" and lived on the income supplied by his numerous siblings in Havana. Still, he never expressed self-pity, even while writing of the death in 1823 of his stepson, Pedro, "whom I loved like a son and my best friend," and of Pedro's inconsolable widow, Pepita, who now focused on their only daughter. After this somber recital, General O'Farrill turned to brighter news. "Madame Merlin," he wrote, "has very much perfected her musical talent and is very much *en vogue* and the toast of the capital."

The contrast between the situations of each sister is remarkable: tragic mourning on the one hand, and social success on the other. Similarly startling is the difference between the resigned and philosophical O'Farrill and the sparkling Mercedes. Yet the contrasts encapsulate the transformation in the lives of Mercedes and her extended family which had occurred over the course of the preceding decade. Roles reversed as Mercedes, previously in the shadow of her closest relatives—father, mother, uncle, and husband—became the dominant or memorable force in the family. Moreover, her role in society would transcend that of a beautiful and fashionable woman. She would, instead, take center stage, both literally and figuratively.

By 1824, Mercedes had spent over a decade in France, with her own share of difficulties. After the near destruction of Merlin's military career in 1816, he had somewhat pragmatically become inspector again later that year and retained employment in that capacity until 1821. Falling short of an actual command, it still amounted to active service, superior to the fate of many comrades. However, in 1820 the government uncovered a rather nebulous conspiracy of diverse antiroyalist groups and became less tolerant of suspected disloyalty.

Some of the men linked to the conspiracy were known friends or associates of General Merlin, including General Foy, General Pajol, and Jacques-Antoine Manuel. General Merlin's continuous police surveillance since 1816 had documented these relationships, and although it is not explicitly noted in his military records, it is probably the cause for his descent into the reserves in 1821. His military career had ground to a halt.

That year was also particularly traumatic for Mercedes and her husband, as they faced the loss of their three-year-old daughter, Annette-Elisabeth-Joséphine. Little Annette was born in June 1818, Mercedes' second daughter and last child. Mercedes always had strong, loving maternal instincts, and throughout her life remained close to her surviving three children. The loss of a little child must have been intensely difficult. The couple buried their youngest in a tomb next to the imposing double monument built by Gonzalo O'Farrill for his Anita. They inscribed a simple yet moving epitaph: "She has reached the port before the storm."

Personal grief aside, the Merlins' troubles included financial concerns beyond the general's employment difficulties. Despite efforts made over so many years and by so many on their behalf, they failed to benefit substantially from the anticipated final resolution of the Cuban estates. The untangling of Joaquín's legacy had stalled in the confusion of the war and its aftermath. Even the presence of Mercedes' brother, Quico, in Cuba since 1814 did not move the matter forward until 1817, when he managed to win royal approval to manage the *testamentaría* despite being four years short of legal age. That right itself had taken almost three years of appeals, and it came at a price. Quico had previously presented in Cádiz a repayment plan for the debt, and attempts were made to settle some of the private and state debt through the sale of numerous properties so that the heirs could move forward.

Further momentum on resolution of the estate had come from Pepita and Pedro's decision to travel to Cuba in 1815, possibly to settle in Havana for the long term. Their decision meant a painful separation from Pedro's mother, Ana, who at the time had just arrived from Spain and was still gravely ill from unknown causes. They were driven by the harsh realities of exile. Pedro had no real prospects in France; his name in Spain was tainted by association with his stepfather O'Farrill, and his entire education had prepared him only for a high-ranking state or diplomatic career. Taking advantage of an 1814 "amnesty" for lower-ranking Afrancesados, Pedro received permission to travel with Pepita and two servants to Cádiz, where they hoped to receive license to continue to Havana. It was a catastrophic journey. Their ship foundered and sank off the coast of Portugal, forcing them to continue their journey by land—under surveillance by officials reporting their every step back to Madrid. They then waited months in Cádiz, funds dwindling, while Pedro saw his petitions and explanations ignored. In late 1816 Pepita gave birth to a daughter, also called Teresa but nicknamed Teranita.

The Santa María family had finally arrived in Havana sometime in 1817. By this date, Joaquín's uncle, the ever loyal Marqués de Cárdenas de Monte-Hermoso, had died and so had Teresa Montalvo's brother, the Count de Casa-Montalvo. It fell to Juan Montalvo, Teresa's surviving brother, to aid the Santa Cruz heirs and represent Mercedes before the courts. "Uncle Juanito," as Mercedes fondly called him, had already proven a loyal supporter over the years, having earlier taken over from his older brother. Besides any affection he may have had for his own sister's children, he had known Joaquín well in Madrid, where he had first been a student and then a cadet in the Royal Guards. Later he had assisted Joaquín in the Guantánamo Commission. He would remain Mercedes' main Cuban confidant until his death.

The surprise appearance of Joaquín's two illegitimate daughters in 1818 prompted the need for Juan Montalvo's advice. Matilde and Merced Valdés complicated the *testamentaría* by demanding "justice" and the share that Joaquín had planned to leave them in his unsigned will. Theoretically, Spanish law granted illegitimate children the right to the fifth of their father's free assets, but obtaining a judgment against such socially prominent defendants was not easy, especially with such a financially troubled estate. As ever in Cuban litigation, a strategy of delay came into play even as the girls' publicly appointed guardian argued passionately about their vulnerability and orphaned state. Ultimately, much to the court's astonishment, the family agreed to a settlement in 1821. The court's comments at this relatively quick settlement noted that while it could see no "legal obligation" from the estate, the ease with which Joaquín's legitimate heirs agreed led it to believe that some "natural" rights must exist. Grand Cuban families always preferred to keep their public image spotless and avoid public airing of shameful secrets. The family offered the young girls eighteen thousand pesos, part in cash and part in a share in some small farms.

Prior to the settlement with the Valdés girls, the heirs and representatives had agreed on a tentative division of the remaining estate and debt in 1819. Whatever the three heirs had previously believed about the original two-million-peso valuation in 1807, the estate now consisted of various sugar mills, farms, and lands valued at just under 900,000 pesos and still encumbered by 480,000 pesos in treasury debt and 151,000 pesos of private debt, leaving a net value of just over 300,000 pesos. Piece by piece, the valuable coffee estates Las Delicias, Neptuno, and Minerva had gone, as had various lands rented to smallholders, and other properties. In dividing the actual assets as well as the associated debts, the various strategies and interests of the respective heirs came into play. Quico was the current Count de Jaruco y Mopox and the main representative of his father's debts before the Royal Treasury. He took the bulk of the assets, including the sugar mills, but he also took the bulk of the royal debt and the private obligations. Pedro, on behalf of his wife, agreed to undertake some 141,000 pesos of Treasury debt, in exchange for more lands—they had clearly decided that their interests lay in Cuba and therefore wanted assets they could administer. Mercedes, living in Paris with her French husband, wanted no administrative entanglements. She accepted an obligation from her brother to pay out her share of capital over approximately twelve years, as well as receiving 5 percent on the outstanding capital. In return for this obligation, Quico took her share of assets.

Joaquín's legacy continued to be problematic. In 1821 the Royal Treasury refused permission to split the estate's debt and the underlying mortgaged assets—the Treasury wanted a single holder of the debt and associated mortgaged properties. Additionally, the Treasury refused to take some land—known as Santa Margarita—in lieu of a partial payment. The objections shattered the Santa Marías's plan to settle in Cuba as landholders. Almost all their portion of lands reverted to Quico (as well as the debt), and both Pepita and Mercedes saw their net share reduced by the value of the rejected Santa Margarita land. Mercedes was left with a legacy worth some ninety-one thousand pesos, relatively little considering that just one of her father's coffee farms (Minerva) had sold for some two hundred thousand pesos.

Although this division was intended to be final and provide some closure, two unresolved items would have significant repercussions in the years to come. One item related to the old sugar mill, Jesús Nazareno, which Pedro took as the bulk of Pepita's inheritance. Joaquín had dismantled the mill, and the current value reflected rents from parcels leased to tenant farmers. Over the years, however, many of the tenants had failed to pay; therefore, Pedro had required the other co-heirs to make up two-thirds of the shortfall until these difficulties were resolved. Nazareno was also subject to ongoing litigation with some O'Farrill cousins regarding a boundary dispute, and it was expressly stated in the settlement that all three heirs would share the cost of litigation. Should the case be lost, Pepita would be compensated. Finally, Quico stipulated that if there were further difficulties with the Santa Margarita property, then his sisters would duly compensate him either in cash or land.

Shortly after signing and ratifying the final agreement in October 1821, the Santa María family returned to Paris, giving up any dream of settling in Cuba. Pedro unexpectedly died soon after, in 1823, to Pepita's devastation. She lived with her daughter and General O'Farrill near Mercedes, who by now lived by the Porte de Saint Martin on 40 Rue de Bondy (now Rue René-Boulanger), considered then part of the fashionable Quartier Chaussée d'Antin.

Nearly constant turmoil and insecurity had dominated Mercedes' life for well over the previous decade. The loss of mother, child, country, fortune—and to a certain extent, social position—created an emotional tide that easily could have swept the overly sensitive Mercedes into the same devastation suffered by her sister. Mercedes would later note, in her memoirs and letters, that she had a natural tendency toward melancholy, her health easily affected by emotional shocks and disappointments. Passionate and self-willed at times, she also could become discouraged and depressed. Over the years, Mercedes would learn to combat these sentiments with frequent distractions and nearly constant activity—like her own father. As she remarked: "reason and force of character helped me to combat [this] disposition." The net result was that her happiness and gaiety often had "the character of fireworks; it rose, shined and finally faded into obscurity."

Mercedes' world had altered from what she had been raised to expect as a child and young woman in her parents' milieu, even from what she had experienced in early married life. Far from being part of the court's inner circle, with a husband who was the confidant of a king or a father who enjoyed the friendship of the first minister, Mercedes and her family endured an internal exile from the seat of power.

On a daily basis, she witnessed her own dear Uncle O'Farrill, ex-minister of war, stripped of his ranks, honors, and fortune, accepting his fate philosophically. He managed on his family's pension, kept meticulous accounts, wrote his political memoir with Miguel de Azanza, his deeply personal *Carta* defending Ana from the old calumnies and slurs, and he often gave away whatever he had to aid old friends in more perilous straits. Mercedes remembered his walking to the observatory, where he attended various courses and lectures—enjoying his lifelong passion for science. He refused all of Mercedes' pleas to take a carriage, not wishing to use his meager funds on himself. Instead, he claimed that walking was good for his health. She regarded him as an almost saintly figure whose deeply religious nature fostered stoicism and held back bitterness. He was a deeply adored reminder of another era.

Mercedes might have persevered along an uneventful path, cherishing her little family and meekly accepting fate's outcome. In that case, she would have remained a passing footnote in accounts of the Peninsular War referring to her great-uncle, her husband, and the Afrancesados. Instead, as when she escaped from the convent of Santa Clara, Mercedes took matters into her own hands.

Her first step toward reshaping her new life was a fairly common one for the era: she opened a salon. Salons, of course, had long been a part of Parisian life. People still recalled the witty salons of the pre-Revolutionary era; Napoleon's Joséphine had held one in her pre-imperial days. Even the elites of the empire, such as the nearly bankrupt Duchess d'Abrantès, continued their salons in reduced circumstances. Unlike the duchess, however, Mercedes had neither been well known nor established in Parisian circles before the Restoration. She had no role—neither formal nor informal—at the Bourbon court that now played an important role in social life. Being a foreigner did not preclude Mercedes from social success, but the foreigners who flourished, like Countess Apponyi, the wife of the Austrian ambassador, generally had ties to important foreign embassies or had great wealth to sustain lavish entertainment.

Mercedes, however, had incredible success. As early as 1823, Merlin de Thionville's son Paul recalled meeting an old school acquaintance, Auguste de Staël, the son of Madame de Staël, at his aunt Mercedes' salon. Given how much Mercedes had admired Madame de Staël's novels during her Madrid youth, hosting her son must have been deeply satisfying.

Mercedes' early success would prove long-lasting. An 1844 article in Madrid's *El Heraldo* marveled about her celebrity (its term) in sophisticated Paris:

> To achieve fame in Paris...is the easiest thing in the world...for one hour, for two, for half a day...[to achieve it] for a week, that is phenomenal. Paris...always needs to be devouring something.... Nonetheless, as we have said, Madame the Countess Merlin is one of the few privileged beings who maintain in Paris a constant and fixed

value, one of those persons whom everyone knows and appreciates, even if only by name.... But how, you may ask? How has a foreign lady...who has not published any masterpieces, nor possesses one of those fabulous fortunes...who is not a celebrated artist...been able to conquer such a unique position?

The answer, according to the journalist, lay in a uniquely French reason for celebrity. Madame Merlin, it appears, was a perfect example of what the French termed a *femme du monde*, an almost untranslatable concept that far transcends its literal meaning of a society woman. In becoming a *femme du monde*, Mercedes united the more obvious gifts of beauty, good birth, and culture with the talents of the artist, the attractions of a witty hostess, and the elegance and stylishness of a trendsetter, along with the nurturing soul of a patroness of the arts.

Mercedes knew what was required to ensure conviviality and pleasure among guests. She had grown up surrounded by two masters in the arts of sociability and entertaining. Mercedes had seen her mother host one of Madrid's most fashionable salons and had particularly noted her mother's talent for drawing out even the shyest guest. Teresa's gatherings had intermingled high-ranking dignitaries with the artistic world—enhancing the attractiveness of the salon while providing pleasure to its hostess. From her father, Mercedes had formed an understanding of grand gestures and lavish hospitality.

Mercedes had also inherited from her parents her mother's startling beauty and her father's good nature and warm heart. Describing Mercedes in his reminiscences, the English man-about-town Captain Gronow noted that she was a Spanish Creole and that "Her beauty was of the very highest order. Her face was one, which, once beheld, could never be forgotten; the perfect oval of the contour, the small regular features, fine brow, and dark flashing eyes were in perfect harmony." The Countess de Bassanville added, "To the poetic grace of the Spaniard she joined the wit and distinction of the French," and said she was sought after not only for her salon but also for herself. Both commentators agreed that she was good-natured and generous-hearted.

All of these qualities, as well as Mercedes' understanding of hospitality, were critical features of her triumph. However, without either her parents' enormous wealth or their political power and court connections, how did she raise her salon to such a level of success? The answer lay, as General O'Farrill noted in his letter to Joseph, in Mercedes' musical talents. Sometime after 1820, Mercedes began perfecting her voice with lessons from the acclaimed Spanish tenor and composer Manuel García. García had achieved success singing in Naples and Rome and had joined the Italian Opera in Paris in 1816. After spending some time in London, he rejoined the Italian Opera and also established his own school. García soon gained renown as one of the preeminent vocal coaches in Europe. Along with his own children—especially his daughters, the divas Maria Malibran and Pauline Viardot—Mercedes would become famous as one of his greatest students.

Mercedes had always had an excellent voice, as noted early on by the nuns of Santa Clara, and she thrived on music. But she had always felt the lack of serious training, and now, with an eminent teacher, she finally achieved her early promise. Mercedes was a soprano, and although there are obviously no recordings of her voice, the descriptions from Parisian music critics are endless. Her voice was supple, expansive, and rich, according to one, while another said it was full of sweetness. Her friend the writer and hostess Sophie Gay echoed these thoughts, adding that it was simultaneously strong and light, and animated by dramatic sentiment. With her mixture of beauty, presence, and vocal talent, she could have succeeded as a professional singer, becoming a great diva of the operatic world—if this hadn't been precluded by her birth and social conventions. Destitution would be the only excuse for a well-born figure taking to the stage as a career. Similar thoughts were expressed about another great amateur, Prince Emilio Belgiojoso, an Italian exile whose extraordinary voice made Franz Liszt wish that financial ruin would force him into a professional singing career.

In a world that adored music, Mercedes' voice amounted to an irresistible attraction. Musical performance and opera constituted key ingredients of *le monde* (high society). Paris at the time was surpassing other European capitals to become that center of the classical music world. By 1824, Rossini, the most successful operatic composer, had arrived and become the director of the Théâtre des Italiens. In 1833, Bellini would arrive, and later, Donizetti. Liszt, Chopin, and countless other iconic performers and composers either spent considerable time in Paris or would adopt it as their base from the 1830s.

Through her singing tuition with the masterful Manuel García, Mercedes came into contact with the professional music world and gained the respect of these artists—all the while maintaining the social proprieties required of a well-born, if less affluent, aristocratic woman. In 1824, through an extraordinary confluence of events, Mercedes met Rossini and performed with Maria García (later the diva known as La Malibran). Rossini had recently composed a cantata for four voices commissioned by one of Mercedes' Cuban Peñalver cousins. Since he had never heard it performed, this cousin, visiting Paris, wished Mercedes and three other singers to perform it, accompanied by a quartet. Rossini flatly refused, having little respect for amateur singers. Peñalver insisted, and Rossini finally consented to an audition. Enchanted by Mercedes' performance, Rossini insisted on a full orchestra—causing Mercedes to remove her doors to bring in the instruments. She found a professional tenor and bass, but the ensemble lacked a contralto. Then García, "who still hid his daughter like a miser concealing his treasure," offered Maria to fill the role.

Despite Rossini's doubts, there existed other talented amateurs in European society, and many took their music tuition and practice quite seriously. Aristocrats widely cultivated music as a desirable achievement, although most amateurs would never perform beyond a private salon. Generally, before the mid-1820s, they would not perform alongside professionals; Mercedes represented a driving force in the change. Amateurs, termed dilettanti in the contemporary press, would not sing or play for a fee but could perform in public for charity. Paris saw the introduction of the benefit concert showcasing society dilettanti and renowned artists. Before, a *dame patronnesse* could lend cachet and sell tickets, but now a talented lady could also perform and even see her name written up in the press afterward.

In this way, Mercedes served as one of the pioneers, perhaps even the very first to undertake this role. Her son Gonzalo recalled that during a trip to Switzerland in 1825, she sang in aid of Greek independence from the Ottoman Empire (then an intensely romantic and popular cause) at a grand concert in Geneva. The following year, she helped organize and direct a similar event in Paris, again for the Greeks. Mercedes was one of only three ladies who sang arias, but many others participated in the chorus, all under the master Rossini himself. Sophie Gay noted that the memory would long remain with those present. Gay especially highlighted the daring of these Parisian ladies in performing before a paying audience—but no one dared criticize them because of the charitable intent. The concert raised thirty thousand francs, an astonishing figure at the time. Throughout the following decade, Mercedes would organize concerts for Polish refugees, the destitute workers of Lyon, and the earthquake victims of Martinique, and would be active in many other charitable endeavors.

Mercedes' involvement with the musical world also played an integral part in her salon. In January 1831, the *Revue de Paris* highlighted one of Mercedes' private concerts, saying:

> Like every year, [it was] composed of a great number of the *dilettanti* of Parisian high society. One goes to Madame Merlin's salon to hear good music. . . . Rossini played the piano. Mme. Merlin, Mme. Rimbault, M. Blanchart and Mme. Sparre were joined by the artists of the *Théâtre Italien*, Mme. Malibran, MM. Davis, Lablache and Donizelli. . . . Mme. Merlin was as brilliant as always; [her] voice powerful and agile.

Mercedes' salon became an obligatory stop for any newly arrived musician in Paris who desired a passport to celebrity. Even established singers vied for the honor of being presented, happy to oblige Mercedes' call. Examples included Giulia Grisi and later the tenor Mario, nobly born Giovanni di Candia, a dilettante who achieved fame and fortune as a professional, changing his name to avoid his family's shame at his public career. Franz Liszt was happy to coordinate rehearsals and recruit other artists for her concerts. Other members of *le monde* would have to pay the artists' rates of up to five hundred francs for each musical piece, but for Mercedes they gladly performed for free.

These concerts, along with balls and other grand soirees, formed the *grand* days of the salons that occurred only a few times during the season. Mercedes held more intimate, *petit* days, generally on Fridays. The Countess of Bassanville explained that the *petits* combined selectivity with fine little suppers harkening back to the days of "our grandmother," in reference to the style of pre-Revolutionary salons, something Mercedes remembered from her mother's *tertulia*. Indeed, in her memoirs, Mercedes lovingly recalled charming late-night suppers and wondered why they had become less fashionable given their magical ambiance. After midnight, one could put away business worries and ambitions to live for oneself. To Mercedes the spirit became more lucid and the heart warmer. Mercedes' regular evenings also might allow for informal music, card games, or charades, and any number of diversions including conversation—although she generally forbade any of a political nature. She avoided conflict, and again drew on her mother's example to make all guests, regardless of rank or character, feel at ease. Captain Gronow wrote, "She was thoroughly independent. The poor way-worn musician...met with as civil and kind a reception as the Duke or Count just arrived from the Faubourg St Germain."

Mercedes hosted her prestigious gatherings in settings rather grander than expected, given the Merlins' economic situation. Society generally believed the couple to be wealthy, but to actually own or even rent an entire *hôtel particulaire* (private townhouse) would probably have been beyond their means—even bolstered by the occasional Cuban income. Here Mercedes benefited from a friendship with the Count and Countess de Lariboisière. It is not clear how exactly the friendship began, but the two families shared enough mutual interests for their affinity to flourish. The count, a former imperial officer, was the son of Napoleon's chief of artillery, who had died on the retreat from Russia. The countess, Elisa Roy, was an immensely wealthy heiress, one of the two daughters of a lawyer and minister of finance under the Restoration. The daughters eventually inherited some forty million francs, one of the largest fortunes in France. Elisa would bequeath over three million francs to establish the well-known Parisian hospital Hôpital Lariboisière. The friendship between the Merlin and Lariboisière families endured for over thirty years, based on a combination of shared Napoleonic sympathies (on the part of General Merlin and the count) and on a shared passion for philanthropy (on the part of Mercedes and Elisa). Mercedes and Elisa Roy served jointly as patronesses on various charitable ball committees, and the count would eventually be a pallbearer at Merlin's funeral.

Close friendship permitted the Merlins to share the Lariboisières' sumptuous *hôtel particulaire* at 40 rue de Bondy from 1818 until 1831. The Merlins later moved with them to an even grander one at number 58, another classic Parisian house hidden between a courtyard and large garden. Their apartment had all the elegant rooms needed to host a fashionable salon, and both ladies held balls and soirees and received visitors at the same house.

Almost two decades after arriving in Paris, after witnessing the fall of an empire, the death of loved ones, and the birth of three children, Mercedes had established a new life for herself. She triumphed in a traditional role in aristocratic society, not unlike her mother's within Joseph's inner circle, but Mercedes' social success also pressed against boundaries. She enjoyed her busy social life. In 1830, however, yet another significant political shift brought Mercedes even more success, while also offering General Merlin a second chance for his career.

Since 1824, the ruling king no longer had been the relatively conciliatory Louis but his ultraconservative brother, Charles X. Upon inheriting the crown, one of Charles X's first acts was to cleanse the senior officer corps by forcibly retiring the remaining republican and imperial-era officers—including General Merlin. Merlin fought against the retirement, bitterly writing to army chiefs that his service in Naples and Spain had counted for nothing except harm to his career. Resistance was futile, however, and he was pensioned off as of January 1825, at age fifty-three, on six thousand francs per year. Such a development would have been difficult for any marriage, but particularly painful when contrasting Mercedes' rising influence to his own extinguished career. In 1830, however, the July Revolution overthrew Charles X. His Orleans cousin, the more liberal Louis-Philippe, ascended to the throne. The July Monarchy had begun— and with it the true splendor of La Belle Créole.

ROMANCING THE PAST

*I*n the days following the July 1830 revolution, Mercedes found herself surrounded by triumphant liberal supporters of the new regime. After all, she had often hosted many of them—some whom she laughingly referred to as the "worst journalists of the kingdom." However, true to her warm nature, she had no qualms in chastising them when she felt they had overstepped the bounds of civility. She recounted one such episode to Count Apponyi:

> The chief editor of *Le Figaro* showed me numerous letters found in Madame's* apartments. This correspondence was highly compromising and these gentlemen wished very much to publish it. However, I managed to prove to them the unworthiness of such a project.

This altered political landscape offered the Merlins new possibilities. General Merlin felt much more affinity with this relatively liberal branch of the Bourbons, and Mercedes could even lay claim to

---

* Madame—the Duchess d'Angoulême, only surviving child of Marie Antoinette and Louis XVI—and an ultra-royalist.

having once helped the new king. Back in 1798, Joaquín had hosted Louis-Philippe, then an exiled prince, and his brothers as they passed through Cuba. In a similar fashion, Mercedes now hosted Louis-Philippe's heir at her balls. General Merlin, along with numerous other former imperial officers, rallied to the new government. Pragmatically, Louis-Philippe accepted their services and reincorporated them into the military. By August 8, 1830, General Merlin carried out an extraordinary inspection, and one month later he received command of the 17th Military Division, based in Corsica. General Merlin would have relished his first military command since the Hundred Days. At the age of fifty-nine, and inactive since 1821, Merlin nonetheless energetically undertook the long journey to his new post. To reach Bastia, the base of the 17th Division, he had to travel south to the Mediterranean coast and then sail 160 nautical miles—finally arriving in Corsica on October 18.

Even with this new command and corresponding salary, financial considerations continued to weigh on Merlin's mind. In 1824, before his forced retirement, he had pleaded with the ministry for special consideration during a month-long leave in Switzerland. Army regulations were clear: officers did not receive their salaries while on leave outside the country, but Merlin cited his long years of service and lack of fortune. He further expressed the wish to please his wife by taking her to see their ten-year-old son François, then studying in Switzerland. He was sufficiently circumspect to omit, however, that they and Mercedes' family would enjoy Joseph Bonaparte's hospitality at his old Swiss chateau of Prangins. Despite Merlin's years of service and his other arguments, the ministry flatly denied his appeal. In retrospect his request is unexpected proof that funds in the Merlin household were not as plentiful as the outside world may have believed.

Finances once again compelled General Merlin to send a bill for his Corsican transport costs to the department in charge of military travel. The bureaucrats in the ministry immediately queried his high travel expenses and heard from Minister of War Marshal Soult that Monsieur le Lieutenant Général Merlin was not authorized to incur them. The rejection particularly stung a senior officer proud "of his own good appearance...representing with dignity a government." He complained that uncompensated extra costs were "extremely ruinous for a senior officer."

Merlin's command began well, although his working relationship with the civilian commander began to deteriorate as the year progressed. Complaints arose between General Merlin and a politically dominant Corsican family led by Mercedes' old suitor, Horace Sébastiani—by then foreign minister. Conflict stemmed from what Merlin considered the Sébastiani faction's "pretention to dictate the laws there." Whatever the specifics, the conflict undermined Merlin's position. In October 1831, Soult decided to transfer him to the 9th Division, based in Montpellier.

Bad luck struck in the form of ill health as the sixty-year-old general suffered an acute attack of gout that left him bedridden and convalescent. He was unable to take up his new command in Montpellier and petitioned to retain his Corsica command. However, in January 1832 Merlin received a double blow; his ill health led to his replacement in both Montpellier and Corsica. Apparently, his experience would now best be deployed as an inspector general. Merlin believed otherwise, and in one of his typically impassioned letters he wrote: "Permit me, Monsieur le Ministre, to open up my heart to you in a circumstance that relates to the honor of a lieutenant general." Merlin had truly wished "to retain a command where I was useful, liked and respected." That last phrase in particular revealed much of the frustration felt by an experienced cavalry commander first placed on reserve, then retired under the previous regime, and now once again losing the chance to exercise a command. Merlin would never cease to hope for another command. Even at sixty-three he would assure the minister that he was as full of vigor as a colonel of hussars.

Merlin left Corsica in March 1832—in perfect health, as he rather bitingly told the ministry. He returned to Paris to await a new assignment. Unlike Ana Carassa, the devoted military wife who gamely accompanied General O'Farrill to all his postings, Mercedes had not joined Merlin in Corsica. The most obvious reasons were their children and her dislike of sea journeys, but other factors may have contributed. In 1825 Pepita had died, seemingly never recovering from the loss of her husband just two years before. She left her orphaned daughter Teranita under the guardianship of O'Farrill, although Mercedes must have undertaken her upbringing as Teranita and O'Farrill both lived in the Merlin household. Then in the summer of 1831, Gonzalo O'Farrill died. His closeness to Mercedes' family, his physical and spiritual resemblance to Mamita, and his status as the last living link to her Cuban past all served to magnify the impact on Mercedes. They buried O'Farrill with Ana in Père Lachaise Cemetery. Their matching double monument can still be seen today, crumbling yet still imposing.

Mercedes now assumed responsibility for Teranita Sáenz de Santa María, Pepita's estate, and the remainder of O'Farrill's financial claims. In 1827, Fernando VII had finally pardoned his old minister of war, restoring his rank and honors. O'Farrill had then managed to obtain a little over half of the ninety-one thousand pesos in assets that had been seized in Cuba in 1809. He and his brother Ignacio petitioned constantly between 1820 and 1829 for the return of the remainder, which had been sent to Cádiz at the height of the hostilities. The multiple petitions met with an intransigent resistance from a Spanish administration divided in its attitude toward the Afrancesados, calling O'Farrill a traitor to Spain who "saw its towns destroyed, temples profaned, [and] its handsome countryside awash in blood." The thankless task now fell to Mercedes, aided by Juan Montalvo in Havana, to secure Teranita's inheritance.

During General Merlin's Corsican assignment, Mercedes' existence followed the rhythms of Parisian social life: winter in Paris for the season, with balls and carnival festivities, concerts through Easter, then summers in the country or at fashionable spa towns such as Néris or Vichy. Mercedes occasionally used the summer months to travel abroad, primarily to Italy, Germany, and Switzerland. Her musical reputation had spread beyond Parisian society, and she sang on numerous occasions at concerts and private soirees. Parisian journals covered these performances, as did foreign newspapers such as

Madrid's *Correo Literario*. Recalling her childhood love for the countryside, Mercedes enjoyed visiting their country property outside Paris. In 1824, General Merlin had bought the seventy-acre domaine Sillery, now located eleven miles south of Paris. The timing coincided with the forced sale of his brother's estate, and it seems likely that Merlin decided to sell the Brunehamel property as well.

During the Parisian winter season, Mercedes' salon continued to flourish and shine. Although known mainly for its music, the salon likewise attracted what the Countess d'Agoult, Franz Liszt's longtime lover, called *"grands hommes"* or celebrated men. According to Agoult, all hostesses craved figures who could add luster to their salons, and society ladies would do almost anything to lure prominent thinkers, politicians, or authors to their homes. To this end, Mercedes penned endless pretty little notes gently prodding and reminding invitees of the next reunion, dinner, or ball: "have you suddenly forgotten, monsieur, that small dinner, so gay and witty."

Lines often merged between writers, journalists, and politicians; hence a man such as Narcisse-Achille de Salvandy could be all three: holding high political positions under the Restoration and the July Monarchy (counselor of state, elected deputy, and later minister of education), writing for the *Journal des Débats*, and publishing novels and books (the historical novel *Don Alonzo*). Popular in the fashionable salons, Salvandy admired Mercedes, lavishly praising her musical talents and once writing that "all voices do not penetrate as profoundly into the heart." Mercedes also attracted eminent men from the intersection of academia and politics, such as the literary historian Abel-François Villemain, the philosopher Victor Cousin, and the legal stars and political players Philippe Dupin and Antoine-Pierre Berryer. Many of these guests were members of the Académie Française (the ultimate authority on the French language) and hence at the pinnacle of intellectual society. In later years, through her numerous friends and webs of acquaintances, Mercedes would host the premier literary critic Charles-Augustin Sainte-Beuve, the writer Prosper Mérimée, the poet Alfred de Musset, and various publishers, editors, and journalists. Despite their intellectual weight, when they attended Mercedes' salon, she created charming, playful situations where one guest might improvise a fable, or two eminent jurists enact a ludicrous mock court case—with the poet de Musset writing the judgment in burlesque verse.

In addition to interacting with the men who attended her salon, Mercedes socialized with women who moved between the literary and social worlds. Her friend Sophie Gay was both a successful novelist and playwright. Mercedes attended Sophie Gay's salon and met her beautiful and talented daughter Delphine. Delphine married the newspaper editor and publisher Émile de Girardin in 1831 and went on to publish novels, poetry, and plays. After 1836, when her husband established *La Presse*, one of the most influential papers of the day, Delphine would write a regular society column, "le Courrier de Paris," under the pseudonym Vicomte de Launay.

Through Sophie Gay's salon, Mercedes met a new writer in the first flush of success, Honoré de Balzac, as well as the rather disreputable aristocratic writer the Marquis de Custine. Balzac enjoyed good music and therefore appreciated Mercedes' salon as well. Custine also shared a love of music and would become a loyal friend even if his notorious private life prevented his complete acceptance throughout society. Mercedes was a frequent guest at his home, Saint-Gratien, where he would host intimate dinners with guests including Sophie Gay, the Duchess d'Abrantes, and novelists Victor Hugo and George Sand, and they would hear Chopin play piano for hours.

Beyond enjoying the delights of various salons, Balzac profited from his attendance in another way. He was known to obsessively plunder friends and acquaintances for characteristics and bits and pieces for his own fictional creations. Seemingly fascinated by Mercedes' Havana birth, creole looks, and passionate nature, he happily pillaged it all. Over the years, her name, physical attributes, and parts of her background—not all flattering or correct—appeared in different forms in various novels. The common theme was always a Spanish or Creole beauty. In *The Maranas*, Juana, the daughter of a beautiful and notorious mother—mistress of an imperial marshal—marries a French officer in French-occupied Tarragona. In Paris "she lived in a fine house, with noble rooms, where she maintained a *salon*, in which abounded artists...a few politicians...and certain men of fashion, all of whom admired Juana." Juana's social success is counterbalanced by her husband's failures, eventually leading to a murderous ending. Balzac wrote that novella in 1832 but dedicated later editions to Mercedes.

Madame Evangelista in *The Marriage Contract* (1835) is a fabulously wealthy Creole widow from the aristocratic family of Casa-Real, whose husband had "indulged even her most extravagant fancies" and struggles to maintain her family's lavish lifestyle and beautiful daughter despite being secretly ruined. Balzac would have had access to Mercedes' initial memoirs and heard about Teresa Montalvo from his intimate friend, the Duchess d'Abrantès. The description of Madame Evangelista carried echoes of both Mamita and Teresa Montalvo: "She had black eyes and hair....Her face, still beautiful, had the fascinating Creole complexion [*sic*], which can only be described by comparing it with white muslin over warm blood-colour, so equably tinted is its fairness." Madame Evangelista had a regal dignity and "combined the ease of indolence with vivacity." Mercedes herself observed that Habaneras united vivacity and languidness in her 1831 memoirs.

Mercedes would continue to appear in nineteenth-century literature. In his 1839 novel *Béatrix*, Balzac forgoes any subtlety by describing Madame Schontz as having the creole beauty of the Comtesse Merlin. In *The Girl with the Golden Eyes*, by far the most melodramatic of these works, Balzac spins a lurid tale of murder, obsession, and depravity with more than a dash of the exotic creole. The Havana-born Mariquita, Marquise de San-Réal, married to an older Spaniard and brought to France, shares a passion for her slave/lover Paquita Valdés with a fashionable Parisian dandy—who is secretly her own half-brother. After the bloody denouement, Mariquita announces that she will return to Spain to the convent of Los Dolores. Since Balzac had never traveled to either Spain or Cuba, certain critics attribute his inspiration to his friendship with Mercedes—La Belle Créole.

Mercedes' salon also found its way into novels. Alexandre Dumas used it as the stage for an encounter between the two protagonists in *Pauline* (1838) with Mercedes herself appearing as a character and interacting in the scene. As late as 1876, the journalist Granier de Cassagnac titled the first chapter of *The Secret of the Chevalier de Médrane* as "A soiree at the home of Comtesse Merlin."

Surrounded by this literary milieu, seeing the preparation for the Duchess d'Abrantès' own memoirs might have inspired Mercedes to organize her own recollections. Perhaps nostalgia moved her, as she reflected on her sister's death in 1825 and her uncle's advancing age. Any longtime exile can become colored by sentiment and wistfulness, especially with constant reminders of the past in correspondence with relatives and streams of visitors. Although Mercedes' closest Cuban relatives were gone, her house became a familiar stop for well-connected and well-traveled Habaneros. Visitors included her extremely wealthy cousins, the future Count and Countesss of Peñalver, who married in Bologna in August 1823 and commissioned the Rossini cantata that Mercedes and Maria Malibran would later perform. Writing in Havana about Mercedes in 1837, the political and literary essayist Domingo del Monte noted the "infinite number of Habaneros who have seen her in France and have had the fortunate opportunity to enjoy her pleasant and sweet treatment." Whatever the motivation, Mercedes began crafting a memoir that she published privately for her friends in 1831. This rather slim volume, called *Mes Douze Premières Années* (*My First Twelve Years*), covered her Cuban childhood, her voyage to Spain, and her early days with her mother.

Romanticism clearly influenced Mercedes' writing, emphasizing as she did passionate emotions, the beauty of nature—the overall supremacy of all sentiments. She focused on the exoticness of Cuba, stressing the Spanish and Creole traits that entranced the French. The heat and the sun equated with passionate natures and slow, languid movements—perhaps even with an unstated sexual allure. The sun's intensity also colored the countryside more brightly, flamboyantly. Mercedes encapsulated in this small book all the longing she felt for her lost paradise and for those that she had loved and could no longer see. She re-created Mamita and conjured up the sense of all-encompassing love that she emanated toward her little Mercedes. Furthermore, the memoir enabled Mercedes to reassert her father's position, or at least define how she wished him to be recalled: loving, generous, jovial, and illustrious. Her memoir reaffirmed the preeminent position of her family and furthered the illusion of enormous wealth that persists today.

Memoirs were incredibly popular in the aftermath of the Napoleonic wars. Seemingly every general and marshal wrote a memoir or had one ghost-written. The Duchess d'Abrantès, facing financial ruin after her husband's suicide and the fall of the empire, made memoirs her entire career. Abrantès used some of the same anecdotes in different ways, providing different angles in multiple editions. Her Spanish journeys, for example, are covered in three different books. So in one sense, Mercedes was not entering an unknown world. But Mercedes, one of the first females to venture into this genre, further distinguished herself by not writing about high society as later authors would do; she wrote instead about her childhood and early years. Delving into childhood was a conscious choice—it played on a particular strength guaranteed to generate public interest, while nourishing the nostalgia for her cherished Cuba and its sights and sounds.

Today, with travel to the Caribbean generally so accessible, it is easy to forget how exotic these distant islands would have been to a nineteenth-century European reader. Cuba then was an almost unknown world, conjuring up images of heat, humidity, brilliant colors, sweet sugars, rum, slaves, and sensual women. The mystique surrounding the island would have been similar to what the French remembered about the old Saint-Domingue and their remaining colonial islands. George Sand had just mined this vein in her first novel, *Indiana*, about a French Creole from Île Bourbon.

Ironically, in a small way—although for very different reasons— many tourists still share this view of Cuba as an unknown. Whether Europeans see romance in the revolution or Americans feel tempted by curiosity for a forbidden destination, the modern world finds Cuba a continual enigma.

Despite sharing a common frontier, the French likewise identified Spain as alien, more passionate, more mysterious than France. Its inhabitants were supposedly more likely to commit acts of passion, to have spectacular fortunes, and to be driven by emotions and jealousies. Writers like Prosper Mérimée and Balzac used these images and ideas in their novels—some based in Spain itself while others merely had Spanish characters.

While not sold publicly and published anonymously, Mercedes' *Mes Douze Premières Années* sold out. Her identity was transparent, and a journal for the publishing sector soon wrote that "this charming work, from the pen of Madame Mercedes Merlin...no sooner appears than it disappears." This "timid" first work reached an even wider audience than her Parisian circle. Her Cuban visitors, including the educationalist and philosopher José de la Luz y Caballero and the landowner José Luis Alfonso, quickly circulated her memoir back home, resulting in a laudatory review in the newly created journal *Revista Bimestre de la Isla de Cuba*.

The *Revista Bimestre* was launched in 1831 and involved influential writers and thinkers on the island, including Domingo del Monte. Del Monte not only created an influential literary and political circle but was fundamental in developing and nurturing a sense of Cuban nationalism and identity. He stressed the *criollo* (creole) character over the Spanish, trying to distance Cubans from their colonial status. Over time he even toyed with abolitionist policies. Given his background, it is not surprising that the review reflected the dual sentiment of pride that a fellow countrywoman had succeeded in sophisticated Paris, as well as pleasure over Mercedes' decision to focus on recollections of her homeland.

> The sweet sentiment of affection for the homeland which this little work emanates...would be in itself enough recommendation.... If to this is added that the interesting author was born in Havana, which she recalls with tenderness, despite living in that capital surrounded by the most select of society, we would be guilty of indifference if we didn't dedicate an article in the *Revista Cubana*.

According to the article, the book got its "mysterious and irresistible attraction" from the warmth with which passages were relayed, a talent for judiciously using and placing these passages in the narrative, and the elegant language with a slight hint of melancholy and tenderness throughout. Domingo del Monte's review highlighted various extracts, translated from the French, including a loving description of Mamita and the tale of Mercedes' escape from the convent (rumors of the escapade had long circulated in Havana). Del Monte agreed with many of her comments, although he did not accept some of her less flattering portrayals of Habaneros as completely under the influence of the fiery sun. Interested in promoting a more advanced vision of Cuban society, del Monte excused these recollections given Mercedes' many years away.

Perhaps having heard hints of another volume, del Monte wanted to read more. He may have expected her continued success in the future and likely would have assumed she would continue to honor her distant native land. Mercedes indeed would write more about their homeland, although perhaps not as del Monte anticipated. This later work would be her most lasting achievement.

14

THE LITERARY
SOCIALITE

Flushed with her first, albeit private, literary success, Mercedes quickly published a second volume in 1832. She had ended her first recollections with the arrival in Madrid of a mysterious package from Florida, delivered by the wife of the American ambassador. The first pages of this second volume revealed that the mysterious package contained the "true" story of Sor Santa Inés, the nun from Santa Clara convent who had befriended the young Mercedes. The story, however, had all the hallmarks of a novel, containing a heartless father, a faithful lover, a harrowing escape from the convent and the island, and the tragic death of the two lovers following a shipwreck. It is difficult to know how much truth remained in the story, but Mercedes would later use this technique in other works: adding a romanticized veneer to a real-life incident, at times crossing into pure fiction. Mercedes always kept the kernel of truth in her work, but her nonfiction shifted time frames for the sake of better narrative, embellishment, or for heightened drama. The challenge today is to unravel the truth from the rest.

After publishing the *Histoire de la Soeur Inès*, Mercedes began to expand her memoirs to incorporate her later years in Spain, including the war years so familiar to many of her close circle. While Mercedes continued the general tone begun in the first memoir, she now drew on new themes designed to interest her audience. Few French readers had known the Cuban characters in her first volume, but this market definitely had familiarity with the main political and cultural players in the Peninsular War. While still stressing the more exotic elements of her tale—the nightly gypsy serenades, Mercedes and Pepita dancing and singing with castanets, Aunt Manuela's peculiarities—she now sprinkled her narrative liberally with recognizable names such as Goya, General Dessolles, and of course, a certain dashing General H.S., whose description would have identified him as Horace Sébastiani. He received a less than flattering portrayal, but whether her depiction exacted a subtle revenge against someone who interfered with her husband's career in Corsica remains unknown.

For this portion of her memoirs, Mercedes supplemented her own recollections with various other sources. Gonzalo O'Farrill had died in 1831 but had left two key documents: his highly personal *Carta* or letter to his stepson that described his life with Ana Rodríguez de Carassa and defended her from public criticism, and his political memoir. In the latter he justified his political actions, focusing on the crucial period between the abdication of Carlos IV and the aftermath of the battle of Bailén. Both documents offer insight into O'Farrill's motivations and decision to embrace the Afrancesado path, and provided Mercedes the opportunity to highlight the contradictory emotions felt by her family as their Spanish patriotism clashed with their support of the French.

In this new volume, Mercedes maintained a subtle practice of reducing her age. Her first book never mentioned the year of her birth. She correctly stated that she was eight and a half years old when her father returned, but upon her arrival in Spain, she claimed to be eleven when in truth she was thirteen. Now she continued shaving years off, declaring that she was fourteen when Napoleon took Madrid in December 1808, when she was actually nineteen. An acute reader might have questioned a fifteen-year-old marrying the thirty-eight-year-old Merlin! She even recounted the celebrated Cuban visit by the then exiled Duke d'Orléans (now the king, Louis-Philippe) in 1798 but then coyly added that she could not have witnessed it as she had not yet been born. She was actually nine years old. Mercedes was never very good with dates, but her slips of memory worked suspiciously in her favor.

Mercedes was forty-seven years old in 1836, when she published the second memoir, but she was still publicly acclaimed as beautiful—even young—in most accounts, and her portraits attest to her youthful appearance. But various events in her life indicated her true age. In April 1834, Mercedes' namesake and niece, Marie-della-Mercédès Merlin—the little girl born shortly after Mercedes' arrival in France—married Marie-Joseph-Alfred Lebarbier de Tinan. The groom was the son of none other than Aunt Manuela's lodger in Madrid, the French officer who had begged for an introduction to Teresa Montalvo so that he could hear Mercedes sing.

Almost a year later, on March 1835, another ceremony united Mercedes' twenty-two-year-old daughter, Teresa, with a forty-year-old widower named Firmin-Désiré Gentien. A landowner and mayor of Dissay, a town near Poitiers, Gentien owned an immense turreted fifteenth-century chateau built by the bishop of Poitiers. Teresa had inherited both her mother's dark eyes and some of her musical talent. Much like her own mother, Mercedes had cultivated her daughter's talents, and occasionally Teresa would sing Italian airs or Spanish boleros with her mother, sometimes accompanied by other guests such as Prince Emilio Belgiojoso.

The Merlins gave their daughter a trousseau containing silver serving pieces and a splendid one hundred thousand–franc dowry. But as their finances could not have sustained such a significant outflow, the marriage contract stipulated that the dowry would only be payable upon the death of the first contributing parent.

Perhaps these various family events delayed the completion of the new memoirs; by their publication date, Mercedes viewed this endeavor in a more professional light. Surviving letters to publishers confirm her desire to earn money from writing, as do the strategies she utilized to publicize her books. The Merlins needed the additional income. By August 1836, General Merlin had once again entered the reserves, but with a salary reduction to just over seven thousand francs. With additional rents and interests, their estimated annual income hovered at less than twenty thousand francs. To maintain her level of entertainment, Mercedes must have relied on her inconsistent Cuban income. Ironically, Mercedes could have earned considerably more had she ignored convention and sung professionally on stage, as did Mario, the *Cavaliere* de Candia. Despite the lack of prior professional experience, his first contract, with the Opéra Français, paid fifteen hundred francs per month. Her friend Maria Malibran received approximately four hundred fifty thousand francs for two seasons during this time.

Mercedes set about ensuring the success of her new memoirs, now called *Souvenirs et Mémoires de Madame la Comtesse Merlin, Souvenirs d'une Créole* (*Remembrances and Memoirs of Madame the Countess Merlin, Remembrances of a Créole*) by using her circle of *grands hommes* and other acquaintances as an effective publicity tool. Well-placed, favorable reviews were as crucial an element in nineteenth-century book sales as they are today. Balzac himself penned (under a pseudonym) one of his own reviews. Already, prior to the release of the first two volumes (*Souvenirs d'une Créole* comprised four volumes, which included the original memoirs as well as *Soeur Inès*), anticipatory notices appeared in numerous journals, including the *Revue de Paris*. There then followed a flattering review by Charles Sainte-Beuve in the *Revue des Deux Mondes* on April 1, 1836. This memoir "without literary pretensions," recounting a youth begun in an "opulent climate," charmed the eminent literary critic. He particularly enjoyed the vivid scenes and concluded by describing Mercedes as someone in whom "joy…is accompanied by an inner strength."

Mercedes also called upon one of her regular salon guests, Count Charles d'Aragon, a popular young man, to secure a favorable review from his good friend George Sand. However, Mercedes was mistaken if she thought that it would be straightforward to obtain the support of the world's best-known woman writer. While Mercedes and George Sand shared a love of music and an interest in writing, their differences probably outnumbered their similarities. Sand had more in common with another noted hostess and writer, the Italian political exile Princess Cristina Belgiojoso, as both adopted gender-defying prototypes—dressing outlandishly at times and championing men or causes to an extreme. Mercedes had independent views but presented a more compliant and "womanly" image.

Sand did not dislike the book—she particularly admired the "simplicity and goodness which breathes through each impression" and applauded the young girl "destined to the social jail like others but who protested with all her imaginative strength against convents, books, slavery, corsets and slippers." However, Sand quickly deviated from her brief and instead of reviewing the entire memoir, she merely evaluated *Mes Douze Premières Années*. She departed further by including a lengthy discussion on a favorite subject: women's intellectual progress. Criticizing Mercedes' tendency to present the intellectual reflections of an adult as the musings of her youthful self, Sand noted that otherwise the book would be a "little poem without fault" and that the "charming work" attested to women's desire to improve their actual condition. Anticipating her editor's annoyance, she wrote several defensive-sounding letters to François Buloz at the *Revue des Deux Mondes* (where it was originally destined) as well as d'Aragon. In them she noted that she had truly liked the book but likewise insisted that Buloz not "change a syllable" of the review. Sand's article eventually appeared in the *Revue de Paris*.

Charles de Bernard's review in the *Chronique de Paris* gallantly alluded to Mercedes' musical talents and renown, but lightly ridiculed many of the events and characters, from Mercedes' overly perfumed mother to Joseph's possible flirtation in the Casa de Campo. The reviewer evidently hoped to find the depiction of a sultry creole but concluded that Mercedes should have named her memoirs *Souvenirs d'une Miss* instead. The reviewer also disliked a woman's depiction of military matters, including battles and the evacuation of Madrid, which filled much of the third volume: "In the midst of all these historians…Madame la Comtesse Merlin does not even fear a little bit to see endangered by the shocks of a melee with no gallantry or quarter given, the flowers and ribbons of a toilette better suited for the conversations of the salon or in the loges of the Italian Opera." The biased male reviewer yearned for something other than military events from a feminine "mouth which must know so many delicious words." That same year, Bernard also ridiculed a novel by Delphine de Girardin, *Monsieur Balzac's Cane*, declaring that he would soon publish *Madame de Girardin's Umbrella*.

Two more flattering articles appeared in June and December 1836 in the *Journal des Débats*, focusing on the femininity, sweetness, and creole essence of the work. "One is astonished," wrote the reviewer Philarète Chasles in the first article, "to see so French a Creole woman and a French woman so Creole." Chasles also reflected a certain condescension, the opposite of Sand's paean to women's advancement, when he praised Mercedes for not having pretensions as a woman of letters. In his view, women should be happy to be talented and surrounded by male admiration but should not enter the domain of serious male writers.

Along with recruiting prominent reviewers, Mercedes took advantage of her memoir's publication to reinforce her family's ties to the remaining Bonapartes. She wrote to Joseph, now living in England, and enclosed a copy of her work. She shared the news of her daughter's recent wedding while excusing her husband from writing due to his military position. Joseph's reply revealed much about his ongoing affection for Mercedes and her family, as well as his own ceaseless defense of his family's reputation. His detailed letter clearly indicates a careful reading of the entire memoir, and he didn't hesitate to chastise Mercedes for depicting his brother in "the colors which were those of his enemies the day after his fall."

While he agreed with her loving depictions of her family, Joseph disputed at length various assertions regarding his relative weakness in handling Marshal Soult's refusal to support Marshal Marmont at Arapiles in 1812 and other military matters. This was not the first time Joseph had minutely critiqued memoirs—he had done so even more robustly and coldly with the memoirs of the Duchess d'Abrantès. However, with Mercedes he alternated between a stern tone and a nostalgic tenderness. He concluded by assuring her of his belief that "under your pen, it [truth] will never be disguised.... So many people speak and write against those who are crushed under fortune's wheel but that cannot be the ambition of a writer such as you." He sent her his pure and tender homage.

Souvenirs d'une Créole sold remarkably in France as well as Germany, and by November 1836 Mercedes entered negotiations with her publisher, Gervais Charpentier, for a second edition as well as for additional volumes of memoirs. Writing to him from Sillery, Mercedes agreed in principal to sell the rights to her existing memoirs but she was unhappy with the terms. Sounding like an accomplished professional, Mercedes indicated that modifications were needed; the payment of five thousand francs was acceptable but she considered the offer for additional volumes unsatisfactory, although Charpentier believed that he could offer similar sums "[as] I have the price of the first edition plus the sales and that the last ones will have two advantages over the first as [their content] will not be known and they will complete the work." Instead, Mercedes dictated an alternative arrangement: altered payment dates, permission to print one thousand copies of her portrait in exchange for two hundred fifty francs worth of books at wholesale, and two thousand francs per new volume payable at delivery.

Unfortunately, Charpentier could not publish the new edition as quickly as Mercedes wished, and in June 1837 she informed him that she would take her memoirs elsewhere. Mercedes wished to publish the new edition by the autumn, one imagines both for financial reasons as well as to maintain the public's interest. Even as she broke off with 262, she began discussions with a new publisher, Pierre-François-Camille Ladvocat, regarding publishing further memoirs on a basis similar to Charpentier's. Their first joint project was not to be a straightforward memoir but rather, according to the publisher, a portrait of society. In the early prospectus, included in Ladvocat's summer 1837 editions, the title given was *Les Loisirs d'une Femme du*

Monde. The two volumes were meant to cover Mercedes' recollections of society, full of fresh and striking portraits and anecdotes.

Ladvocat announced the publication for January 1838, but it didn't appear until July. The delay was most likely due to Mercedes' ongoing tension between her hectic social life and her literary obligations, a challenge for Mercedes that she never really overcame. Ladvocat sensed this conflict with Mercedes already in Vichy for part of the summer and planning to continue to another spa town, Néris-les-Bains. He therefore sent her a copy of the Duchess d'Abrantès' newest book, "to make you think a little on the engagements you have undertaken with your editor." He also hoped that she would find enough leisure time far from Paris to work. One wonders how much leisure she found, as *Le Ménestrel* reported on the brilliant concerts held in Vichy, Néris, and Aix-les-Bains during the summer of 1837. Mercedes and other luminaries from Paris all attended.

Mercedes' new publisher was not the only one to note that her good intentions toward work sometimes clashed with social engagements and travels. Since early 1837, Domingo del Monte had been trying to secure some pieces from Mercedes for the 1838 edition of the recent literary venture *Aguinaldo Habanero*. Their mutual friend in Paris, José Luis Alfonso, had repeatedly presented this request, and although she happily promised, Alfonso doubted that anything would be available before 1839. Mercedes, Alfonso confided, had gone off to Vichy and other travels and had forgotten—as happened "nine times out ten." From her country home, in October, Mercedes contritely promised to set to work immediately.

As some point between June 1837 and January 1838, Mercedes changed the focus of her planned work and rather surprisingly decided to dedicate the bulk of her book to a biography of her friend Maria Malibran. La Malibran had died unexpectedly in September 1836 from complications following a riding accident, aged just twenty-eight, at the height of her celebrity. Her accidental death in England caused worldwide consternation. Mercedes' intimate acquaintance with the García family placed her in a privileged position to recount Maria's life. The new book varied substantially from what she had planned.

However, the choice evidenced a remarkably shrewd decision calculated to leverage the public's enormous interest in the tragic story of the popular singer. As one reviewer lamented, the cult of the singer or artistic performer had surpassed that of even noteworthy statesmen who "would be forgotten the day after his death."

Mercedes' account was generally well received, even by that particular commentator who conceded that La Malibran had been a remarkable character, adding that Mercedes "had a charming style well made to recreate such a portrait, full of grace and freshness." Similarly, *Journal des Débats* thought the Malibran biography the best segment of the two volumes, since her story was dramatic and full of eccentricities.

Mercedes chose to focus on the personal aspects of Malibran's life, using additional information and anecdotes garnered from their mutual acquaintances. That public use of intimate letters and other details, such as financial contracts, commonplace in any modern-day biography, brought a vicious attack from one reviewer in the newly founded *La France Musicale*. The anonymous reviewer labeled Mercedes vulgar for providing this personal perspective and accused her of publishing the biography for her own vanity. Interestingly, it went further, conjecturing as to why a rich and socially prominent woman would violate the privacy of her supposed friend, even suggesting that she desired to create a new career because of the lessening of her vocal talents with age. It was an odd accusation at a time when Mercedes commanded much respect among great opera singers and could still delight her friends by improvising Spanish airs with Chopin, singing and clicking her castanets. The reviewer appeared ready to forgive these transgressions against La Malibran's personal life if Mercedes had been a professional writer—and generally dismissed all her publishing endeavors. One of Mercedes' earlier biographers suggested a particular enmity from the founder of this journal, Léon Escudier, who was later Verdi's publisher, but no explanation exists as to the cause.

The remainder of *Loisirs* consisted of some short pieces ranging from Mercedes' *Pensées* (Thoughts) to some short sketches. The most interesting of them is one called *L'Evasion* (the Escape), which recounted the brutal incident with her grandmother the Countess de Casa-Barreto and her young aunt Conchita. As usual with Mercedes, she did everything possible to imbue the episode with drama; saturating the senses with color, sounds, and emotions. Nevertheless, the choice to reference it again in later works underlines the trauma lying at its heart. As ever with Mercedes, the truth could be dressed up, but its essence survived, with her Cuban heritage never far below the surface.

PART IV

Cuba, Spain, and France

→ 15 ←

DAUGHTER OF HAVANA

*O*n January 11, 1839, a massive earthquake shattered the French possession of Martinique. The devastation prompted a public outcry in France, and by mid-March an official central committee sent out a general appeal throughout the nation. But another announcement reached the press even before the appointment of the committee members; the Comtesse Merlin, "always faithful to her self-appointed mission to come to the aid of the unfortunate," would be spearheading a grand benefit concert. Only six weeks lay between the announcement and the planned concert on April 25, so frantic efforts began to recruit performers from among the dilettanti and the ranks of the professionals, as well as patrons who could lend their prestige and sell tickets.

Mercedes worked tirelessly, and the press regularly provided updates on the forthcoming gala: she hoped to use the grand salon of the Louvre by royal permission; the singers Duprez and Mario demanded to sing; the premier artists led by the composer Meyerbeer and Mario were uniting with all the talents of the Parisian salons; they would transform the Théâtre de la Renaissance for one day into the most elegant of salons. Among the thirty-two *dames patronesses* were Princess Belgiojoso and Delphine de Girardin.

The press deemed the evening a great triumph and praised it extensively, although *Le Ménestrel* ironically noted that Parisians had spent some eight hundred thousand francs on their toilettes to raise twenty-five thousand francs for Martinique. Still, they noted that a second earthquake might be warranted if it produced a comparable evening. Delphine de Girardin's column described the superb choruses organized in "double rows of women in white dresses, crowned with camellias and heather" behind flower-filled golden baskets. More flowers and countless candles decorated the hall. The performances all drew praise, but Mercedes' stood out. Delphine heralded her duo with Mario from *Roberto Devereux* as the highlight of the concert: "Never has Madame Merlin had more brilliance and lightness in her voice." *Le Ménestrel* concurred, saying that Mercedes "sang an air with a remarkable purity and talent, and many persons felt regret that she was a countess."

All in all, it was another triumph for La Belle Créole.

Mercedes' public achievement was all the more remarkable given the trying circumstances in her private life. All the while she marshalled her charitable forces, her husband's health was failing. Just thirteen days after the Martinique benefit, on May 8, 1839, Christophe-Antoine Merlin died following a "long and painful illness." He had long suffered from severe attacks of gout, a condition which over time can lead to renal failure and possibly contributed to his death.

Mercedes found herself a widow at fifty, putting on mourning and entering into an altered world. The funeral occurred within two days, with a service at Saint-Laurent Church and burial at Père Lachaise. The funeral had a decidedly military air due to the pallbearers Marshal Clauzel, two generals, and the Count de Lariboisière. Despite the rain, the *Journal des Débats* reported many comrades in arms, deputations from diverse regiments, numerous deputies and peers, and other notables. Marshal Clauzel, himself the nephew of another Conventionnel, recalled past republican and imperial glories, lamenting the passing of the old soldiers who had served their homeland since the "dawn of our glorious revolution." Running through General Merlin's military achievements, he noted the inspiration that young Christophe had drawn from his older brother—a poignant reference to the death of Merlin de Thionville in 1833. Marshal Clauzel offered a last farewell as the coffin descended: "*Adieu*, dear comrade! *Adieu*, dear Merlin!"

Two days later, the relentless progress of estate law took over, much as it had when Mercedes' father had died in 1807. In French law, every death required a notary to take a formal inventory as an initial step in settlement of an estate, called the *succession*. Walking through every room of their apartment at 58 Rue de Bondy, assessors placed a value on each celadon vase, decorative bronze and marble clock, damask-covered mahogany divan, rosewood Pleyel piano, and even Mercedes' own gowns and jewels. Beginning with the *caves* full of wine, including the sweet Spanish Jerez that Emilio Belgiojoso asked her to provide as a gift to the Austrian statesman Prince Metternich, and finishing in Mercedes' boudoir, the assessors missed nothing. They did not even exempt the servant quarters housing General Merlin's valet, Mercedes' lady's maid, the footmen, housekeeper, kitchen maid, and coachman.

In the main part of the apartment, the assessors inspected the grand salon, with its three windows overlooking the gardens, filled with various sets of furniture covered in red damask or white satin, the ornamental musical clock, and the piano. Moving along to the adjoining room, also overlooking the garden, they found Mercedes' bedroom—the *chambre à coucher*—a seemingly private chamber but in the French style also a public room, filled with more elegant furniture sets and another piano. Mercedes' truly private room was her boudoir, housing her writing desk as well as a traveling desk, and more rosewood furniture. Surprisingly for so stylish a person, Mercedes' wardrobe was not so extensive, but it did include two highly desirable (and expensive) long cashmere shawls—at six hundred francs each, worth more than any single dress. Likewise, the bulk of her jewelry consisted of lovely, delicate gold bracelets encrusted with pearls, rubies, emeralds, topaz, and opals—but none surpassing a worth of one hundred francs. However, she did own several substantial pieces: a set containing a bandeau, three brooches, and earrings in gold with sapphires, topaz, rubies, emeralds, and opals; various other brooches embellished with precious stones; two jeweled diadems, and a spectacular tiara composed of over three hundred diamonds and four pearls. The crown was the most valuable item by far—worth over ten thousand francs.

Upstairs, the general's rooms contained his cavalry sabers, austere iron bed, and books. He owned numerous military journals—as expected—but more surprisingly, Ovid's *Metamorphoses* and Lord Byron's poems. The apartment contained another reminder of the past: an excellent art collection probably accumulated in Spain, comprising works by some of the great Spanish painters: Velázquez, Zurbarán, and Ribera (*Lo Spagnoletto*).

After the completion of the inventory, the arduous process of dividing the estate commenced—particularly complicated by a Spanish marriage contract, lost Spanish properties, the guardianship of Pepita's daughter, and the dowry promised to Teresa. The family notary, Monsieur Delapalme, advised Mercedes to reject her joint ownership of the estate due to the onerous obligations claiming it would entail. Instead, Mercedes accepted eighty-six thousand francs as the value of her old dowry—including the now useless Spanish state bonds. The remaining net assets would be split as required under French law: half to the widow and the rest to the children. In total, Mercedes received approximately 109,000 francs. The residual in Teranita's trust account was transferred to François Merlin, as the two cousins had married in late 1838. It is not clear whether Teresa collected any portion of her one hundred thousand–franc dowry, although at the very least she would have to wait until her mother's death for the bulk of it. Reviewing the estate's total assets, it became clear that General Merlin had attempted to make his financial position as liquid as possible—he had sold Sillery in July 1838 and had placed the proceeds in notes or loans to various individuals or even in investment accounts with their old notary.

Merlin's legacy was a far cry from the chaos that Joaquín had left over thirty years ago, but there simply wasn't that much left—especially in terms of income-producing assets. Mercedes, for example, took the bulk of her share in the seventy-five thousand francs worth of furnishing and personal property, the cash balances in the notary accounts, and merely twenty-one thousand francs in notes payable and shares. It is difficult to imagine how Mercedes could continue to support her lifestyle, even considering the Cuban income and any possible pension from the military. To give some context, in Balzac's novel *The Marriage Contract*, the fashionable newlyweds begin with sixty-seven thousand francs in income per year but quickly over-spend by an additional two hundred thousand francs a year. Mer-cedes wrote in her memoirs that "when unforeseen events separated me from my family and friends and launched me into a foreign land, my happiness became for him [Merlin] a sacred mission." Merlin not only "surrounded her with care and tenderness," he sometimes fondly called his eternally youthful wife his eldest daughter. A pic-ture emerges of the struggle he must have had throughout the years to ensure this vow, and it is nearly miraculous that the estate lacked any noticeable debts. Mercedes' Cuban income would be more important than ever.

To raise some cash and settle the fifteen thousand francs in funeral costs, taxes, and legal fees, Mercedes placed some of the best of the art collection for sale. The nation was enthralled by all things Spanish in 1839, so it was the right year to try to sell Spanish art in Paris. Paris at the time had quite a few renowned Spanish art collec-tions, including the finest of all, belonging to Marshal Soult. Many French officers left Spain with valuable art, some purchased from the nationalized assets, others seized as prizes. Joseph had awarded both Sébastiani and General Dessolles valuable paintings from the royal collection, but Soult became notorious for both the quantity of art he amassed as well as for his ruthless acquisition methods. Further spurring interest, in 1838 Louis-Philippe opened his Musée Espagnol at the Louvre, publicly showcasing over four hundred magnificent works collected by Mercedes' Rue de Bondy neighbor, Baron Taylor.

The catalogue for the Merlin sale spoke excitedly of the charming portrait of a young Spanish Infanta by Velázquez, and of a hooded Franciscan monk in prayer by Zurbarán—a painter "whose works at the Musée Espagnol were so admired." The Velázquez sold for fifty-five hundred francs and the Zurbarán, a dramatic figure half in darkness, kneeling holding a skull, was quoted at twelve hundred francs, while four smaller evangelists by Ribera were eighteen hundred francs. In total, Mercedes offered fifteen paintings, but strangely enough she seems to have kept the most valuable ones. In the end she sold only the Velázquez and a few other lesser pieces. Perhaps she still couldn't bear to part with her cherished possessions.

Shortly after the sale, Mercedes retreated to Germany, first to the spa town of Baden and then later onto Stuttgart. She had previously enjoyed visiting friends in Germany, and her son François was a young officer based in nearby Metz (in Lorraine). She was still there in September when she asked M. Delapalme for some five thousand francs in funds, as she intended to stay for some months more. Contradictory press reports arrived in Paris. Some had her delighting in concerts and balls in Baden, but her loyal friend Delphine de Girardin testily refuted those stories in her own column, telling the journalists to "lie...if lying is your style, but at least ensure that your lies are not so bad." Far from being the "queen of pleasures," Mercedes was in deep mourning and received no one. Still, when she returned to Paris that winter, the *Revue de Paris* claimed that "in Stuttgart, one dances and plays music all night long, because Madame Merlin carries with her and leaves after her a taste for the arts and distinguished pleasure."

During Mercedes' stay in Germany, worrying financial news began to arrive from Havana. The first development appeared in the form of Joaquín's illegitimate daughter, Merced Toledo (formerly called Valdés). Now a thirty-four-year-old widow with several children, in late 1839 Merced Toledo renewed her requests for financial assistance through the legal settlement of the long-promised share of Joaquín's estate. While never formally acknowledging the kinship, the heirs agreed to donate eighty-five hundred pesos to Merced Toledo, "who is said to be...Don Joaquín's daughter out of wedlock," since the siblings wished to improve her fortune. Sadly for Merced Toledo, although she thanked her half-siblings effusively, she would spend several years in a futile court case for a portion of this income, as Joaquín's Barreto family refused to recognize the transferred shares.

Then in the winter of 1840, the highest appeals court in Spain finally ruled against the Santa Cruz heirs in their ongoing dispute over the Santa Margarita lands. This was now the third judgment; the first negative judgment by the Royal Treasury in 1821 had forced the redistribution of Joaquín's estate and an appeal failed in 1835. The heirs had pressed on, although it seemed that Mercedes and her niece had the most to gain by appealing. With no more legal recourse, Quico exercised his right to compensation from his co-heirs. Mercedes and Teranita would each have to repay some thirty thousand pesos in capital plus interest on that amount (approximately one hundred fifty thousand francs each).

Mercedes was appalled and felt she faced ruin. The effect on her niece and son would also be devastating, as they feared the loss of a portion of their Nazareno lands as a consequence. The ongoing litigation over Santa Margarita had been a source of tension between Mercedes and Quico, with constant disagreements as to how much Mercedes should receive. Other factors further aggravated tensions, including deductions for legal costs arising from the Nazareno boundary dispute with their O'Farrill cousins—the co-heirs had agreed to share these costs, and in Mercedes' case it meant a reduction in income. Although they ultimately secured a favorable judgment, Spanish law did not permit the recovery of their legal expenses. The strained sibling relationships also emanated from an underlying resentment on Quico's part at having been, in effect, left to pick up the pieces and fight the numerous legal battles on his own. On Mercedes' part, there was a deeply held belief that she was somehow entitled to more and that bad faith was involved.

Compounding Mercedes' financial concerns, she faced difficulties obtaining her widow's pension from the French military for typically bureaucratic reasons: the lack of a birth certificate from Havana. While the pension was not a huge amount, it certainly stood to help her financial position. All of these events took their toll on Mercedes' fragile nerves, and she ultimately took the momentous decision to return to Cuba and seek a solution for her financial woes, securing her future through a voyage into the past.

Mercedes began her journey in early April 1840, traveling first to London and then onward to Bristol, on the southwest coast, to board the steamship *Great Western*. The wooden paddle-wheeled steamships offered cutting-edge technology. The *Great Western*, designed by the legendary British engineer Isambard Kingdom Brunel, began its first regular transatlantic service in March 1838. To reach Bristol from London efficiently, Mercedes would have used the new Great Western Railway, another Brunel creation, part of the way. The entire transatlantic voyage to New York would take approximately two weeks, considerably less than the journey on Admiral Gravina's flagship in 1802.

Although she had numerous acquaintances in London, having visited previously in 1838, there was one resident in particular she wished to see: Joseph Bonaparte. The ex-king of Spain had left his beloved estate in New Jersey in 1839 and settled in London, as he was banned from France and Italy. Mercedes found him in poor health. As she left London on April 12, he said his farewells by letter, enclosing some missives for friends in New York and Philadelphia and encouraging her to visit the latter city. His health never really recovered, and he died in 1844 in Florence, finally reunited with his family.

Mercedes sailed for New York on April 16 along with some 112 other passengers, one of whom happened to be one of the world's most sensational celebrities, the dancer Fanny Elssler, about to premier in New York. News quickly reached Paris about the exceptional passenger list, including the "most elegant dandies of English society" who had paid up to three thousand francs for their tickets at auction. The normal fare was six hundred francs.

Once in New York, Mercedes had some days to see the city and even traveled to Philadelphia and on to Washington. Escorted by the Spanish ambassador and his wife, she also met President Martin van Buren. The French newspaper in New York, the *Courrier des Etats-Unis*, reported back to Paris that Mercedes was the toast of the city, as anyone with claims to being a lady or a gentleman sought an introduction.

Mercedes completed the final part of her journey to Havana on the *Christopher Columbus*, a sailing ship traveling along the American coastline. As much as she anticipated seeing her homeland, Havana society eagerly awaited her arrival. In the meantime, local society, hungry for news, consumed the *Courrier* article and José de la Luz y Caballero commented on the flattering reception awaiting Mercedes in a letter to their mutual friend José Luis Alfonso.

Mercedes finally arrived around the seventh of June. Already, as the ship passed the Bahamas, she delighted in the warm and fragrant air of the tropics, which also elicited a rush of memories and emotions. She wrote, "The sun, the stars...all seems to me grander, more diaphanous, more splendid!...My vision cannot absorb it all nor enjoy it all; my breast cannot contain my heart! I cry like a child, and I am crazed with happiness!" Even after thirty-eight years away, Mercedes still felt a passionate love for this land: "I recognize that neither the distance nor the years have been able to cool my first love."

As the *Christopher Columbus* entered the fabled Havana harbor, Mercedes thought she recognized houses, churches, and other familiar sights. But the harbor she entered would have been significantly busier than the one she had left in 1802. The overall impression was one of movement and confusion; songs mixed with yelling by an assortment of people of every shade and type. No matter how much she remembered from the past, the reality was, as she wrote, "animated and ardent like the sun." Her uncle Juanito and his sons welcomed Mercedes by meeting her boat in the harbor. Eventually, she disembarked in front of the old basilica of San Francisco de Asís—almost facing the house where her father had died.

The Montalvo family lived in an immense house on Calle de Cuba, built by Mateo Pedroso in 1780 and still known by his name. Juan Montalvo had married his cousin María Antonia Calvo de la Puerta, the daughter of the same Marqués de Casa-Calvo who had accompanied Mercedes and her family throughout their Spanish adventures and into exile. The couple had eleven children, not unheard-of in Cuba. Stepping through enormous wooden outer doors into the soaring gateway, how could Mercedes not have felt nostalgic seeing the flower-filled, vast central courtyard, and looking up at the two upper galleries with their graceful columns and airy, interconnecting rooms? From its balconies and windows, Mercedes could see and hear the harbor. The family enjoyed the fabled breezes by dining on the gallery itself, spreading out a table to include all the children, grandchildren, and guests. The numerous younger cousins surrounded her, asking her coquettishly, "Do you know me?" Over-whelmed, Mercedes mixed up relatives, causing laughter all around. She particularly awaited the arrival of her brother, who often resided outside of Havana, as well as her great-uncle Rafael O'Farrill, Mam-ita's son and Gonzalo O'Farrill's brother. When Mercedes finally saw him, his poignant resemblance to his mother brought forth a rush of memories: "Mamita, her house...my adoration for her gen-erosity, my childhood life, all was there again in this living reminder of the past."

The numerous reunions also included the various slaves and ex-slaves related to her family. In a similar fashion to her young cous-ins, they presented themselves and asked if she recognized them, and they reminded her of their connection. Mercedes saw her "milk brother," the son of her old nurse Mama Dolores, as well as Agueda, her own mother's nanny.

Mercedes was feted everywhere—the Montalvo house filled nightly with visitors, entertainments, and opulent meals. Lavish and flowery poems in her honor appeared in the local press, a typical Cuban custom for special occasions. Mercedes' cousin the Count de Peñalver hosted a special concert and ball in her honor, where she also performed arias from *Lucia di Lammermoor* and a duet from Bellini's *Norma*. Press coverage immediately followed, with the author noting that outside, crowds gathered under the moonlight on the Alameda de Paula to enjoy the "harmonious accents" emanating from within.

Uncle Juanito provided Mercedes with her own carriage and coachman for use throughout the city, and she escaped the ever-present heat by going on regular early evening carriage rides like most other Habaneros, enjoying the coolness, the sociability, and even music in the Plaza de Armas. In this relatively compact and walled city, there were memories wherever she looked: the Convent of Santa Clara, Mamita's old home, and even her father's house. That house seemed filled with the echoes of her past: Catalina lulling her to sleep, the table where her father had shown her the elaborate family tree, which in turn elicited a deep longing for her father: "Oh—where is my father? I can find no trace, just a pile of lifeless stones and an eternal remembrance." With those sentiments in mind, Mercedes also ventured out to the city cemetery, built after her departure when Habaneros stopped burying their dead under the church floors. Mamita and Joaquín had been some of the earliest burials.

Along her rides through the city and her conversations with her relatives, Mercedes discovered the great changes that had occurred in Cuba in her long absence. Over these years, sugar production had exploded, along with the number and locations of sugar mills. Joaquín may have left a disastrous legacy, but he had been farsighted in other ways. Steam engines now appeared regularly in mills, and a new railroad existed where Joaquín had once traced a canal from the sugar-rich Güines area to Havana. But Mercedes could not have failed to see the less-attractive consequences of that growing wealth: an increase in slaves.

From Mercedes' birth to her visit, Cuba's population had shifted from majority white to just over majority black, including many free black citizens. Spain had bowed to English pressure and officially banned the slave trade in 1820, so in theory no new slaves could enter Cuba. However, corrupt officials blatantly tolerated an illegal trade that generated enormous fortunes for slave traders, who with other merchants often financed the landowners to support the expense of producing sugar. In some cases these "new men" became landowners themselves, and their names now could be found alongside those of Cárdenas, Peñalver, O'Farrill, and Montalvo. There were also many more titles—counts and marqueses abounded, and with them the opulence that Cubans loved. Even in 1830, the visiting son of

Marshal Ney noted the astonishing cost of the Count of Fernandina's new home: 1.5 million francs.

Relations with the Spanish government had grown more uncomfortable compared with past times. Cuba was famed for its loyalty to Spain after most of the American empire had collapsed, but part of that faithfulness reflected a constant fear of slave uprisings—the specter of Haiti. Cuban landowners may have wished for more political freedoms, but they needed a powerful army. It was a complex situation, not helped by what many viewed as oppressive captain-generals.

During her stay, Mercedes saw some of the liberal intelligentsia, including del Monte and Luz y Caballero, who resented heavy censorship in Cuba and wanted to ensure the end of the slave trade, if only in some cases to avoid the continued increase in the slave population. They constantly feared exile from their beloved homeland but cherished a goal to develop its cultural institutions and society. They happily greeted Mercedes, recalling her warm Parisian hospitality and appreciating the appeal of a Cuban native with Parisian sophistication. Del Monte had never met her (although he had publicly praised her memoirs), but after visiting with her various times he felt assured of his long-held high opinion. Others did not have the chance to meet her, such as the Matanzas-based Félix Tanco, but eagerly wrote to del Monte offering to give Mercedes various pieces of writing because she "is educated and…being almost a stranger in her homeland, her observations are disinterested." Tanco was also incredibly curious about this "high ranking personality": what did she think about the state of Cuba, the blacks, and customs?

Mercedes was equally curious about this altered yet familiar place. Motivated on her journey by financial pressures, she now recognized the prospects for a new and potentially lucrative literary endeavor—an account of her Cuban journey. Mercedes had witnessed the recent success of her close friend Custine's book *Spain Under Fernando VII*. This book, an account of his own travels while exploring the native character and customs using an epistolary format, could have easily inspired Mercedes. She began requesting useful information from knowledgeable friends, especially del Monte, and she also collected all sorts of local literature. Del Monte had a sense of her plan when he wrote to Alfonso just after Mercedes' departure. He had given her various notes in part because he "supposed that she would publish her voyage to Havana and it was more convenient that the facts she based her observations on be true." He wanted to ensure that she not publish anything "contrary to the truth or our interests."

Mercedes' final public event was a concert for the Casa de Beneficencia, the local charity home for women, in the Teatro Tacón, outside the city walls. A sumptuous Havana society event, it featured Mercedes singing several arias and a duet with her cousin Teresita Peñalver as well as performances by another singer, María de Jesús Martínez. The event received fulsome coverage in the *Diario de la Habana*; Mercedes was once again acclaimed. However, as del Monte reported in a letter to Alfonso, the evening may have revealed more complicated attitudes than publicly admitted. While the newspaper had called Mercedes an illustrious Habanera, it seemed that other Cubans viewed her more as an outsider. Del Monte observed that while she was well received at first, her "eccentricities had roused our people, who are the most intolerant in the world." Whatever these perceived eccentricities were, when rumors spread that Mercedes had not listened to Señorita Martínez in rehearsals, the audience expressed its displeasure by applauding the local girl excessively, to the distress of Mercedes.

Perhaps Mercedes was disconcerted for other reasons. On the same day as the concert, July 18, she had finally signed an agreement with her brother, Quico, and Juan Montalvo had signed another on François Merlin's behalf. The grueling negotiations required all of Uncle Juanito's diplomatic tact and involved Mercedes' overwrought emotions. Quico would later state that he agreed to certain terms only after the tearful pleas of a sister he had not seen in some thirty years. The final document is extraordinary in its avowals of fraternal sentiment. The siblings recognized their differences, now concluded "fraternally," Quico expressed his "fraternal love and appreciation" for Mercedes undertaking the "long and arduous journey."

Motivated by his "truly tender affection" and cognizant that the final settlement was insufficient to maintain Mercedes' rank while his own fortune was greater (as appropriate in the natural order of things), Quico supplemented her income. Mercedes in turn recognized the love and generosity that she always expected from her brother and gave "the most expressive thanks."

Away from the niceties, the agreement resulted in the reduction of Mercedes' remaining seventy-three thousand pesos in capital to just over thirty-two thousand pesos, and then supplemented it by various sources, including contributions from Juan Montalvo and Quico. The contract resulted in fifty thousand pesos in capital at 5 percent interest. Mercedes would immediately receive ten thousand pesos of capital plus the two thousand pesos annual income on the balance. The rest would be payable after her death. Quico's final gesture was an extra two thousand pesos annually for life.

Now ready to depart, Mercedes made her final farewells, receiving visitors and gifts that included two silky, long-haired miniature dogs. Accompanying her on the journey to France on the *Le Havre-Guadeloupe* were two young cousins: one of her uncle Juanito's younger sons, and the eight-year-old son of Luisa Calvo. Both traveled under her care for their education, extending a familial link that she savored. Overall, Mercedes' trip had netted mixed results. She had obtained some stability in her finances. She had retraced her childhood paths, and perhaps found the basis for a new and profitable literary venture. But this journey into the past had also raised questions: was she Cuban or French, and did her heart lie in the Americas or Europe? Did an exile have the same right to comment or criticize as the fellow countryman who had stayed? All these questions would long haunt Mercedes and are still asked to this day.

16

A SONG FOR HAVANA

*M*ercedes sailed serenely into Le Havre on August 17 after a little more than three weeks at sea. She returned with the Havana project in mind and with some respite to her financial concerns, but she also returned to some developments of a more personal nature.

At fifty-one years old, Mercedes could still bewitch men as in the past. At some point, possibly when they coincided in Baden during the summer of 1839, she beguiled a youthful admirer: the son of Jérôme Bonaparte, youngest brother of Napoleon and ex-king of Westphalia. Also named Jérôme, the prince quickly fell madly in love with this alluring older woman, and soon rumors flew among *le monde* of a possible marriage—raising the ire of Prince Jérôme's father over a possible misalliance. Mercedes laughed at the absurdity, crying indignantly, "God knows I have never had that ambition!— a misalliance with me...." Her reaction was not only at the ludicrous suggestion and her own self-regard, but also perhaps at the irony, given the ex-king's own past. As a junior officer, Bonaparte had defied his brother Napoleon and married the daughter of a wealthy Baltimore merchant. Napoleon's fury knew no bounds, and after unsuccessfully pressing for an annulment from the pope, he finally dissolved the marriage in France and forced Jérôme to marry a German princess. Napoleon never even acknowledged Jérôme's son from the American marriage, although a grandson later became Teddy Roosevelt's secretary of the navy and attorney general.

Her passing flirtation with a Bonaparte meant nothing to Mercedes, but she soon commenced a tumultuous and ultimately unsatisfying relationship that would last the remainder of her life. Philarète Chasles, a journalist and literary critic almost ten years younger than Mercedes, was a surprising choice for a reigning beauty. He had an abysmal amorous history and no fortune. Although married with two children, Chasles's marriage began as an affair with a woman whose first husband, Baron de Presles, was in a mental institution. Chasles waited almost ten years, until 1836, before regularizing his relationship, and was not even faithful then.

A socially ambitious man, Chasles first met Mercedes through the 1826 Greek benefit concert for which he had written the lyrics for the chorus. An early friend of Balzac's, Chasles wrote the preface to Balzac's 1831 *Romans et Contes Philosophiques*, and together they attended various salons. Chasles later secured a position as professor of Germanic literature at the College de France and became librarian of the prestigious Bibliothèque Mazarine. Despite their earlier meeting, it was not until 1836, when Chasles wrote the two complimentary reviews of *Souvenirs*, that Mercedes and he became better acquainted. Accepting her thanks for the articles and her dinner invitation, Chasles responded with an obsequious letter—clearly in 1836, Mercedes was the superior, almost untouchable queen. The liaison's dynamics would later evolve.

At times charming and always appearing erudite, Chasles could also be cold, aloof, and demanding. In character he bore a striking resemblance to the Marqués de Cerrano who had so shattered Mercedes' young heart. He often failed Mercedes, yet felt no qualms in casting recriminations, perceived insults everywhere, and seemed full of self-pity. Responding to one of his letters, Mercedes asked him "why... that hostile and menacing attitude against all the world?... I swear that I would have judged you otherwise: it seems to me that you had a better heart when I met you." Yet something appealed to Mercedes. Perhaps she admired his learning or his culture. Given his apparent success with women, Chasles must have emanated a charming seductiveness or, like the Marqués of Cerrano, his initial appearance belied his true nature. Chasles' feeble character repeatedly disappointed Mercedes, yet to be fair, he may have felt profound emotions, as he described her as "incapable of being tamed, dominated or understood; with a unique, wandering imagination and guided by caprices…a being that moves you, attaches you and shocks you at the same time….That woman was the *Comtesse M…* only love of my life."

Mercedes quickly followed her impulsive and warm heart. Her letters, while still full of the passionate sentiments she displayed to Merlin, now revealed a more mature emotion rather than the lightly coquettish tone of her newlywed days. "You know how to make the fibers of my soul tremble! I am like you, I can predict you, I understand you so well! It seems to me that I can see through your eyes, that I can feel through your heart….I write to you, dear soul, in the middle of the night, with love's fever intensified by the silence and the solitude….I call [you] the tenderest of names."

When they became lovers is unclear, but by Mercedes' return from Havana they were apparently more than mere acquaintances, and their surviving correspondence reveals a level of literary collaboration from late 1840. Earlier letters express a businesslike rather than passionate tone. "It is me again, Monsieur, but you must be resigned and continue to exert the obligingness and activity…so that we can reach the goal." She signs another related note as "grateful and affectionate M. Merlin."

What Mercedes had in mind for her new literary project was not just a light travel account evoking the sights and sounds of Cuba, although she certainly did wish to capture that essence. She aimed higher, with a more ambitious goal. Remembering the complex political scene, the tense standoff emerging between creole landowners, liberals, and Spanish government officials, the pressure from the international abolitionist movement as well as her frustrating negative experience with the judicial system, Mercedes felt there was more to cover. Her good friend Custine, building on the success of his very thoughtful 1838 travel account of Spain, ventured to Russia in 1839. The resulting project, *La Russie en 1839*, when it finally appeared in 1843, highlighted not just the cultural differences and perceived eccentricities of that land but also evinced a deeper understanding of its government and character. Custine's text became a bestseller and became required reading in the West over a hundred years later, during the twentieth-century's Cold War. Given Mercedes' close friendship with Custine and her frequent stays at his home, she must have known some details of the work. How much Custine's groundbreaking endeavor in this genre informed Mercedes own work is not clear, but she chose an epistolary style—similar to how Custine organized his Spanish account. Written to various prominent or close friends, each letter allowed Custine the freedom to include or exclude all sorts of information or topics. In a similar fashion, Mercedes addressed her "letters" to numerous friends and acquaintances from her salon—each specifically chosen for the theme of each letter. She also expanded the breadth of topics, including local customs, law, government, agriculture, history, and slavery. Both she and Custine placed themselves in the narrative, and both espoused romantic sensibilities.

This ambitious oeuvre became *La Havane*, ultimately published in 1844. But before the finished product appeared, Mercedes confronted numerous obstacles. She began her project with probably the most difficult subject matter: slavery. The topic split opinion in Europe, striking close to home in France, which still allowed slavery in its colonies. Here Mercedes entered into a primarily masculine environment not previously broached by a Cuban woman. She wrote an essay addressed to Baron Charles Dupin, a renowned mathematician and member of the Upper Chamber. Its publication, on June 1, 1841, in the *Revue des Deux Mondes*, under the title "Les Esclaves dans les Colonies Espagnoles" (The Slaves in the Spanish Colonies), coincided with the appearance of the first published Cuban slavery novel, *Sab*, by Gertrudis Gómez de Avellaneda.

Mercedes founded her arguments on the essay supplied by del Monte regarding the population of Cuba as well as on the writings of José Antonio Saco, the influential exiled Cuban polymath. In essence, Mercedes conveyed to Europe the opinions of the liberal and more forward-thinking Cubans on this crucial question. Following their lead, she espoused a strict enforcement on the ban on slave trade along with the recruitment of white agricultural workers to ultimately replace the enslaved population. However, while Mercedes passionately exclaimed "nothing more just than the abolition of the slave trade," she did not champion the abolition of slavery itself. She argued against the liberation of the existing slaves, out of respect for the property rights of landowners.

Mercedes highlighted a commonly held belief among Cuban landowners, that Britain's drive for abolition was based on their own trade interests rather than any moral scruples. Mercedes shared these anti-British sentiments, as she later confirmed to her friend, the society physician Dr. David-Ferdinand Koreff. Delighting in a royal union between a Spanish princess and a French prince in the face of British government opposition, Mercedes called them the most immoral, hypocritical, and egotistical government "that has conducted the affairs of a nation in the past, present and I hope, the future." Continuing her arguments, Mercedes also reflected the traditional view of Spain's more "humane" law relative to the French *Code Noir* and the Cuban landowner's own more lenient approach and paternalistic ties with domestic servants. Mercedes' essay contained echoes of her great-uncle Monte-Hermoso and his fellow landowners' 1789 defense of their treatment of slaves and the organization of work in the sugar mills. She supplemented her reasoning with anecdotes gleaned from her family regarding recent slave uprisings. In one story, her cousin Rafael Montalvo's household slaves faithfully defended his family from attack by other, newly arrived slaves on their estate. Mercedes also recalled how her cousin Matilde Calvo de la Puerta's cook Antonio refused to serve Captain-General Tacón out of loyalty to the family, as Tacón had exiled Matilde's father. The celebrated cook proudly spurned the lucrative offer, saying that he preferred poverty with his masters than riches and freedom with Tacón.

Overall, Mercedes adopted the language from the 1817 Royal Decree ordering the abolition of the slave trade, which claimed that slavery had offered benefits to the captives. The old flawed logic asserted that prisoners from African inter-tribal wars would otherwise be killed were it not for the slave market, and that the slaves would be introduced to Christianity. Mercedes also repeated the fears of a reduction in sugar output, since freed slaves would not wish to work and to force them would lead to internal bloodshed.

Given Mercedes' well-known philanthropy and her early experience with the harshness of slavery, it is particularly disappointing that she failed to demand the emancipation of Cuban slaves. Her background, upbringing, and family ties proved too strong and constrained her to a much more modest step of advocating the abolition of the trade itself. Indeed, a large number of her fellow Cubans would have perceived her as a bold liberal. In 1841, many Cuban landowners did not yet recognize the need to address this issue, and Cuban slavery only ended in 1886.

Mercedes and Chasles collaborated on the slavery letter, as fragments of surviving correspondence show: "You have committed me... to cite the good articles of the *Code Noir*, since I had already cited the bad ones, I concede." She charged Chasles with editing the final piece and inserting certain information either in the text or as notes. But given the importance of the underlying issue for her homeland, she remained firm on one point—"Above all, do not permit the least omission, because I prefer to withdraw my article, if M. B. [Buloz] insists on demanding that sacrifice."

Since the piece concerned such an emotive topic, the *Revue*'s editor added a disclaimer: "Having expressed our reservations, one should not be astonished either to see us accept these documents necessary for the great debate raised by the question of slavery, or by the enthusiasm with which the author, creole by birth and origin, speaks of her homeland." Other newpapers also covered *L'Esclavage*, including *Le Voleur* and *La Presse*, which regretted its inability to reprint the entire essay given that it "stands out by its great moderation, rare good faith, touching accounts, colorfulness and the accuracy of its insights."

Mercedes' essay reached a wide audience, drawing strong attacks from abolitionists, including the author of a pamphlet on the transition from slavery in the British possession of Demerary (part of Guayana), as well as favorable coverage in the German press. Using this positive reception in Germany, she would later even try to encourage German emigration to Cuba. The essay was published as a Spanish-language pamphlet in Madrid, where the introduction recognized the seriousness of the slavery question to the Spanish colonies—yet in Cuba itself it could not be published due to the political climate and censorship.

Prior to publication in June 1841, Mercedes had reopened her salon, holding regular Friday evenings and concerts with the usual host of talented singers and flattering coverage. That summer, she traveled to Baden again, once more taking the spa cure and breathing the fresh air she so loved. She wrote to one friend that she planned to meet more than twenty persons from Paris in Baden, as well as friends from Stuttgart, and would take her castanets and copies of her *Esclaves*. Once in Baden, Mercedes wrote often to Chasles, constantly reassuring him not to be jealous of Prince Jérôme, also in Baden—"the dead do not return."

Mercedes and Chasles' relationship stood at a passionate beginning, and Mercedes thought it still "incomplete." She "still did not know if she addressed the friend or the lover." Mercedes stayed through August in Baden, but despite the hectic social life, she appeared beset by her perpetual melancholy. "The fact is that at the bottom of my heart a deadly melancholy....I need above all else to be loved." Sometimes she worked surrounded by vases full of "the most beautiful flowers in the world," yet other times she could barely write.

After Baden, Mercedes proceeded on to see her son and niece in Metz, and finally to Teresa in Dissay. Back in Paris in 1842, she requested additional materials for her Cuban project from Saco and

Alfonso. Alfonso gladly provided an essay on political and administrative affairs, while Saco also furnished her with accounts on the government of Cuba. Saco saw Mercedes frequently upon her return—he dined regularly at her rented home in Versailles that summer. But Saco didn't wish his name associated with her actual project, explaining to Alfonso that he didn't want responsibility for what a third party wrote. Expressing a similar concern, del Monte had asked Alfonso in 1840 if he could get an early glimpse of anything she wrote—to ensure she expressed sentiments favorable to their cause. Saco did wish Mercedes well in her project, however—he liked her and suspected that she needed a success due to her deteriorating financial position.

Saco's suspicions uncovered the truth. Despite the Cuban settlement and the eventual concession of a fifteen hundred–franc annual military pension, Mercedes suffered from insufficient funds. Her difficulties resulted from three factors: her own expensive lifestyle, her desire to save Chasles from insolvency, and his monumentally inept handling of her financial affairs. Mercedes recognized her role in her money problems: "It is possible, that I have been a bit slow in losing my opulent habits and that manner of largesse which arises from a character which detests the little miseries of life…but I learn by necessity." From early in their relationship, Mercedes offered Chasles what little she had available to pay his debts and avoid prison—to no avail. Chasles spent at least part of November and December of 1842 in debtor's prison—nicknamed l'Hôtel des Haricots—causing Mercedes great stress and sorrow. By that date, Mercedes no longer could save Chasles from his "labyrinthine" situation, as her own financial burden had become intolerable.

In an attempt to reduce her expensive lifestyle, Mercedes left Paris, spending time in more economical places: a small rented home in Versailles, her daughter's chateau in Dissay, and her son's home in Metz. Mercedes also took on a seven thousand–franc loan from a merchant-moneylender to tide her over until either she sold her book or received more Cuban income. She also began selling various possessions, including the horses in her stable, and offered, anonymously, several of her more valuable pieces of jewelry to a dealer, including her diamond and pearl tiara. Before leaving Paris, she dismissed "her people," including her cook, and entrusted the payment of their wages and other smaller debts to Chasles. He handled the matter miserably, seeming incapable of transacting the simplest matter. He failed to use appropriately the 1,250 francs that *La Presse* paid for serialization of selected Havana letters. Always imprecise, he claimed she owed more money, he failed to pay the cook despite false assurances, he never obtained receipts nor provided clear accounting, he undersold her jeweled diadem despite Mercedes' insistence on a minimum price, and he generally placed her in embarrassing predicaments with former servants and friends. Chasles always tried to evade or force Mercedes into more debt. Mercedes' requests and instructions fell on deaf ears, with a prickly Chasles often taking offense. Exasperated, Mercedes finally wrote: "Now I bitterly repent having accepted your obliging intervention into my affairs." Despite her problematic monetary situation, Mercedes' business sense far surpassed her beloved Chasles' ability.

Amid the chaos between 1842 and 1843, Mercedes attempted to finish the Havana book, obtain an English translation, conclude a deal for a French version with Adolphe Granier de Cassagnac, and raise funds by organizing a literary subscription among friends and relatives in Cuba to publish a privately issued, limited-edition book about the journey. Her correspondence with Chasles implies that they continued to collaborate on the project—Mercedes gathered material from her various sources and initially wrote the pieces, then sent them to Chasles for revision and editing.

The English publication never happened, despite expressions of interest from two established publishers. Mercedes pleaded countless times for Chasles to obtain the necessary translation and to select the most appropriate letters for the market, both reasonable requests given Chasles' expertise in English literature. He never fulfilled any task satisfactorily, even losing the manuscript at one point. The English contract delayed the French, as Mercedes insisted on completing the English version first—in part under pressure to assist her Cuban friends by presenting their case in English. A possible German deal also failed.

Mercedes had hoped to raise fifteen hundred francs from the Cuban subscription for a 150- to 200-copy edition, but despite her cousin José Ricardo O'Farrill's attempts, there just wasn't enough interest. She seemingly also blamed the duplicitous Cassagnac for this failure. Her erstwhile collaborator became a competitor— arranging the publication of his own travel chronicle and its successful subscription throughout the Antilles. Interestingly, one Martinique planter privately noted that Cassagnac would have as easily written against their interests if enough money were involved.

Finally despairing of the Cuban subscription, Mercedes issued a selection of ten letters translated into Spanish under the name *Viaje a la Habana* (Voyage to Havana), which came out in 1844. That same year, the publisher Amyot released *La Havane* in French with the full thirty-six letters. Mercedes restricted the Spanish-language edition to those letters deemed uncontroversial to the Spanish political establishment—no slavery, legal system, or other politically charged topics.

The French critics generally gave *La Havane* a favorable reception, although some grumbled regarding the length and heaviness of the more serious parts, preferring the more colorful and picturesque accounts. One critic wrote that it would be preferable to omit all by "officious bureaucrats...leav[ing] only, in a word, that which *Madame la Comtesse Merlin* has really written." Some expressed astonishment at a *femme du monde* addressing serious topics. Still, the historian and diplomat Alexis de Saint-Priest was charmed by the book and especially praised the biographical sketches of Hernán Cortez and others. In Spain, the *Revista de Madrid* published fragments and the biographical note by Gertrudis Gómez de Avellaneda that appeared in *Viaje* as a preface.

Cuba was a different story altogether. In 1843 the local press picked up Letter XXV from *La Havane*, addressed to George Sand, on the women of Havana (ironically, not included in the Spanish version). It created an immediate negative furor. There soon appeared a critique of the letter under the cover of a correspondence between two fictitious friends, Chucha—a very Cuban nickname—and Sera-fina. The anonymous author of "Letters to Chucha" attacked the depiction of languid creole women eating fruit while lounging in *butacas* (Cuban-style armchairs) or lying in a bath, overcome by the heat. Once again, as in the last concert in Havana or even in the early reviews of her memoirs, what irritated Habaneros—at least literary ones—was Mercedes' depiction of a creole stereotype as opposed to a more cultured and advanced individual. Mercedes did indeed often exaggerate or highlight the exotic for her European audiences, but several of the offending descriptions echoed previously published accounts by other travelers. Indeed, some of the attacks against Mercedes ignored reality. "Serafina" ridiculed as untrue Mercedes' statement that young Cuban women married their cousins for the sake of family bloodlines, yet while possibly uncommon in bourgeois or new-money circles, it was certainly the case—even in 1843—within the old aristocratic milieu. Mercedes' mistake, perhaps, lay in generalizing the representation of her own insular world as the broader Cuban reality.

When the entire book came out in 1844, the Cuban response was harsh. Leading the attack was Félix Tanco, the writer and friend of del Monte who had at one point praised Mercedes and eagerly sought to present her with his works. Since 1843, possibly as a result of the "Women of Havana" letter or other available fragments, Tanco planned an attack on "*la Vieja Merlin*" (the Old Merlin). When *Viaje a la Habana* came out, Tanco published a relentlessly negative thirteen-part review in the *Diario de la Habana* under the pseudonym Verafilo and later compiled the articles into a pamphlet: *Refutation on a Voyage to Havana*. Tanco challenged Mercedes on almost every word; finding exaggeration or error everywhere. Some of his complaints seem petty: the galleries in her uncle's house were not so long as to be lost from view (although he agreed it was one of the largest homes in Havana). He protested that the graceful use of fans was not necessary if the breeze was blowing. Tanco even decried Mercedes' finding a memory on every corner. He seemed especially offended by Mercedes' comment that Havana buildings had no history (as compared with Europe) and cuttingly determined that Mercedes had dared view Cuba through Parisian eyes.

Tanco also bitterly complained about the use of a short novel by a young Cuban *costumbrista* (writer focused on local manners and customs) named Ramón de Palma that Mercedes wove into her own narrative without attribution. Mercedes had actually used other pieces from Cirilo Villaverde (who later wrote *Cecilia Valdés* and used Mercedes' own family details in his plot) as well. In some cases, Mercedes had even rewritten parts. It has never been fully explained why Mercedes did not name the sources, but from 1842 to 1843, in at least four separate letters to Chasles, Mercedes pleaded for the names of those "young authors" so that she could write to them. In one letter, she explicitly told Chasles to mention Palma and Villaverde as "charming writers and poets" with an explanatory note referencing her usage. It seems that once again, as with the sale of her jewels, the payment of her servants' salaries, and even the handling of the English manuscript, Chasles failed Mercedes miserably.

In the middle of Tanco's onslaught, José de la Luz y Caballero stepped in to defend her. Writing under the pseudonym Fairplay, he strongly rebuked Tanco for his lack of gallantry in attacking an absent lady. While Luz agreed that the text contained numerous errors, he considered some quite pardonable. Nothing was heard from del Monte, who happened to be abroad with his family when the book appeared. Soon other events overwhelmed him. Mercedes' *Viaje* unfortunately coincided with the repercussions of the Escalera Conspiracy, related to the discovery of a massive coordinated slave uprising and the colonial government's bloody and ruthless reprisals. The government arrested countless blacks—free or slave—and whipped many until they provided information. These "confessions" implicated many leading liberals including Tanco, Luz, and del Monte. Tanco spent months imprisoned in La Punta fortress and then left Cuba, while Luz was eventually acquitted. Friends and relatives warned del Monte to consider himself exiled, and he never returned to Cuba. Mercedes warmly welcomed del Monte to dine in Versailles and commiserated with his sad fate. Privately, del Monte explained to his American correspondent, the politically connected Alexander Everett, how Mercedes had pieced together her *La Havane*, calling the fracas the work had created in Cuba "risible" since they seemed to be trying her for every innocent exaggeration. He excused her geographical or chronological errors as understandable given her long absence. Most important, del Monte stressed the value of the work to Cuban patriots as it "contains revelations and political facts of extreme importance to us, it inculcates sound governing principles, it denounces the slave trade."

Yet despite the censure, *Viaje a la Habana* has survived. Together with her early memoirs of her Cuban childhood, *Viaje a la Habana* is frequently quoted today, and several editions are still available. The historian Hugh Thomas considered it "one of the best accounts of contemporary Cuba" available, and cited Mercedes numerous times in various works. Mercedes' lyrical descriptions continue to evoke her aristocratic creole milieu.

17

FINALE:

ADAGIO CANTABILE

By late 1845, Mercedes once again needed new funds as a matter of urgency. Throughout 1844 and into 1845, despite her previous financial difficulties, she had slipped back to her old, lavish hospitality and entertainments. During the 1844 carnival, Mercedes hosted a magnificent costumed ball. She wore a splendid Grecian gown sewn throughout with gemstones, while other guests appeared as huntsmen from Louis XVIII's court and American Indian chiefs complete with their own interpretation of native ornaments: eagle's beaks and rhinoceros horns. One incident at the ball garnered extensive coverage in the press: a masked woman followed Baron de Rothschild all night, constantly shouting, "Give me money!" Perplexed and frustrated, the banker finally snapped back, "Why do you always ask me the same thing?" The mysterious guest replied, "Because you have nothing else to give."

Mercedes also continued her concerts and soirees throughout the 1845 season, as well as her participation in the Prince de la Moskowa's newly formed Concert Society. Her Friday evenings continued to thrive in popularity. She organized at least two major concerts in March and April, offering her guests the privilege of hearing duos by the famous Giulia Grisi and her (off-stage) companion, Mario, as well as her own daughter, Teresa. The musicians were also top drawer, featuring one of her current favorite composers, Giulio Alary, who accompanied many of the singers himself. Mercedes planned her entertainments meticulously, even printing her concert programs on expensive, delicately pink, iridescent stationery. These were special evenings, and some of her guests saved their programs as mementos that have survived to this day.

Brilliant appearances notwithstanding, Mercedes did not have the income to maintain her lifestyle. Her brother was not always reliable in fulfilling his financial obligations, and Mercedes sorrowfully told Chasles that "it is a cruel thing, an existence that depends on...the goodwill of those who don't like to pay." An ongoing bitter dispute between Quico and his nephew François further strained familial ties. According to their 1840 agreement, François and Teranita needed to repay Quico some 27,900 pesos in either cash or land. Therefore, the parties ordered a survey of Nazareno, but the subsequent valuation was disastrous. From its 1821 value of 105,600 pesos, its worth had plummeted to merely 31,970 pesos, barely enough to clear the debt. François refused to relinquish the Nazareno lands and Quico sued. The case dragged on—mainly due to François' delay tactics. Uncle Juanito died in March 1844, leaving the two nephews without their natural mediator.

Mercedes then looked for other financial solutions, hoping to find one in another journey to the past: Spain. According to her son François, Mercedes believed that something remained of her aunt O'Farrill's estate, and Mercedes certainly still hoped to obtain O'Farrill's remaining confiscated forty-three thousand pesos (approximately 215,000 francs). With these hopes in mind, Mercedes embarked on her journey in the autumn of 1845. Despite the cloud that had accompanied the departure of the Afrancesados in 1813, Mercedes had many contacts and friends in Spain to smooth the way, including Francisco Martínez de la Rosa, a playwright, former first minister, and ambassador to France and Rome. Mercedes even managed to revive her friendship with the Dukes de Osuna—all was forgotten regarding their old palace on Cuesta de la Vega, which she had effectively enjoyed for years as her husband's prize of war. By 1844 Mercedes had entertained the current Duke de Osuna in Versailles—also signing his membership certificate (as *dame patronnesse*) in the new musical society, along with its president, the Prince de la Moskowa—Marshal Ney's son. Her social prestige preceded her, thanks to the coverage of her concerts and literary works in the Spanish press.

Taking advantage of the hospitality offered by another friend, Manuela Kirkpatrick, who was Countess de Montijo and mother of the future Empress Eugénie (wife of Napoleon III), Mercedes found a flatteringly warm welcome in Madrid society. Mercedes may have been a petitioner, but "never, it must be acknowledged has a petitioner been more spoiled than me. Instead of going to the ministers, I give them an audience; they spoil me and become my advocates against themselves." She found some things changed from her girlhood days; no one wore a *basquiña* anymore, instead wearing a lace *mantilla* over French-style gowns. But overall, she thought the country still the Spain of Cervantes. Mercedes couldn't resist recording colorful local sights and sounds for her Parisian friends, describing the "solemn loneliness of the Somosierra," the mountain pass in the Guadarrama, and the overall magnificence of bullfights, with "all the popular wild and generous instincts manifested spontaneously and at the same time with the brilliance of Mediterranean passions." Although she made these descriptions in private letters, Mercedes might have thought to publish them in one of the journals, as there is some evidence that she also wrote simultaneously to Buloz, the editor of the *Revue des Deux Mondes*.

Retracing her past life, she once again climbed the steps of the royal palace for a grand event—this time a concert in honor of the Spanish queen, Isabel II, Fernando's daughter. Isabel II gave Mercedes an opal and diamond bracelet as a memento. Mercedes also agreed to assist Cuban-born Gertrudis Gómez de Avellaneda with a new literary journal for women, *La Ilustración, Album de las Damas*.

Avellaneda, who had written the biographical sketch contained in *Viaje a La Habana*, would visit Paris the following year and enjoy one of Mercedes' musical evenings. Mercedes charmed Avellaneda with her "elegant writing" and vocal talent, worthy praise from a woman considered today one of the great nineteenth-century Cuban writers.

Despite all outwardly gracious welcomes and apparent forgiveness, Mercedes failed to retrieve O'Farrill's remaining estate, mainly due to the "bitter fruits of hatreds... and of the anarchy that has long reigned over this country." The Countess de Montijo, whose intimate friend Prosper Mérimée was also visiting, arranged for him to escort Mercedes back as far as Bayonne. Mérimée is perhaps best known outside France as the author of *Carmen*, but to his contemporaries he was a great man of letters, a member of the Académie Française, and a high-ranking civil servant. He knew everyone and went out widely in society—including frequenting Mercedes' dinners or concerts. In the middle of his successful 1844 candidacy for the Académie, he wrote a charmingly apologetic letter to Mercedes, begging forgiveness for missing a social engagement. However, as with many in *le monde*, appearances could often be deceptive. While his letters to the Countess de Montijo are quite deferential and obliging, they are also often filled with vicious gossip and disparaging comments about mutual acquaintances—including Mercedes. He seemed particularly obsessed with the fifty-four-year-old Mercedes' still relatively youthful appearance, acidly noting that she had previously plucked her grey hairs and now must either use a dye or perhaps wear a wig. He was less than pleased to be her traveling companion and wrote to Montijo that he would have "preferred the company of the *mayoral* or the postilions" managing their carriage. Mercedes, believing she traveled with a friend, innocently complained of her disappointment with the outcome of her trip and the discomforts of the road—Mérimée later confided all to Montijo, adding that Mercedes had forty-five bags and brought too much food.

The hypocrisy often found in the fashionable world probably did not shock Mercedes, although she came to find distasteful the "frivolities and vices" of *le monde*. Although her disenchantment would crystalize in following years, it would also partially explain the theme of her first full-length novel, *Les Lionnes de Paris* (*The Lionesses of Paris*), published anonymously as *Feu le Prince de*..., which followed various society figures who scandalously resembled certain well-known Parisians. Some thought that the character of Giuditta depicted Princess Cristina Belgiojoso, Mercedes' friend and fellow hostess. Mercedes' nature did not generally tend toward public ridicule; instead, she was well regarded for her tolerance and kindness. The German poet Heinrich Heine, friends with much of the literary world, once wrote that Mercedes, who "always speaks well not only of her enemies but even of her friends, can likewise be insulted without danger." But Mercedes' novel might also have been driven by the urgings of Chasles as well as reflecting her staunch support for her friend Delphine de Girardin. From 1843, there had been a lively fight among several literary women (primarily George Sand, Delphine, and Belgiojoso) for the presidency of a proposed Académie de Femmes, a parallel to the all-male academies. Mercedes enjoyed a strong professional relationship with Émile and Delphine de Girardin and *La Presse*—in 1844 it serialized her novella, *Lola* (set in Peninsular War–era Spain), and she often figured favorably in Delphine's column. Still, Mercedes appeared somewhat ambivalent about *Les Lionnes*, only mentioning it in letters in a discouraging manner: "I will try to do something with [*les*] *lionnes*, since you wish it, but I have no more faith in anything."

Mercedes might not have been pleased with *Les Lionnes*, but she needed to work and therefore searched for fresh topics. She was already recycling material, repackaging *Lola* with her Maria Malibran biography as *Lola et Maria* in 1845. She ultimately focused her energies on a new project—*L'Expiation*. She found pleasure in researching the historical period—fourteenth-century Florence—borrowing books from the Bibliothèque Mazarine through Chasles. She strategically planned her contract negotiations in the late summer and autumn of 1846 with publisher Anténor Joly, addressing such issues as serialization, reversion rights, and various other details. She even accepted a tight submission deadline of January

1847. She also sought advice from Chasle, sending him a manuscript, which he annotated. However, Mercedes soon encountered difficulties in meeting the submission date.

When Prosper Mérimée had next seen Mercedes after Spain, in March 1846, he told the Countess de Montijo that Mercedes "looked less well preserved [and] limped a little." Mercedes blamed the limping on their long carriage ride from Madrid, but it seemed to be something more serious. She returned to the social whirl after her Spanish adventures but hid a general deterioration in her health. Once more she held musical evenings, introducing new popular performers during the spring season and later in her small Versailles hideaway, adding to the "brilliant" musical ambiance and disputing the musical scepter with other renowned hostesses. Balzac particularly enjoyed her evening card games, making an exception to go there even when in the middle of his creative obsessions. However, she spent much time in the summers of 1846 and 1847 in various spas—Aix-la-Chapelle, Néris— undertaking cures, hoping to find relief. Spa society generally bored her, and her life there consisted of bathing in the "boiling" water, cold and hot showers, drinking two or three glasses of the local water, and nothing much more. Although these cures were extremely fashionable in the nineteenth century, Mercedes had a serious ailment. The exact source of the suffering is unclear, but she confessed to her friend Dr. Koreff that she had difficulty walking, and she complained of aggravation from cold weather. Contemporary doctors recommended Aix-la-Chapelle for all rheumatic problems, noting that those who suffered from cold climates particularly benefited. Even today, the French spas are still considered helpful for soothing anxiety and stress. Mercedes required rest, and she was unable to work for long periods of time.

Although Mercedes continued to work on *L'Expiation* throughout the fall of 1846 and into the early winter of 1847, the book failed to materialize. She submitted the first volume in late December and received praise from Joly as well as specific comments to enhance the dramatic action and find interesting "exotic color." He also requested the second volume in order to fully assess the work. However, it is unclear if Mercedes continued with the project. By late 1847, she no longer referred to it in her correspondence. In September she admitted that she "detested" the pen, explaining that "when one was unfortunate [enough] to plan [something] beautiful and when one failed to attain it, one must quit the field."

Her relationship with Chasles continued in a wearisome cycle of work collaboration, brief meetings, tender words, and mutual recrimination. Mercedes constantly expressed deep concern for his health (Chasles always seemed on the verge of a dramatic illness from overwork) and still looked to his literary advice. He often referred to her as his "dear and terrible friend" or as my queen or her majesty, and would decry her silence or her leaving Paris without a word. From a distance it is difficult to know which party's complaints have greater merit, but Chasles more often failed to fulfill his promises, while Mercedes appeared to tolerate his petulance. As late as December 1847, she still felt deeply enough to trust him with her most intimate thoughts and fears. She opened her heart in a letter, admitting extended concerns about the future. She felt menaced in her daily existence by "the indifference...and possibly the bad faith" of others. She lost pleasure in society, ceasing to admire it "after having seen up close the glories of that world." She faced "disappointments" in her own family and feared "imminent ruin without it being possible to stop."

Amid these distresses, Mercedes turned to religion for consolation—a bit of a surprise, given her previous intense dislike for the cloistered life in the Convent de Santa Clara. She confided to Chasles her hope for divine mercy and her consolation from reading the Gospels. She chastised Chasles for his skepticism, and urged him to follow the examples of great Christian thinkers such as St. Augustine.

Concerns for the future were perfectly understandable given the building national crisis. The previous January 1847, Mercedes had expressed disappointment that Teresa might not spend the winter in Paris due to her husband's worries regarding discontent in the countryside. Political turmoil was simmering in France. In February 1848, the tensions erupted into a revolution that brought down the

Orleanist monarchy and introduced a Second Republic. June saw more violent clashes in Paris involving a workers' uprising that resulted in much bloodshed. Mercedes fled the city, finding refuge with her friend Custine. Spending months at his home Saint-Gratien, Mercedes saw the world of the July Monarchy disappear. By the end of the year, France had elected a new president: Louis Napoleon Bonaparte, Napoleon's nephew and Josephine's grandson.

While these tumultuous changes encompassing the nation affected all French citizens, Mercedes also undertook a momentous—albeit personal—step. In 1848 she left her longtime home on Rue de Bondy, the site of so many social triumphs and memorable evenings. She moved into a smaller apartment in a relatively newer neighborhood—le Quartier de l'Europe, at 18 Rue de Berlin (today known as Rue de Liège).

Adding to this turmoil, Mercedes' emotional life continued in a chaotic state. Two undated letters, probably from 1846 to 1848, imply infidelities by Chasles. Mercedes was outraged: "You have tricked me—I don't wish more from you." In the second letter she affirmed that she "had always acted towards you loyally, purely." Now she angrily told him farewell—"I no longer wish to hear your name pronounced...no more excuses, no more lies....Return my letters...not one more word from you!"

However, the relationship continued in some form. Subsequent letters indicate the transformation of a passionate if unsatisfactory liaison into a longstanding friendship. Chasles continued harassing her about missing books and cajoled her with possible projects, while Mercedes invited him to him to dine and converse wherever she happened to be.

Domestic upheaval continued as Mercedes' son-in-law Firmin Gentien died in May 1849, leaving Teresa a widow at thirty-seven with three young daughters. The following year, Teresa decided to sell the Château de Dissay, and Mercedes lost one of her most treasured refuges. That summer of 1849 she spent three months at Saint-Gratien. Custine had his own financial concerns—staving off ruin by selling property and even considering selling Saint-Gratien—and with his love of all things exquisite, he perhaps understood better than most the constant terror that Mercedes felt in contemplating her future. Custine admired Mercedes, praising the finesse and expansive wit she deployed as an unrivaled hostess in a letter to Balzac. Their friendship endured even though Custine's fairly open homosexual lifestyle (unprecedented for the era) seemed to run counter to Mercedes' general views.

Reviewing her options and convinced of her brother's bad faith in fulfilling his contractual obligations to her, Mercedes decided once again to journey to Cuba. This time, her younger son Gonzalo accompanied her on the British ship *Teviot*, stopping at various points in the Caribbean. She arrived in late September 1849 along with nineteen Italian singers from London's Royal Italian Opera House, who upon their arrival in Havana received more notice than Cuba's own renowned singer. The quiet arrival marked a very different visit from her earlier triumphant return; this time Uncle Juanito did not welcome her, and there were no flattering poems or gala concerts. Despite her second visit, lasting seven months, much longer than the more celebrated 1840 voyage, not a word appeared in the press until her departure on April 21, 1850, on the steamship *Ohio*, bound for New York. Mercedes seemed merely to disappear into her family's homes for an intensely private visit. She may have attended the eagerly anticipated opera performances or enjoyed her cousin the Count de Peñalver's end-of-year soiree before departing for his estates. She might have even accompanied her cousins, the Señoras Montalvo de O'Farrill and O'Farrill de Montalvo—both ladies noted for their diamonds, to see the captain-general's palace decorated in the latest European style in honor of the Spanish queen's birthday. But if Mercedes participated in these events, the papers didn't cover it. Then again, Mercedes might have been mourning the tragic death—really suicide—of Quico's only son in late October. According to press reports, a depressed Joaquín de Santa Cruz took poison and left a note to his father stating that he had carried around the poison in his pocket for two years.

By late November, despite this latest family tragedy, Mercedes managed to reach an agreement with her brother. The new accord reflected "changed" circumstances—although these circumstances were never explained. Mercedes once more deferred receipt of her capital until after her death and in turn received a set three thousand pesos per annum.

A more joyous family event occurred on March 16, 1850, when Mercedes witnessed the marriage of her son Gonzalo to one of her Cárdenas relations. It is impossible to know whether Mercedes had planned a Cuban marriage all along or if opportunity merely stepped in. But Mercedes, who had always rejoiced at these close family alliances, would have been delighted—not least by the bride's dowry. Gonzalo married Juana Cárdenas y Cárdenas, the daughter of the Marqués de Campo—Florido and widow of the Count de San Fernando de Peñalver. This marriage stirred up memories, since Juana's grandmother was possibly the Aunt Paquita from Mercedes' Cuban childhood. At the very least, Mercedes would have recalled those long lazy days on the Cárdenas properties by San Antonio de los Baños, when she had swum so happily in the river with her cousins and waited for the fireflies to light up the tropical dusk. All her business finally transacted, Mercedes, her son, her new daughter-in-law, and their servants left Havana the following month. Gonzalo would one day sail back to live and eventually die in this city, but Mercedes would never return to her birthplace.

Back in France on the Rue de Berlin, Mercedes retreated from fashionable society. She turned more toward her religion, receiving regular visits from the parish priest of Saint-Louis d'Antin. Perhaps an underlying faith had unknowingly throughout the years helped her accept the shocks and reverses of her earlier days as well as more recent difficulties. She had a loyal group of friends who often dined with her—Mercedes still loved her cozy dinners, a legacy of her mother's Madrid evenings. She still maintained a relation of sorts with Chasles, although he seemed to offer as little comfort as before. Mercedes chided him for criticizing her little circle, whose only offense was the "assiduous care that they have given me during my long malady." Inviting him to dine in 1851, she wrote: "I warn you will only find those that you disdain—I have no others to offer—

neither academician nor high-level officials." The English society beau Captain Gronow touchingly recalled Mercedes as her beauty and talent diminished: "She did not feel her declining powers.... She was one of those who will not grow old.... [But] she possessed what is much rarer than we all imagine, a truly kind heart; and she reaped the reward for though Madame Merlin had not always a great regard for appearance, no one had the courage to fling a stone at the generous-minded, warm-hearted woman."

Mercedes focused on her children and their families. Shortly after Mercedes' return from Cuba, Teresa remarried and initially came to live in Paris with her new husband, Alfred de Ferry. In November 1850, Juana gave birth to a son, Michel-Gonzalve-Christophe Merlin. For Mercedes, always close to her children, these happy family events would have offered some solace and distraction. She would have welcomed the new grandchild—as she had lamented her niece Teranita's numerous miscarriages. Although Mercedes could no longer find refuge in Dissay, she longed to escape the city for her health, and in April 1851 began searching for a small country rental, carefully outlining her available budget. She found in the village of Saint-Léger on the western outskirts of Paris "all that tranquility and fresh air in a charming and modest residence can offer."

Mercedes' love of music continued, although her voice had lost that lightness and purity of her heyday. She still participated—at a distance—in philanthropic activities, lending her name as a *dame patronnesse* for a musical benefit for the deaf in February 1851. She also encouraged young musicians, such as the New Orleans–born Louis Moreau Gottschalk. He would later travel to Cuba and Puerto Rico, writing classical pieces full of island rhythms and bearing lyrical creole names such as *Souvenir de La Havane*. She also kept working on literary projects, although the only new piece to be published was a serialized version of the *L'Expiation*, now called *Flavia*, in a Spanish newspaper in November–December 1850.

It was in this much quieter world, far from the Cuban countryside, Napoleonic political upheavals, and sparkling masked balls, that Mercedes died from heart complications on March 31, 1852, aged sixty-three. Her son Gonzalo would later say that she had long been prepared to die.

After her death, Mercedes' three children found her personal possessions considerably reduced, worth only 21,500 francs. No significant jewels remained—not a diadem nor the fabulous tiara. Mercedes had sold or pawned most of these valuables to cover her expenses or help literary acquaintances such as the writer Alphonse Karr—and Chasles. A depository held several thousand francs worth of silver serving pieces as collateral, and her correspondence revealed the extent of the cash loans, furniture, and other goods given to Chasles. Her three children declared to the notary that they would pursue a claim against Chasles for these missing items. Overall, Mercedes' debts exceeded her assets. Her creditors ranged from merchants to old friends or relatives including her cousin the Count de Casa-Montalvo, the Spanish minister Martínez de la Rosa, her doctor, and her dressmaker. At her death, Mercedes owed back wages to her personal maid Pauline and her long-serving housekeeper, Madame Pio, totaling nearly nine hundred francs. The family decided to auction the contents of her apartment as well as the remaining Spanish art collection. Miraculously, it seemed, Mercedes had managed to retain her beloved Zurbarán and Riberas as well as additional pieces she had brought back from her 1845 Spanish journey. Mercedes' collection stirred interest among connoisseurs, but it was somewhat overshadowed by another recent event. Marshal Soult's death in late 1851 caused a sensation in the art world as his fabulous collection—including some of the finest Spanish art work—went on sale May 19 through 22, 1852, forcing the postponement of Mercedes' more modest sale. Mercedes' final book, *Le Duc d'Athènes* (a retitled *L'Expiation*), also appeared in 1852.

More surprisingly, the legal inventory also uncovered a final secret handwritten will. Strangely reminiscent of her father Joaquín, Mercedes' final concerns focused on the females of the family: her three Gentien granddaughters and Teresa. Mercedes called on her sons' "fraternal tenderness" to ensure the fulfillment of Teresa's dowry since they had "more than enough resources." She further bequeathed particular gifts to each granddaughter: to her goddaughter Marie, "a bracelet with an opal surrounded by diamonds which I had from the Queen of Spain and my lace veil," to Marie Louise and Carmen, "all my other lace." Mercedes further gave Carmen five thousand francs in agreement with the girl's godfather over the satisfaction of a debt. Her son-in-law Alfred de Ferry wished to note the will in the estate proceedings, but both sons forcefully argued that this will had no validity. This response echoed uncannily the fate of Joaquín's last desperate will.

Mercedes' funeral service took place on April 2, 1852, at La Trinité, then located on Rue de Clichy. The French, Spanish, and Cuban newspapers all widely reported Mercedes' passing and recalled her past triumphs. *La France Musicale* added that members of the literary, artistic, and social world thronged her funeral. However, Chasles—faithless, difficult Chasles—left an intriguingly incomplete account of her burial at Père Lachaise cemetery. Really an unfinished sketch, Chasles indignantly counted only a dozen mourners around the open grave and wondered how this could be the tomb of the "Queen of Society." He continued, "One would have counted thousands if all those that she had welcomed, charmed, celebrated with her charitable generosity had come to address their final homage....Poor vanished star!" Among the dozen tearful mourners was the Prince de la Moskowa, Marshal Ney's son, who mirrored Mercedes' varied past: his father had been in Napoleonic Spain, his mother's family tied to Merlin de Thionville, and his brother had left a travel account of Cuba, while Moskowa himself personified her beloved musical world through his musical endeavors.

According to the cemetery *conservateurs*, Mercedes was buried in the same tomb as her uncle O'Farrill—where she officially rests to this day. Anecdotally, however, her old biographer Figarola Caneda thought she lay under the more modest tombstone of her daughter Annette. That marker, broken and almost illegible, now stands yards away from the original site. Recently, a historian of Père Lachaise claimed that the neglected grave was moved to make way for a new concession and that the bones of Mercedes, General Merlin, and their daughter were placed in the cemetery's ossuary. If this story is true, it echoes what Mercedes wrote in *La Havane*, when she fruitlessly searched for the tombs of her father and Mamita only to find their bones discarded to allow new burials.

Wherever she finally lay, she slept, semiforgotten, to be resurrected periodically in a gossipy article about French salons, Napoleonic Spain, or upon the reissue of her *Viaje a la Habana* or *Souvenirs et Mémoires*. Her highly personalized accounts offer a unique perspective far removed from the usual military or political histories and provide rich material for modern social historians. While her musical attainments may seem ephemeral as no technology existed to capture them, the surviving descriptions provide a glimpse of an extraordinary musical talent and confirm that her luminous soirees helped launch countless great artists. The nurturing of other musicians places Mercedes firmly in an unbroken chain of musical history.

Undoubtedly, however, her Cuban writings provide the most tangible legacy today: visit Old Havana and one finds traces of Mercedes everywhere—in the sign outside the palacio of the Counts of Jaruco; in the carriage rides she portrayed so well; in the beautiful countryside and Havana bell towers. Her triumph lies in the sweet seductiveness of her creole descriptions. At their best, they bring entirely to life the essence of a Cuban evening: the air, the light. The oven-hot heat of the day and the luxuriant foliage of the countryside, the cacophony of bells, songs, and cries, the mélange of colors—she captured it all. She immortalized her class, her strata of society beautifully, but she ventured beyond the limits that very society imposed on women. Bound by her family's decisions and subject to the chances of fortune in a turbulent time, Mercedes found the strength to carve out her own celebrated place in a new society.

In reading her surviving works, one can also glimpse her passionate love for her birthplace even across her long-ago exile, and she echoes the sentiments felt by any exile living far from a homeland.

ACKNOWLEDGMENTS

A historical biography inherently relies on the preservation of old paper in archives and libraries, in this case scattered all over the world. In each place the collaboration and contributions of numerous people have been indispensable for the completion of this project. Mercedes' life had three distinct parts—Cuba, Spain, and France—and although the research did not fall so easily into these categories, they provide a good framework for the many acknowledgments.

For all things Cuban—rare books, newspapers, prints, advice, and enthusiasm—the staff and resources of the University of Miami's Cuban Heritage Collection are second to none. I began my search there for Mercedes' true life after my cousin María Antonia Masvidal-Visser introduced me to the collection. My deepest thanks go to director emeritus Esperanza de Varona, librarian emeritus Lesbia Varona, director María Estorino, and their staff, particularly Annie Sansone-Martínez, Meiyolet Méndez, and Rosa Monzon-Alvarez. Not only did they facilitate my work and offer a beautiful setting for research, but they have striven to salvage and nurture Cuban culture and history outside of Cuba.

My family in Cuba and other friends there searched out what they could on Mercedes and happily accompanied me around La Habana Vieja. My dear friend Gerry Smurfit also cheerfully chased Mercedes' heritage in Havana and took beautifully evocative photographs of the buildings and the people. I wish I could have used them all! Her companionship gave me the courage to return to Cuba for the first time in almost thirty years.

Two wonderful Cuban historians of the colonial era, Aisnara Perera Díaz and María de los Angeles Meriño Fuentes, contributed so much to the Cuba chapters. They helped locate materials, answered countless questions, offered opinions and insight into the world of the sugar oligarchy, and also introduced me to their own passion: the microhistory of slaves. Their efforts at long last permitted me to disentangle Joaquín's legacy and the reasons underlying Mercedes' celebrated 1840 journey. Special thanks also to Araceli García-Carranza at Havana's Biblioteca Nacional.

Like Mercedes, I also went to Spain. My thanks go to the staff at the Archivo Histórico Nacional in Madrid and the Archivo de Indias in Sevilla, as well as all the other Spanish archives. In Madrid, María Ruiz Sastre relentlessly besieged the historic churches as well as the diocesan archive and Archivo Histórico de Protocolos to find everything from Mercedes' marriage contract to her daughter's baptismal record. María became another Mercedes devotee along the way. Thanks also to Isabel Lapuerta Amigo for help in tracking down sources and introducing me to María. Isabel's friend Concha Beltrán, a Valencian economist, answered queries on eighteenth- and nineteenth-century Cuban and Spanish currencies and introduced me to Antonio Santamaría García, a specialist in the field who provided even more answers and explanations. Natalia Figueroa answered questions regarding her father's discovery of Mercedes' 1810 letters to Merlin.

France proved to be rich in sources and archival materials—not surprising given Mercedes' many years in her adopted homeland. In Paris I had the privilege of working in the library of the Institut de France, and I would particularly like to thank the director,

Madame Mireille Pastoureau. She patiently answered queries and provided guidance. Monsieur Xavier Darcos, Secrétaire Perpétuel de l'Académie de Sciences Morales et Politiques, graciously sponsored my petition for access, and Monsieur Pierre Kerbrat, the secrétaire général at the Académie, facilitated the matter. The Institut de France also houses the Bibliothèque Mazarine, where Philarète Chasles worked—a particularly apt coincidence.

Two marvelous persons offered incalculable assistance in Paris: Sime Massot and Marine Cornuet. Sime took on countless administrative tasks—making phone calls, writing e-mails and letters, and organizing various matters. Marine undertook transcriptions and photography of pages and pages of archival material. She happily hunted down the Merlin wills in the Archives Nationales as well as General Merlin's military dossier at Château de Vincennes. When she moved to New York, her mother, Madame Andrée Cornuet, stepped in and completed the task.

Although England was never Mercedes' home, four institutions proved essential resources. The London Library's open access stacks are a researcher's dream, and finding the almost untouched 1808 Diario de Madrid prints was an incredible moment. The staff is always helpful. The Rare Books and Manuscripts Reading Room at the British Library became indispensable, while Elspeth Hector at the National Gallery's library not only allowed me access but offered an explanation for the postponement of Mercedes' 1852 art sale. Jill Hughes at the Taylor Institute at Oxford University kindly provided copies of the Salvandy letters, which are used here with permission.

One of the most satisfying aspects of this project was finally meeting some of Mercedes' numerous French descendants. Not only did they offer their own "souvenirs et mémoires," they also supported the idea of a new biography of Mercedes. Particular thanks go to Jean-Pierre Binder, husband of Mercedes' great-great-great-granddaughter Françoise, who has diligently re-created the family genealogy and shared many years' worth of work.

Jacques Mercier du Paty de Clam and his lovely wife, Pasquale, opened up their home to me, my husband, and many previously unknown Merlin cousins, and arranged a visit to Teresa's old home at Dissay. The beautiful family portraits are also available here through their kindness. Olivier Merlin, a direct descendent of Merlin de Thionville and an admirer of Mercedes, patiently corresponded with me and offered information on his illustrious ancestor as well as on General Merlin. Antoine Barbry, related to General Merlin through his maternal family, also shared his own research on the Merlin siblings.

My understanding of the complex nineteenth-century Parisian musical scene was substantially aided by Oliver Davies, formerly with the Royal College of Music in London, a musical historian and pianist par excellence and cofounder of the Museum of Music History. His devotion to music history has safeguarded the rare examples of Mercedes' concert programs. He also gave me the chance to hear Mercedes' own composition—played for probably the first time in decades, if not longer.

My father-in-law, Dr. Leopoldo Lapuerta, fielded all questions medical as well as the fine points of the Spanish language. Likewise, his brother, Francisco Lapuerta, a Spanish notario, shared his deep knowledge of Spanish legal history and made many things understandable. Monsieur Domenico Gabrielli, a historian of Père Lachaise Cemetery, provided details for the mystery of Mercedes' grave. Father Rupert McHardy of the London Oratory kindly offered details on the baptismal liturgy. Artemis Kirk, University Librarian at Georgetown University, has also supported my efforts in numerous ways.

My good friends Laura Aldir-Hernández and Nadine Badra Renom each in their own way adopted Mercedes and this biography as their own cause. Laura read every chapter, offering wonderful insights and ruthless critique and (thank goodness!) much encouragement. She has never, throughout the years, let me lose heart or perspective.

Nadine offered all help French and musical. Not only did she ponder the best translation or meaning of French words, she has unraveled General Merlin's handwriting, found obscure books on French ordinances, and always offered a friendly ear to my many complaints. Nadine also deserves credit for introducing to me Professor Francis Pomponi, Corsican patriot and historian.

I owe an enormous debt to my family, especially my husband, Carlos. Little did my husband know when he helped me find a 1905 copy of *Viaje a la Habana*, how entangled he would become. My husband reviewed numerous drafts, supported my research, writing, and travel, and the endless conversation beginning with "Did you know that Mercedes…" My children spent holidays playing "spot the missing tomb" in Père Lachaise as well as scouting out Madrid, Aranjuez, and Paris, looking for Mercedes' old haunts.

Carole Sargent at Georgetown University's Booklab helped transform an idea into a real proposal that led to my agent, Don Fehr at Trident Media. Thanks also to my editor Lisa Reardon and everyone at my publisher Chicago Review Press.

And finally, thanks to Domingo Figarola Caneda, the first librarian of the Biblioteca Nacional de Cuba, who salvaged anything he could find on Mercedes and many other Cuban historical figures. He and many other authors too numerous to mention provided a foundation for this new work.

NOTES

ABBREVIATIONS

AdP	Archives de Paris (Paris, France)
AGI	Archivo General de Indias (Sevilla, Spain)
AHDM-SM	Archivo Histórico Diocesano de Madrid, Parroquia de San Martín (Madrid, Spain)
AHN	Archivo Histórico Nacional (Madrid, Spain)
AHN-SN	Archivo Histórico Nacional—Sección de Nobleza (Toledo, Spain)
AHPM	Archivo Histórico de Protocolos de Madrid (Madrid, Spain)
ANC	Archivo Nacional de Cuba (Havana, Cuba)
ANF	Archives Nationales de France (Paris, France)
AP-Almudena	Archivo Parroquial de Santa María la Real de la Almudena (Madrid, Spain)
AP-Santiago	Archivo Parroquial de Santiago y San Juan Bautista (Madrid, Spain)
BAD	Bibliothèque des Arts Décoratifs (Paris, France)
BINHA	Bibliothèque de l'Institut Nationale d'Histoire de l'Art (Paris, France)

BHVP-PC Bibliothèque Historique de la Ville de Paris—Archives
                  Philarète Chasles (Paris, France)
    BIDF Bibliothèque de l'Institut de France (Paris, France)
    BNC Biblioteca Nacional de Cuba (Havana, Cuba)
    BNF Bibliothèque Nationale de France (Paris, France)
      BS Bibliothèque de la Sorbonne (Paris, France)
    CM-M *Souvenirs et Mémoires de Madame la Comtesse Merlin* (1836)
  CM-VH *Viaje a la Habana* (Condesa de Merlin 1844)
  CM-LH *La Havane* (Comtesse Merlin 1844)
  MOMH Museum of Music History (London, United Kingdom)
      NG National Gallery Library (London, United Kingdom)
    SGU Archivo General de Simancas (Simancas, Spain)
    SHD Service Historique de la Défense (Vincennes, France)
    TIL Taylor Institution Library—University of Oxford
                  (Oxford, United Kingdom)

All translations from French and Spanish are mine unless otherwise noted.

CHAPTER 1: *Havana*

Along the cathedral square: Many of the houses of Old Havana are today known by particular names that, in some cases, were only acquired in the nineteenth century. In the case of the Peñalver family, they received the title of Marqués de Arcos in 1792, and the house is better known by the name Casa del Marqués de Arcos, while the Pedroso home is now better known as the Palacio del Conde de Casa Lombillo.

Music set in Stone: Alejo Carpentier, quoted in "The Many Lives of Old Havana," *National Geographic*, vol. 176, n. 2 (August 1989), p. 282.

Mercedes' baptism: February 16, 1789, ANC Escribanía de Guerra Legajo 887, No. 12 237.

Havana's Cathedral: José María de la Torre, *Lo que fuimos y lo que somos*, p. 90.

Of such marvelous beauty: Quoted in Hugh Thomas, *Cuba or the Pursuit of Freedom*, Prologue title page.

For general history of early Havana see: de la Torre, pp. 5–23; Thomas, *Cuba*, pp. 1–71.

Estimated sugar mills: Based on Alexander von Humboldt, *The Island of Cuba—A Political Essay*, p. 166. There were 473 mills in 1775 and more than 780 in 1817; grandfather is Ignacio Montalvo, Count of Casa-Montalvo, whose estate was known as the Macuriges estate: Thomas, *Cuba*, p. 63.

Life for the early settlers: de la Torre, pp. 20–23.

Mercedes and mosquitos: CM-LH, vol. 1, pp. 314–315.

Law of the Indies: de la Torre, pp. 7–8.

Knee-deep mud: Humboldt, p. 79.

The Real Arsenal and *Santísima Trinidad*: de la Torre, pp. 108–113.

As a port city: Emilio Roig de Leuchsenring, *La Habana—Apuntes Históricos*, pp. 81–84; Sherry Johnson, *The Social Transformation of Eighteenth-Century Cuba*, pp. 21–22; Thomas, *Cuba*, 12–13.

The first slaves: Levi Marrero, *Cuba: Economía y Sociedad*, vol. 1, p. 213.

Slave trade concession: Hugh Thomas, *The Slave Trade*, p. 31; Johnson, p. 26.

First newspaper: Roig, p. 211. There were two other short-lived attempts at newspapers, but this is recognized as Havana's first.

Richard O'Farrill naturalization: Real Cédula de Ricardo O'Farrill in César García del Pino and Alicia Melis, *Documentos para la Historia Colonial de Cuba*, pp. 200–201.

Cuban elites in military: Johnson, pp. 13, 63–64. For general discussion on creole elites and military service, see Thomas, *Cuba*; and Johnson.

Mercedes' family's military connections: Based on review of Montalvo, Cárdenas, O'Farrill, Santa Cruz, and Herrera entries in Francisco Xavier de Santa Cruz y Mallén, Conde de Jaruco, *Historia de Familias Cubanas* (hereafter Jaruco). This includes those related by marriage as well as blood.

Increase in sugar cultivation: From 1762 to 1792 cultivation grew from approximately 10,000 to 160,000 acres, Manuel Moreno Fraginals, *El Ingenio*, p. 10.

Population increase: Based on census figures in Ramón de la Sagra, *Historia Económica-Política y Estadística de la Isla de Cuba*; racial balance, Thomas, *Cuba*, pp. 65–66.

Oven-hot sun: quoted in de la Torre, p. 23; one languishes: CM-M, v. 1, p. 113.

Voluptuous delicacy: CM-M, vol. 1, p. 115.

System of numbering: de la Torre, p. 52.

Advertisement 1795: *Papel Periódico*, reprinted in de la Torre, p. 130.

Luxuries in demand: Ibid., p. 63; José Martín Félix de Arrate, *Llave del Nuevo Mundo*, pp. 92–93.

Santa Cruz arcades: quoted in Arturo G. Lavín, "El Palacio de los Condes de San Juan de Jaruco, Muralla 109," p. 54.

Countess of Jaruco's house: María Teresa Cornide, *De la Habana, de Siglos y de Familias*, pp. 134–135.

Lorenzo Montalvo burial: Rubén C. Arango, *La Sacarocracia*, p. 336.

The Obra Pía was established in 1669 by Martín Calvo de la Puerta with a gift of 102,000 pesos. Under the articles of foundation, the revenue would annually dower five poor orphan girls, enabling them to marry or enter a convent. They were chosen by lot and had to fulfill certain criteria. Control of the Obra Pía was inherited and in 1789 was held by Mercedes' Cárdenas great-uncle. It lasted into the twentieth century.

Montalvo and O'Farrill links: Montalvo and O'Farrill entries, Jaruco.

Montalvo sons in Madrid: Ignacio Montalvo petition to king, June 30, 1790, SGU, LEG 6844, 87.

Montalvo and Arango mission and shipwreck: Alfonso W. Quiroz, "The Scientist and the Patrician: Reformism in Cuba," p. 119.

Real Sociedad and Real Consulado: Roig, pp. 233–242.

Prussian rents: Humboldt, p. 214.

Uniting all the natural charms: CM-M, vol. 1, p. 4.

Joaquín intelligent and restless: Thomas, *Cuba*, p. 79, note 34.

Joaquín's uncle: The Jesuit priest was Gabriel Santa Cruz y Santa Cruz, Santa Cruz entry in Jaruco.

CHAPTER 2: *Mercedes and Mamita*

The O'Farrills: Details from O'Farrill entry in Jaruco; Ricardo O'Farrill's Real Cédula in García and Melis; an O'Farrill "clan" is also mentioned in Cornide, p. 495.

One tender look: Gonzalo O'Farrill, *Carta de su Padre Político*, p. 7.

Luisa Herrera: biographical details from Herrera and O'Farrill entries, Jaruco; Mercedes descriptions, CM-M, vol. 1, pp. 6–10.

Luisa's burial: Domingo Rosaín, *Necrópolis de la Habana*, p. 34.

Mother's old nanny, Agueda: CM-LH, vol. 1, pp. 302–304.

Mercedes no thought for studies: CM-M, vol. 1, pp. 10–11.

Corinthian capital: Sophia Peabody Hawthorne, "The Cuba Journal," p. 12.

Ceiba: Ibid., p. 34.

Melancholy beauty: Ibid., p. 35.

Running in the countryside: The entire description is taken from Comtesse Merlin, "L'Evasion," in *Madame Malibran*, vol. 2, pp. 229–241.

Mama Dolores: CM-M, vol. 1, p. 127.

First Conde de Jaruco: Eugenio Sarrablo Aguareles, "La Fundación de Jaruco en Cuba y los Primeros Condes de este Título," p. 471. There were other similar cases throughout Cuban society.

Catalina: CM-LH, vol. 1, pp. 331–333.

San Ignacio slaves: Inventory 1808, ANC Escribanía de Guerra, Legajo 8824, No. 13 203.

Slave burial ground: CM-M, vol. 1, p. 98.

Old-fashioned slavery: For a fuller discussion of the changing nature of Cuban slavery see Moreno Fraginals, *El Ingenio*; Jamie Holeman, "A Peculiar Character of Mildness," in Navarro and Cuartero, *Francisco Arango y la Invención de la Cuba Azucarera*. For the landowners' perspective see Marqués de Cárdenas de Monte-Hermoso and sugar mill owners, February 5, 1790, AGI, ESTADO 7, N. 5. Many commentators note that the rules were often ignored.

María Josefa de Cárdenas: Cárdenas and Barreto entries, Jaruco.

Black legend: Cornide, pp. 263–275. Salvador Bueno, "El Temporal de Barreto," in *Leyendas Cubanas*, pp. 291–296.

Distressing incident: The entire description taken from Mercedes' "L'Evasion," *Madame Malibran*, vol. 2, pp. 229–241. Mercedes also referenced it in *La Havane/Viaje a La Habana* but changed the location to Havana. Mercedes often took real incidents and heightened the dramatic description. Conchita was probably older than indicated. Mercedes' age is difficult to judge, but a probable date is before her reunion with her father in summer of 1797, making Mercedes less than nine.

CHAPTER 3: *Joaquín*

Joaquín de Santa Cruz and Guántanamo Commission: Governor of Cuba
[Santiago] to Prince de la Paz, February 3, 1797, AGI, ESTADO, 1, N.
12; General Commander of Navy, November 1, 1797, AGI, ESTADO, 15,
N. 49; Cabildo of Santiago to King, February 15, 1797, AGI, ESTADO,
13, N. 41; Francisco de las Barras de Aragón, "Noticias y Documentos de
la Expedición del Conde de Mopox a la Isla de Cuba"; P. Barreiro (Agus-
tino), "Documentos Relativos a la Expedición del Conde de Mopox a
la Isla de Cuba"; María Dolores Higueras and José Guío (eds.), *Cuba
Ilustrada: Real Comisión de Guantánamo 1796–1802*, vol. 1–2.

License to Spain: petitions 1787–1789, SGU, LEG, 6874, 13.

He said our time: CM-M vol. 1, p. 252.

Coffee: Ibid., p. 118.

"[Jaruco] is wet behind the ears": Minister of Indies to Count de Floridablanca, February 5, 1790, SGU, LEG 6874, 13.

Illuminate the spirit: Joaquín to king for license to Italy, February 10, 1790,
Ibid.

Decorous distinction: Joaquín to king, February 18, 1790, Ibid.

Generally for all his petitions, honors, and related costs: SGU, LEG 6874,
13; SGU, LEG 6846, 2; SGU, LEG 6846, 82; SGU, LEG 6844, 9; and
Sarrablo.

Spent months: Joaquín to king, Duke de Alcudia, and others as well as
responses regarding salary, expenses, and rank for sub-inspector general,
June–October 1795, SGU, LEG 6874, 13.

Joaquín's letters to Arango were first published in *El Curioso Americano*
between December 1894 and September 1900 and were later republished
in Conde de Vallellano, *Nobiliario Cubano*.

This poor boy: Joaquín to Arango, May 2, 1794, *Curioso Americano*, year 2,
n. 3 (December 1894), pp. 41–46.

House in Madrid: Their daughter, Pepita, was born in 1791 on Calle del
Avemaría but another child was born in late 1792 on Calle de la Luna.
By 1793, a newspaper mentioned the Jaruco home as Calle de la Luna, in
front of the Marqués de Branchiforti [*sic*], in the house of the Marqués de
Llano—the same referenced by Mercedes; María Josefa baptismal certifi-

cate January 8, 1791: ANC Escribanía de Guerra, Legajo 887, No. 12 237; María baptism November 7, 1792: Matías Fernández García, *Parroquias Madrileñas de San Martín y San Pedro el Real*, p. 316; *Diario de Madrid*, April 7, 1793.

Musical soirees: Manuel Juan Diana, *Memoria Histórica-Artística del Teatro Real de Madrid*, p. 28.

Our Teresa: José de Jesús Arostegui y Herrera to Arango, February 25, 1797, *Curioso Americano*, year 5, n. 3 (January 1920), pp. 80–81.

Travel to Paris and London: Arrival in London from France, *Morning Post and Fashionable World*, January 20, 1796, and letter from Joaquín to Arango, September 16, 1795, *Curioso Americano*, Epoca 3, n. 10–11 (April–September 1900) pp. 148–150.

Teresa's health: Ibid. Teresa had given birth in March 1795.

Letter to Spain and new projects: Joaquín to Administrator of Mail, February 5, 1797, AGI ESTADO, 15, N. 35; Higueras and Guío, pp. 210–212.

Joaquín's duties: Orders to Brigadier Conde de Mopox y Jaruco, August 14–November 25, 1796, SGU, LEG 6856, 31.

Movement through Cuba: Joaquín's itinerary based on review of various documents. Joaquín to Count de Santa Clara, June 3, 1797, SGU, LEG 6861, 41; catalogue of documents in Higueras and Guío, pp. 195–214.

Delight meeting father: CM-M, vol. 1, pp. 12–13.

Murió Manuel Conde: Story told in Carlos Venegas Fornias, "Un Conde Habanero en el Siglo de las Luces," pp. 25, 27, note 5.

Joaquín's letter: Joaquín to Prince de la Paz, quoted in Higueras and Guío, p. 201.

Joaquín's business interests compiled from "Los Privilegios del Conde de Jaruco," *Curioso Americano*, year 7, no. 2 (March–April 1929), pp. 99–101; Marqués de Branciforte to Prince de la Paz, December 27, 1796, AGI ESTADO 25, N. 96; Marqués de Arcos to Prince de la Paz, November 29, 1796, AGI ESTADO, 16, N. 9; Moreno Fraginals, El Ingenio; Marrero, "El Conde de Mopox y Jaruco: Noble, Cortesano, Empresario y Mercader," in *Cuba: Economía y Sociedad*, vol. 13 and "Cuba Impone Su Libre Comercio," Ibid., vol. 12; Correspondence between Joaquín and Carlos Martínez de Irujo, Spanish minister to the United States, BNC, Colección Pérez No. 1053; San Juan de Jaruco, Joaquín Beltrán de Santa

Cruz conde de, Correspondencia con Carlos Martínez de Irujo Habana-Filadelfia, 1797-1798, 5 cartas (Irujo).

My father loved me: CM-M, vol. 1, p. 13.

Mercedes began her reign: Ibid.

The Havana palace was entailed to Joaquín's great-aunt, the widowed Countess de Jaruco. Even with a new palace in the Plaza de Armas, the strong-willed countess was unlikely to release it (see Lavín). José María de la Torre in his 1857 history of Havana claimed that Joaquín lived in two homes, one on San Ignacio and Chacón belonging to the Chacón family, and another belonging to the Marqués de San Felipe y Santiago, on Oficios and Amargura. The first was next to his grandfather Pedro Santa Cruz's house near the fortress of La Punta, and, in those days, located steps away from the water. The second home was a large palace on the Plaza de San Francisco facing the bay where ships landed cargo. Joaquín died in the San Felipe house in 1807 but Mercedes' description of her room overlooking the water corresponds more to San Ignacio and Chacón.

Joaquín's house contained: Inventory, June 1807 and Delivery of Assets, July 1808, ANC, Escribanía de Guerra, Legajo, 1128, No. 15 624 (Testamentaría).

Passion for dancing and Mamita's company: CM-M, vol. 1, pp. 28–29.

Details of Joaquín's properties: Inventory 1808; Rafael Montalvo against Conde de Mopox, 1801, ANC, Escribanía de Varios, Legajo 749, No. 12 619. Convent of Santa Clara claim on Mopox estate: ANC, Escribanía de Guerra, Legajo 887, No. 13 297; Humboldt, *The Island of Cuba*, p. 214.

Steam: Moreno Fraginals, El Ingenio, pp. 30, 106; Olga V. Egorova, "Agustín de Betancourt y la Primera Máquina de Vapor en Cuba." Steam engine ordered through his father-in-law, Ignacio Montalvo, while on his extended trip with Arango.

Cuban slave owners: Humboldt, "The Nature of Slavery," p. 256.

Remembered being horrified: CM-M, vol. 1, p. 15.

Alleviation of suffering and awakened at dawn: Ibid., pp. 16–19.

Cangis' story: Ibid., pp. 19–23.

Slave queens: Thomas, *The Slave Trade*, p. 397.

Mercedes and the horses: CM-M, vol. 1, pp. 24–27.

CHAPTER 4: *Behind the Convent Walls*

Exact dates for Joaquín's movement are difficult to establish. He often discussed plans and applied for licenses yet inexplicably didn't travel. Knowing the date of his planned Madrid journey would help date Mercedes' entry into convent as she attributes it to the combination of her father's travel plans and her grandmother's influence. Joaquín initially applied to travel in mid-1799 and his mother died in March 1800. Mercedes also mentions the feast of Santa Clara (August 11). Therefore a likely date is summer of 1799.

Joaquín's privileges: Moreno Fraginal, El Ingenio, pp. 34–37; Sagra, pp. 134–137; Jacobo de la Pezuela, *Ensayo Histórico de la Isla de Cuba*, chapter 22. Catalogue of documents, Higueras and Guío, pp. 195–214; Irujo. Contract with the Count de Mopox, (1804–1805), AGI, ULTRAMAR, 123, N. 11; Marrero, vol. 12, pp. 59–74. Joaquín's trading privileges are incredibly complex and the focus of much discussion in Cuban studies. Accusations of corruption, false billings, and smuggled contraband exist at all levels from Madrid to the United States and a full discussion is beyond the scope of this biography. Moreno Fraginals and Levi Marrero provide a good analysis.

Mercedes' marriage: Joaquín to Arango, May 9, 1794, *Curioso Americano*, year 2, n. 3 (December 1894), pp. 41–46.

Mercedes secretly hoped: CM-M, vol. 1, pp. 30–31.

The most prudent path: Ibid.

General background on convents: John James Clune, "A Cuban Convent in the Age of Enlightened Reform: the Observant Franciscan Community of Santa Clara 1768–1808"; Lyding Rodríguez Fuentes, "Santa Clara de Asís: El Esplendor de un Convento para Doncellas de Elite 1644–1780"; Asunción Lavrin, "Ecclesiastical Reform of Nunneries in New Spain in the Eighteenth Century"; Lina Valmont/Alejo Carpentier, "Tras los vetustos muros del Convento de Santa Clara"; Waldo Lamas and Osvaldo Valdés de la Paz, *Historia del Convento de Santa Clara*.

They availed themselves: CM-M, vol. 1, p. 38.

Aunts: María Loreto de San José and María de los Dolores de Santa Teresa, based on Santa Cruz entry, Jaruco and Pedro de Santa Cruz y Aranda will, AHN, ESTADO-CARLOS_III, Exp.529; Joaquín's mortgage in favor of aunts: ANC, Escribanía de Guerra, Legajo 887, No. 13 297. Mercedes calls the eldest the abbess, but this has not been verified. She also says she was placed in the care of the younger.

Enclosure measures: Clune, pp. 314–315.

The account of Mercedes' stay in convent: CM-M, vol. 1, pp. 39–79.

Moratorium 1797: Clune, p. 325.

Conchita's permission: Year 1806 leg. 1987-2 in Santiago Montoto, *Catálogo de Los Fondos Cubanos del Archivo General de Indias*, t. I, v. II, Consultas y Decretos, 1784–1820.

Early biographer is Francisco Calcagno.

Aunt Paquita, Marquesa de Castelflor, is supposedly her grandmother's sister, but there is no corresponding person in the family genealogy. Mercedes was often imprecise with details and possibly meant the wife of her great-uncle Miguel de Cárdenas, whose son became Marqués de Campo—Florido, or even another Cárdenas relative. The Cárdenas family founded San Antonio de los Baños.

Mercedes' stay with Aunt Paquita: CM-M, vol. 1, pp. 79–105.

Famed Alquízar región: Cirilo Villaverde, *Cecilia Valdés*; "Ramillete," *Gaceta de la Habana*, December 23, 1849; Cornide, p. 139.

CHAPTER 5: *Adios, Cuba*

She learned nothing: CM-M, vol. 1, p. 111.

Family tree: Ibid., pp. 118–119.

Inquiry for Grandeza: AHN, CONSEJOS, 5315, Exp. 4; AHN, OM-EXPEDIENTILLOS, N. 12460.

Desk: Inventory June 1807, Testamentaría.

Joaquín entertained: CM-M, vol. 1, pp. 119–121.

Details Guantánamo report: Barreiro, pp. 13–14.

Complex business affairs: Joaquín to Arango, July 22, 1802, *Curioso Americano*, Epoca 3, n. 8–9, (Feb/March 1900), pp. 120–125.

Enterprising: Humboldt, *The Island of Cuba*, p. 191.

Purchase of Jesús Nazareno: Rafael Montalvo against Conde de Mopox 1801, ANC, Escribanía de Varios, Legajo 749, No. 12 619.

Great plans: Joaquín to Arango, July 22, 1802, *Curioso Americano*, Epoca 3, n. 8–9 (Feb/March 1900), pp. 120–125.

Royal debts: Ibid. Sale 1799: Representation of Factoría, April 13, 1807, Testamentaría.

Sweet idleness: CM-M, vol. 1, pp. 110–111.

Neptuno: Joaquín's Report, May 25, 1802, Higueras and Guío, p. 197.

Ship details: Todo a Babor Revista Divulgativa de Historia Naval en Internet, www.todoababor.es/listado/navio-neptuno3.

The Havana breeze: CM-M, vol. 1, pp. 113–117 and 121–124.

Greatest evil: Humboldt, "Nature of Slavery," p. 256.

Manumission: Humboldt, *The Island of Cuba*, p. 136.

Mama Dolores: CM-M, vol. 1, pp. 127–132. These were probably the lands he was selling off to tobacco farmers.

Saint-Domingue revolution: Ada Ferrer, "El Mundo Cubano del Azúcar frente a la Revolución Haitiana," in *Francisco Arango y la Invención de la Cuba Azucarera*, pp. 105–116.

Cuban landowners: Marqués de Cárdenas de Monte-Hermoso and sugar mill owners, February 5, 1790, AGI, ESTADO 7, N. 5.

April 22, 1802: Joaquín's Report, May 25, 1802, Higueras and Guío, p. 197.

As they sailed out: CM-M, vol. 1, pp. 132–136.

CHAPTER 6: *Madrid*

Journey to Cádiz: CM-M, vol. 1, pp. 136–143.

Arrival date: Joaquín's Report, May 25, 1802, Higueras and Guío, p.197.

Lifelong aversion: CM-M, vol. 2, p. 145.

Had built it expressly: CM-M, vol. 1, p. 143.

Sad olive trees: Ibid., p. 148.

Spanish roads: Duchesse d'Abrantès, *Souvenirs d'une Ambassade*, vol. 1, pp. 14–16.

Foreign dress: Elizabeth, Lady Holland, *The Spanish Journal*, pp. 5–7; Duchesse d'Abrantès, *Ambassade*, vol. 1, pp. 90–91.

Mules: CM-M, vol. 3, pp. 47–48.

Madrid coach service: Charles E. Kany, *Life and Manners in Madrid 1750–1800*, pp. 134–135.

Mail service: María Luisa, *Cartas Confidenciales de la Reina María Luisa y de Don Manuel Godoy*, p. 214, note iii.

Ravishing spot: Kany, p. 138.

Good but slow-witted: Martin Armstrong, *The Spanish Circus*, p. 12. There are numerous sources describing Carlos IV and María Luisa including: Lady Holland; Henry Richard, Lord Holland, *Foreign Reminiscences*; Armstrong; Marqués de Villa-Urrutia, *La Reina María Luisa*.

The French ambassador (Alquier) and mentor (Escóiquiz): Villa-Urrutia, pp. 28–30.

Celebrated anecdote: Lord Holland, p. 73.

Letters: Generally see María Luisa, *Cartas*; Villa-Urrutia, *La Reina María Luisa*. Quoted: Sly coward and venemous viper: Villa-Urrutia, p. 87. Judas: María Luisa, p. 269. True friends: Ibid., p. 271.

Mother's acquaintances: CM-M, vol. 1, pp. 149–150.

Meeting her mother: Ibid., pp. 153–156.

There was in Madrid: Duchesse d'Abrantès, *Souvenirs Historiques*, vol. 8, pp. 21–22.

Wrote to Paris: Duchesse d'Abrantès, *Ambassade*, vol. 1, p. 274.

Extremely voluptuous: Lady Holland, p. 199.

The girls have the measles: Joaquín to Arango, June 11, 1794, Vallellano, pp. 125–126. Joaquín only mentions one girl in a letter to Arango dated September 16, 1795 (Ibid., pp. 134–137). María isn't mentioned in the October 1796 will (Testamentaría) when Joaquín describes his four children.

O'Farrill and wife: Andrés Muriel, *Notice sur D. Gonzalo O'Farrill*; O'Farrill; Elisa Martín Valdepeñas Yagüe, "Ilustración, Jacobinismo y Afrancesamiento: Ana Rodríguez de Carasa (*sic*)."

María Felicitas de Saint Maxent, widow of Bernardo de Gálvez: Gálvez supported the American colonies and by winning Pensacola, helped block British southern supply lines. Galveston is named after him. Eric Beerman, "El Conde de Aranda y la Tertulia de la Viuda de Bernardo de Gálvez."

María Luisa detested intellectuals: Marques de Villa-Urrutia, *Fernando VII Rey Constitucional*, p. 29.

Mercedes' education: CM-M, vol. 1, pp. 157–159.

Blas and Tomás: Blas Montalvo and Tomás Santa Cruz petition freedom, ANC, Intendencia de Hacienda, Legajo 1064, No. 1.

American counsel: Letter from Vincent Gray, October 29, 1802, *The Papers of James Madison: Secretary of State Series*, vol. 4, pp. 62–65. During this period the US dollar and the Cuban peso were equal. Hence Gray quotes identical figures to Joaquín.

Details of Joaquín's privileges and quotes: Joaquín to Arango, July 22, 1802, *Curioso Americano*, Epoca 3, n. 8–9 (Feb–March 1900), pp. 120–125.

Their joint will: March 30, 1789 and October 16, 1796 wills, Testamentaría.

My father oldest ally: CM-M, vol. 1, p. 162.

CHAPTER 7: *A Sense of Loss*

The word tú: CM-M, vol. 1, pp. 164–167 and 206–209.

Mercedes' studies: Ibid., pp. 169–173.

Dancing: Ibid., p. 265; CM-M, vol. 2, pp. 188–190.

Strict routine: CM-M, vol. 1, p. 202.

Tertulia: Ibid., pp. 162–163.

Goya episode: Ibid., pp. 182–185.

Teresa and Paris: Ibid., pp. 253–311; O'Farrill, pp. 21–22. I have diverged from Mercedes' timeline since O'Farrill's highly precise *Carta* is more reliable. Mercedes occasionally changed the chronology of events to aid the narrative. Spanish novelist is Fernán Caballero in *Un Servilón y un Liberalito*.

The best of mothers: O'Farrill, p. 26.

Mercedes' imagination: CM-M, vol. 1, pp. 197–200.

Joaquín's debts: Representation of Factoría, April 13, 1807, Testamentaría.

Income: Report for Grandeza, March 20, 1807, AHN, CONSEJOS, 9987, EXP. 13. Joaquín inherited the Jaruco entail at his great-aunt's death in 1804. He received little else: two crystal chandeliers, religious paintings/altar from her oratory, and cancellation of 8,000-peso debt: Condesa de Jaruco's will, ANC, Escribanía de Varios, Legajo 253, No. 3 834.

We lost him: CM-M, vol. 1, pp. 251–253. Joaquín died on April 5, 1802. Captain-General Someruelos, Testamentaría; R.O. June 1807 Testamentaría.

The various wills: March 30, 1789 and October 16, 1796, Testamentaría; Intestate: AHN, OM-Caballeros_Alcantara, MOD. 311.

Monte-Hermoso's statement: Testimony of Marqués de Cárdenas de Monte-Hermoso, June 4, 1807, Testamentaría.

Witness statements: Luis Frances and Domingo Polo demand freedom, ANC, Escribanía Guerra, Legajo 893, No. 13 401.

Matilde and Merced Valdés: Claim, February 11, 1818, Testamentaría; Claim by Convent of Ursulines, January 1809, ANC, Escribanía de Guerra, Legajo 891, No. 13 369.

Auction: Almonedas, July 1807, Testamentaría; Villaverde, *Cecilia Valdés*, vol. 1, pp. 276–277.

Joaquín's slaves: Genoveva *lucumí*, ANC, Intendencia de Hacienda, Legajo 1012, No. 24. Blas y Tomás, ANC, Intendencia de Hacienda, 1064, No. 1. Luis Frances y Domingo Polo, ANC, Escribanía Guerra, Legajo 893, No. 13 401.

R.O. June 1807: Testamentaría.

R.O. March 1808: Testamentaría.

CHAPTER 8: *Treason, Hatred, Vengeance*

Most magnificent: Lady Holland, p. 199.

Incomparable Teresa: Duchesse d'Abrantès, *Souvenirs Historiques*, vol. 8, pp. 21–22.

Two romances: Quesada, CM-M, vol. 1, pp. 321–340; and Cerrano, ibid., pp. 318–321; CM-M, vol. 2, pp. 3–28. Exact dates are difficult to judge since Mercedes occasionally shifted events to aid the narrative.

Gonzalo O'Farrill and wife: O'Farrill, pp. 15–26.

King and queen considered O'Farrill: María Luisa, *Cartas*, p. 214.

Lady Holland recalled: Lady Holland, p. 159.

Very fat, very chattering: Catherine Bearne, *A Royal Quartette*, p. 354.

Admired French Revolution: O'Farrill, pp. 36–37.

The clouds: Ibid., p. 26.

For Spanish-French relations, the royal feud, and political events 1807–1808: CM-M, vol. 2; Conde de Toreno, *Historia del Levantamiento, Guerra y Revolución de España* vol.1; Miguel de Azanza and Gonzalo O'Farrill,

Memoria de D. Miguel José de Azanza y D. Gonzalo O'Farrill; Manuel Esquivel y Castañeda, "Memorias Inéditas"; Rafael Pérez, *El Relato de un Actor*; Miguel Artola, *Los Afrancesados*; Charles Esdaile, *The Peninsular War*.

Russia or Prussia: Lord Holland, p. 135.

The palace was: Ibid., p. 127.

Fernando responded: Toreno, vol. 1, p. 83.

Attacks on Godoy cronies: CM-M, vol. 2, p. 43; Esquivel, pp. 380–381; Pérez, pp. 76–77; Toreno, vol. 1, pp. 89–90.

O'Farrill's illness and night of March 19: CM-M, vol. 2, pp. 43–48.

Looked like devils: Esquivel, p. 382.

Civility of crowd: CM-M, vol. 2, pp. 48–49.

Murat called O'Farrill: Azanza and O'Farrill, pp. 26–28

Dos de Mayo: CM-M, vol. 2, pp. 84–96; Azanza and O'Farrill, pp. 41–46; Toreno, vol. 1, pp. 144–155; Esdaile, pp. 37–40.

Possible kings: Artola, pp. 102–104.

O'Farrill and the Junta: Azanza and O'Farrill, pp. 74–76.

My O'Farrill: O'Farrill, p. 52.

Decision to evacuate: Azanza and O'Farrill, pp. 100–142.

Ana's diary records fear: O'Farrill, p. 40.

So finished the first: CM-M, vol. 2, pp. 97–98.

CHAPTER 9: *The Good Devils*

Their exile through Vitoria: CM-M, vol. 2, pp. 118–144. A romance: O'Farrill, p. 41.

The Emperor Napoleon arrived: CM-M, vol. 2, p. 151.

The sensation: Azanza and O'Farrill, pp. 145–151.

A frustrated Joseph: O'Farrill, pp. 41–42.

Devastation of Burgos: CM-M, vol. 2, pp. 152–162. Mercedes' descriptions are corroborated by other accounts. André-François Miot de Melito, *Mémoires du Comte Miot de Melito*, vol. 3, pp. 22–23; Paul Thiébault, *Mémoires du Général Baron Thiébault*, vol. 4, pp. 284–287; Charles-Alexandre Geoffroy de Grandmaison, *L'Espagne et Napoleon*, vol. 1, pp. 365–369.

Asset seizures, Gonzalo O'Farrill, Condesa de Jaruco, and Marqués de Casa-Calvo: AHN, CONSEJOS, 9395, EXP. 1, 3, 88, 89, and 90.

Quintana's disillusionment: Manuel José Quintana, *Obras Inéditas del Excmo. Señor D. Manuel José Quintana*, pp. 165–236.

Family's return to Madrid, society, and Sébastiani: CM-M, vol. 2, pp. 174–221.

General Bigarré recalled: Auguste-Julien Bigarré, *Mémoires du Général Bigarré*, p. 262.

Portrait of Joseph: CM-M, vol. 2, pp. 107, 212, 218–219; Geoffroy de Grandmaison, vol. 2, pp. 321–326; Bigarré, pp. 213–214.

Joseph told Mercedes: Joseph to Mercedes, September 1, 1836, BIDF, Ms 7917, f23–24.

Joseph loves all beautiful: Bigarré, p. 214.

Particular predilection: Ibid., p. 252.

Joseph's mistresses: Geoffroy de Grandmaison, vol. 2, pp. 327–331.

Condesa de Jaruco liaison: Ramón de Mesonero Romanos, "Las Calles y Casas de Madrid," in *Semanario Pintoresco Español*, November 20, 1853, and *Memorias de un Setentón*, p. 34.

Other historians: Marqués de Villa Urrutia, Geoffroy de Grandmaison, etc.

Teresa dissolute: "Primera Vindicación que hace al Publico el Teniente de Navío Retirado D. Ramón Ortiz Canelas y Esteller 1812," quoted in Domingo Figarola Caneda, *La Condesa de Merlin* (FC), p. 15.

Perceived insult: Salvador Bueno, *Cuba, Cruzero del Mundo*, pp. xiii–xiv; "Los Amores Secretos de José I con una Habanera," *Carteles*, year 37, n. 17 (April 22, 1956), pp. 64–65, 102–103.

Concurred with portrayal: Joseph to Mercedes, September 1, 1836, BIDF, Ms 7917, f23–24.

From early dawn: Miot de Melito, *Memoirs of Count Miot de Melito* (English), vol. 2, pp. 336–340. Mercedes' comments: CM-M, vol. 2, pp. 222–224.

Compensation: Comte de La Forest, *Correspondance du Comte de La Forest*, vol. 2, pp. 421–422, 426; Ibid., vol. 3, p. 58; Joseph to Napoleon, January 21, 1809, Joseph Bonaparte, *Mémoires et Correspondance Politique et Militaire du Roi Joseph*, vol. 5, pp. 390–391. At the time twenty reales de vellón were equal to one peso.

O'Farrill's sugar mill: AGI, ULTRAMAR, 42 No. 32.

Teresa: CM-M, vol. 2, pp. 269–274. The state bonds were known as *cédulas hipotecarias*.

Mercedes, the king: CM-M, vol. 2, pp. 275–278.

Joseph's inner circle: Geoffroy de Grandmaison, vol. 2, pp. 331–332.

O'Farrill's motives: La Forest, vol. 2, p. 422; Ibid., vol. 3, p. 58.

General Merlin: Roger Merlin, *Merlin de Thionville*, vol. 1–2; Paul Albert, *Une famille Lorraine, les Merlin de Thionville*.

Career: Etat de Service 1825, SHD, MERLIN Christophe-Antoine GDI 7YD 623 (SHD Merlin).

Bilbao: La Forest, vol. 1, pp. 222–223; Geoffroy de Grandmaison, vol. 1, pp. 324–325; Joseph to Napoleon, August 22, 1808, Joseph Bonaparte, *Mémoires et Correspondance*, vol. 4, pp. 435–436.

Always perfect: Joseph to Mercedes, September 1, 1836, BIDF, Ms 7917, f23–24.

CHAPTER 10: *Adios, España*

His exterior appeared: CM-M, vol. 2, p. 280.

Garden at Burgos: Ibid., p. 163.

Marriage Contract: Contract October 21, 1809, AHPM, T. 23498, folios 54 r.–57 r.

Marriage: October 31, 1809, AHDM-SM, Libro 34, folios 337 r/v.

Diamonds: La Forest, vol. 3, p. 58.

Pardon of condemned: CM-M, vol. 2, pp. 296–310; La Forest, vol. 3, pp. 57–58. La Forest's report to Paris describes the pardon.

Letters published in Agustín de Figueroa, *La Condesa de Merlin, Musa del Romanticismo*, pp.78–108. First letter, p. 80. Figueroa, Marqués de Santo Floro, found the letters in Madrid's famous street market, El Rastro, and was moved to write a biography. His daughter, Natalia Figueora, confirmed this account but knew nothing of their whereabouts. They may have been lost in the Spanish Civil War.

What will happen: Ibid., p. 107.

Tension between Joseph and Napoleon and demoralization: La Forest, vol. 4, pp. 20–23.

Palace de Osuna and Villaviciosa: Figueroa, p. 86; José Galiano to Duquesa, August 12, 1812, AHN-SN, Osuna, CT 194, D. 87–88.

Musical evenings: Bigarré, p. 262.

Mercedes and Joseph: CM-M, vol. 2, pp. 319–326.

Claimed no memory: Joseph to Mercedes, September 1, 1836, BIDF, Ms 7917 f23–24.

Emissaries returned: Miot de Melito, *Memoires*, vol. 3, pp. 161–165.

Royal Guards and Imperial Decree: La Forest, vol. 5, pp. 279–280; Ibid., vol. 6, pp. 73–74 and pp. 124–127; Joseph to Berthier, October 1, 1811, Joseph Bonaparte, *Mémoires et Correspondance*, vol. 8, p. 94.

General Merlin's jealousy: La Forest, vol. 5, p. 262.

French charity: Bigarré, pp. 289–291.

Ana Rodríguez de Carassa and *La Inclusa*: Elisa Martin-Valdepeñas Yagüe, "Afrancesadas y patriotas: la Junta de Honor y Mérito Real Sociedad Económica Matritense de Amigos del País," pp. 354–356; O'Farrill, pp. 46–48. O'Farrill published a moving condolence letter from Ana's former colleagues acknowledging her invaluable help.

Joaquín's half-brother: Marqués de Cárdenas de Monte-Hermoso, September 30, 1811 in attachment to Testamentaría; CM-M, vol. 2, pp. 269–270.

Quico in Madrid: Joseph to Mercedes, September 1, 1836, BIDF, Ms 7917 f23–24.

Quico to Cádiz: CM-M, vol. 3, pp. 67–69, 82; *El Conciso de Cádiz*, July 17, 1813; Quico petitions Regency, April 11, 1813, AGI, ULTRAMAR, 128, No. 41.

Teresa's death: CM-M, vol. 3, pp. 70–85; O'Farrill, p. 45; April 17, 1812, AP-Santiago, Libro 24, Folio 419. According to the parish records, she was buried in the cemetery just outside the Fuencarral gate.

Teresa's legend: Mesonero Romanos, *Setentón*, p. 34.

Mercedes' daughter: CM-M, vol. 3, pp. 87–96; Teresa's birthdate, June 17, 1812 in baptismal record, July 20, 1812, AP-Almudena.

Emissaries to Soult: Joseph to Mercedes, September 1, 1836, BIDF, Ms 7917 f23–24.

I fear so many things: Mercedes to Merlin, July 1812, quoted in Charles Oman, *A History of the Peninsular War*, vol. 5, p. 614. The original is in the National Archives, Kew, WO 37/2/15.

Resulting convoy: Joseph Léopold Hugo, *Mémoires du Général Hugo*, vol. 3, p. 95.

Evacuation of Madrid: CM-M, vol. 3, pp. 147–197; Hugo, vol. 3, pp. 94–101, Miot de Melito, *Mémoires*, vol. 3, pp. 234–241.

Fate of Deslandes: CM-M, vol. 3, pp. 43–64; Thiébault, pp. 565–566 and 574–576; La Forest, vol. 4, pp. 193–194; Miot de Melito, *Mémoires*, vol. 3, pp. 223–224. Mercedes gives a highly romanticized account in her memoir.

Evacuation to France: CM-M, vol. 3, pp. 239–246, 310–328, 361–375; date from Miot de Melito, *Mémoires*, vol. 3, p. 242.

CHAPTER 11: *Starting Over*

Merlin arrives in France: Joseph confirmed to Mercedes that Merlin was in France by mid-November: Joseph to Mercedes, September 1, 1836, BIDF, Ms 7917 f23–24. Tensions within his staff: La Forest, vol. 7, pp. 10–11. Two thousand men: Geoffroy de Grandmaison, vol. 2, p. 304. A stranger to French: Merlin to President of the War Committee, February, 4, 1825, SHD Merlin.

Terrible for his fierceness: Merlin, vol. 2, pp. 653, 770; Les Tuileries: Ibid., pp. 55–57.

Commenchon and marriage: Rose: Ibid., p. 739; Commenchon: Ibid., pp. 731–732; Mercédès Merlin: Ibid., p. 738.

Aftermath of Vitoria: Miot de Melito (English), pp. 606–613.

Art collection: Wellington to Sir Henry Wellesley, March 16, 1814, Duke of Wellington, *The Dispatches of Field Marshal The Duke of Wellington*, vol. 11, pp. 586–587.

Joseph regarding supporters: Joseph to Napoleon, June 30, 1813, Joseph Bonaparte, *Mémoires et Correspondance*, vol. 10, pp. 338–339.

Ana Rodríguez de Carassa: O'Farrill, pp. 49–57; Wellington to Ana O'Farrill [*sic*], September 18, 1813, p. 151 and November 8, 1813, p. 263 in Wellington, vol. 11; Joseph to Napoleon, March 10, 1814, Joseph Bonaparte, *Mémoires et Correspondance*, vol. 10, p. 192.

Spanish property: José Galiano to Duchess de Osuna, August 12, 1812, AHN-SN, Osuna. CT. 194, D.87, 88.

The Merlins' Spanish losses: Documents inventory from Succession du Général Merlin, ANF, MC/ET/XCIII/579 (ANF Succession Merlin).

Defending France: Etat de Service 1825, SHD Merlin; M.C. Mullié, *Biographie des célébrités militaires*, vol. 2, p. 289.

Battle of Paris: Details from Rapetti, *La Defection de Marmont en 1814*; Jules-Alexis Lucotte, *Notice Historique sur le Lt. Général Comte Lucotte*; French Order of Battle February 1 and March 30, 1814, U.S. Army Command and General Staff College, www.cgsc.edu.

Merlin chevalier Saint-Louis: Mullié, p. 289. Inspector: Etat de Service 1825, SHD Merlin. Plight of officers: Henry Houssaye, *1815 La Première Restauration*, pp. 16–20.

Merlin properties: Merlin, vol. 2, pp. 793–794.

Marriage: March 17, 1814, AdP; Permission to marry January 1814, SHD Merlin.

Back pay: Lucotte, p. 17.

Ruinous costs: Merlin to Minister, February 9, 1814, SHD Merlin.

Commenchon pillaged: Merlin, vol. 2, pp. 768–769.

Appeal for title: Merlin to Minister, September 29, 1814; to Beaufort, January 31, 1815; to Général Durrieu, January 31, 1815, SHD Merlin.

Married daughter: Merlin to President of War Committee, February 4, 1825, SHD Merlin.

Count Merlin: Rafael Nieto y Cortadellas, *Dignidades Nobiliarias en Cuba*, pp. 326–327.

Choosing sides: Houssaye, pp. 269–272.

Merlin claimed: Exposé on the Conduct of Lt. General Merlin, SHD Merlin.

Sire: Merlin to Napoleon, May 14, 1815, SHD Merlin.

Napoleon's earliest supporters: Ordonnance July 24, 1815 in J.B. Duvergier, *Collection Complete des Lois, Décrets, Ordonnances, Règlements et Avis du Conseil d'Etat*, vol. 20; La Bédoyère and Ney, Henri Houssaye, *1815 La Seconde Abdication*, pp. 508–510, 566–585.

Merlin back in Paris : Merlin to minister of War, October 8, 1815, SHD Merlin; Commission established: Ordonnance October 12, 1815 (Commission); November 6, 1815 (Instruction), in Duvergier.

Merlin's review: Exposé on the Conduct; Review Commission Report, February 8, 1816; Report on General Merlin, SHD Merlin.

Surveillance: Travel permissions, SHD Merlin. Surveillance confusion: *Le Livre Noir de MM Delavau et Franchet*, vols. 2–3; Albert, p. 36.

Casimira: CM-M, vol. 3, pp. 153–154.

Full house: Merlin, vol. 2, pp. 770–771.

CHAPTER 12: *The Rise of La Belle Créole*

Quote from Alexandre Dumas, *La Salle d'Armes—Pauline*, pp. 174, 178–179.

Impoverished exile: O'Farrill to Joseph, March 24, 1824, Joseph Bonaparte, *Mémoires et Correspondance*, vol. 10, pp. 273–275.

Royal approval: Quico's petition May 12, 1814, approval January 16, 1817, AHN, CONSEJOS, 9987, Exp. 13.

Pedro and Pepita: O'Farrill, pp. 57–69; Pedro requests license, May 5, 1815, AGI, ULTRAMAR, 329, N. 59.

Matilde and Merced Valdés: Approval of settlement November 9, 1821, Testamentaría.

Estate Settlement : Agreement September 18, 1820, ANC, Protocolo Notarial de José Ortega 1820 Escritura, f 655 vto; Cuadernillo July 27, 1820, ibid.; Agreement between Mercedes and Quico, October 2, 1820, ibid., Folio 699; Agreement October 12, 1821, Protocolo de José Ortega 1821, Tomo II, Folio 729.

Reason and force: CM-M, vol. 2, pp. 33–35.

Dear Uncle O'Farrill: CM-M, vol. 1, pp. 255–259.

Background on salons and society: Anne Martin-Fugier, *La Vie Élégant*; Steven Kale, *French Salons: High Society and Political Sociability*; Also numerous contemporary memoirs cited below.

Auguste de Staël: Merlin, vol. 2, p. 741.

Mercedes' success: "Folletín: Cartas sobre la Habana," *El Heraldo*, October 16, 1844.

Femme du monde: Ibid.

Spanish Creole: Captain R. H. Gronow, *Celebrities of London and Paris*, p. 84.

Grace of the Spaniard : Comtesse de Bassanville, *Les Salons d'Autrefois*, vol. 2, p. 112.

Manuel García: F. J. Fétis, *Biographie Universelle des Musiciens*, p. 262.

Mercedes' voice: "Concert en faveur des Grecs," *Le Constitutionnel*, April 30, 1826, p. 1; "Nouvelles," *Revue et Gazette Musicale de Paris*, January 31, 1836, year 3, p. 39.

Strong and light: Sophie Gay, *Salons Célèbres*. p. 160.

Emilio Belgiojoso: Cited in Charles Neilson Gatley, *A Bird of Curious Plumage*, p. 35.

Mercedes and Rossini: Comtesse Merlin, *Madame Malibran*, pp. 36–40.

Her son Gonzalo: FC, p. 42; Gay, pp. 161–162, concert: "Concert en faveur des Grecs," *Le Constitutionnel*, April 30, 1826, p. 1.

Private concert: "Concert chez Merlin January 7," *Revue de Paris*, vol. 22, 1831, pp. 199–200.

Passport to celebrity: Comtesse de Bassanville, vol. 2, p. 111; "Chronique," *Revue de Paris*, vol. 14, 1835, p. 154; Liszt to Batta, n.d. (1834/1835), Musée Royal de Mariemont, via www.europeana.eu; Concert Program March 26, 1845 in *Mr and Mrs Tudor's Engagement Album*, MOMH.

Price of performance: Martin-Fugier, pp. 421–422.

The *petits*: Comtesse de Bassanville, vol. 2, p. 113.

Suppers: CM-M, vol. 1, pp. 222–224.

No politics: Comtesse de Bassanville, vol. 2, p. 135.

She was independent: Gronow, p. 86.

Lariboisière: Elise Roy: J. P. Martineaud, *Une Histoire de l'hôpital Lariboisière*, pp. 21–23; Comtesse Dash, *Mémoires des Autres*, pp. 195–196. Social: Charles Bocher, *Mémoires*, p. 406; "Bal de l'Opéra—Dames Patronnesses," *Journal des Débats*, January 15, 1832. Comte Lariboisière: *Annuaire Historique et Biographique de Souverains, des chefs et membres de maison princières*, Part 2, pp. 82–86; "Les obsèques du lieutenant-général comte Merlin," *Journal des Débats*, May 12, 1839.

Pension: Merlin to President of War Committee, February 4, 1825, SHD Merlin; Ordonnance No. 129, December 1, 1824, *Bulletin des Lois du Royaume de France*, Series 8, vol. 1, Bulletin 9, pp. 104–105; Ordonnance No. 18, February 16, 1825, ibid., vol. 2, Bulletin 22bis, pp. 72–81. Merlin's retirement was based on years of service, including Naples and Spain. These were not counted for benefits or promotions.

CHAPTER 13: *Romancing the Past*

Mercedes and the bad journalists: Comte Rodolphe Apponyi, *Vingt-Cinq Ans à Paris*, vol. 1, p. 314.

Letter to Ministry: Merlin to Minister of War, July 14, 1824, SHD Merlin.

Pragines: O'Farrill to Joseph, June 1825, Joseph Bonaparte, *Mémoires et Correspondance*, vol. 10, pp. 281–282.

Ministry rejects: Bureau of Transports to General Staff, April 14, 1831, SHD Merlin.

High expenses: Merlin to Minister of War, March 6, 1832, SHD Merlin.

Sébastiani brothers: Summary of Corsican politics circa 1831 and identification of "Corsican family" provided by Prof. Francis Pomponi, University d'Aix-en-Provence.

Faction: Merlin to Minister, January 17, 1832, SHD Merlin.

Reassignments Corsica and Montpellier: Merlin to Minister: November 2, 11, December 10, 1831, January 17, March 6, 1832, Circa 1834, SHD Merlin.

Teranita's inheritance: O'Farrill's petition rejected, January 15, 1829, AGI, ULTRAMAR, 42, No. 32; Documents Inventory, ANF Succession Merlin; Mercedes' petition rejected March 26, 1841, ANC, R.O.C., Leg 121, Exp. 101.

Sillery: Assets, ANF Succession Merlin; www.quartiergare-epinay.pages-perso-orange.fr/historiqueepinay. While this site offers accurate details regarding property transaction, it confuses General Merlin with Count (General) Eugène Merlin, son of Merlin de Douai. It also confuses Mercedes with the other Countess Merlin. In the same year Merlin de Thionville was forced to sell Commenchon and Merlin probably sold Brunehamel. Merlin, vol. 2, pp. 794. Numerous letters exist starting from 1824 addressed from Sillery. Sillery is located in Epinay-sur-Orge.

Grands hommes and witty letters: Daniel Stern (Comtesse d'Agoult), *Mes Souvenirs*, p. 348; Mercedes to Victor Cousins, Monday April 14, BS MSVC 239 (Correspondance General Victor Cousins Tome XXVI) 3465.

All voices: Narcisse-Achille de Salvandy to Mercedes, undated, TIL, MS.F/Salvandy.2. The Académie Française is the oldest of the five academies of the Institut de France. Membership is life-long and limited to forty elected members. In Mercedes' day, the candidates for open seats would have to pay formal calls on the other members and elections were quite contentious.

Eminent men: Comtesse de Bassanville, vol. 2, pp. 113–118.

Balzac appreciated salon: H. Blaze de Bury, *Alexandre Dumas, sa vie, son temps, son œuvres*, p. 67.

Dinner at Saint-Gratien: Adam Zamoyski, *Chopin: Prince of the Romantics*, pp. 153–154.

Lived in fine house: Balzac, *The Maranas (Juana)*, pp. 49–50.

Madames Evangelista: Balzac, *The Marriage Settlement (Le Contrat de Mariage)*, pp. 15, 20; Mercedes' descriptions of Mamita, Teresa, and Habaneras: CM-M, vol. 1, pp. 7–8, 29, 154–155.

Certain critics: Guy Le Prat, Introduction to *La Fille aux yeux d'or*, pp. 313–320. For an interesting discussion on Mercedes' impact on Balzac, see Carmen Vásquez, "Historia de Soeur Inès."

Nicolás de Peñalver y Cárdenas. Extremely wealthy (he paid 100,000 reales for his title) and received permission to be married in Italy by the cardinal-archbishop in 1823. (Nieto, Conde de Peñalver).

Infinite number of visitors: Domingo del Monte, "Una Habanera en Paris," from *Aguinaldo Habanero 1837*, quoted in Salvador Bueno (ed.), *Ensayos Críticos de Domingo del Monte*, p. 196.

Timid: Three major reviews of her full work in 1836 used that phrase.

Visitors: Mercedes socialized with both José Luis Alfonso and José de la Luz y Caballero, Luz to Alfonso, May 26, 1831, José de la Luz y Caballero, *De la Vida Íntima*, vol. 1, pp. 171–173; Mercedes to Luz, circa May 1831, ibid., vol. 2, pp. 113–114; Domingo del Monte, "Mes Douze Premières Années/Mis Doce Primeros Años," *Revista Bimestre*, vol. 1, n. 3 (Septiembre/Octubre 1831), pp. 346–360.

CHAPTER 14: *The Literary Socialite*

Spanish sources: Mercedes also used the newly published chronicle by Count de Toreno.

Teresa's marriage: March 28, 1835, AdP. Firmin-Désiré Gentien: details courtesy of M. Jean-Pierre Binder from the Gentien descendants. Mercedes' namesake: April 23, AdP.

Italian airs: "Chronique," *Revue de Paris*, vol. 14, 1835, p. 154; Concert Program April 17, 1845 in *Mr and Mrs Tudor's Engagement Album*, MOMH.

Dowry and income: Documents Inventory, Assets, Partage in ANF Succession Merlin. Reserves: Service July 1841, SHD Merlin. From 1822 Mercedes received approximately 18,000 pesos of capital and an unknown amount of interest: Accounts, July 18, 1840, ANC, Protocolo Notorial de Manuel Fornari, 1840, folios 591–593vto. (ANC 1840 Contract).

Mario and Malibran: Ellen Creathorne Clayton, *Queens of Song*, pp. 354–355, 375–376. Malibran income @ 25fr/sterling based on published exchange rates in Galignani's New Paris Guide (1839 and 1883).

Balzac's own review: Graham Robb, *Balzac—A Biography*, p. 180.

Sainte-Beuve: "Souvenirs de Madame la Comtesse Merlin," *Revue des Deux Mondes*, April 1, 1836, pp. 123–125.

George Sand: "Souvenirs de Madame Merlin," *Revue de Paris*, April 17, 1836, vol. 28, pp. 184–188; George Sand to Charles d'Aragon, January 21, 1836; to François Buloz, January 20, April 14, 1836; George Sand, *Correspondance*, vol. 3, pp. 251–252, 255–256, 338–339.

Chronique de Paris review: Charles de Bernard, *Nouvelles et Mélanges*, pp. 252–275.

Philarète Chasles: "Variété," *Journal des Débats*, June 30, December 9, 1836.

Joseph's reply: Joseph to Mercedes, September 1, 1836, BIDF, Ms 7917 f23–24; Joseph to Duchesse d'Abrantès, August 29, 1834, Joseph Bonaparte, *Mémoires et Correspondance*, vol. 10, pp. 394–398.

Business with Charpentier: Mercedes to Charpentier, November 29, 1836, FC, pp. 326–327.

Publisher Ladvocat: Ladvocat to Mercedes, June 20 [1837], BIDF, Ms 7916 f.242–243; Prospectus, "Les Loisirs d'une Femme du Monde," in Duchesse d'Abrantès, *Salons de Paris*, vol. 1.

Make you think: Ladvocat, ibid.

Concerts: "Chronique," *Le Ménestrel*, July 23, 1837.

Alfonso petitioned: Alfonso to Domingo del Monte, October 21, 1837, Domingo del Monte, Centón Epistolario, vol. 3, pp. 201–202.

Reviewer lamented: "Revue Critique des Livres Nouveaux," July 1838, in *Bulletin Littéraire et Scientifique*, year 6, pp. 214–215.

Dramatic eccentricities: *Journal des Débats*, July 3, 1838.

La France Musicale: "Madame Malibran," *La France Musicale*, December 30, 1838, pp. 5–7. Chopin: Zamoyski, pp. 144–145. Zamoyski quotes at length from an account of an evening at Custine's describing Mercedes setting the lead for Chopin as she sang and danced, castanets in hand. Animosity Escudier: FC, p. 147.

Chapter 15: *Daughter of Havana*

Concert for Martinique: *Journal des Débats*, March 13, 26, 1839; *La Presse*, March 21, 23, April 22, 27, 1839; *Le Ménestrel*, May 5, 1839.

Funeral: "Les obsèques du lieutenant-général comte Merlin," *Journal des Débats*, May 12, 1839. Painful illness: Journal Politique et Littéraire de Toulouse, May 12, 1839.

Gout: Théodore Boubée, *Mémoire sur le traitement de la goutte et des rheumatism*, pp. 29–30. Mercedes first mentions his gout in her July 1812 letter before the Battle of Salamanca.

All information regarding the inventory, assets, and division of estate: ANF Succession Merlin; Jerez: Leone Séché, *Alfred de Musset*, vol. 1, pp. 165–166.

Sacred mission: CM-M, vol. 2, pp. 295–296.

Eldest daughter: Prosper Mérimée to Countess de Montijo, March 25, 1843, Prosper Mérimée, *Lettres de Prosper Mérimée à la Comtesse de Montijo*; pp. 58–60.

Spanish Art in France: Ilse Hempel Lipschultz, *Spanish Painting and the French Romantics*.

All details regarding sale: Catalogue de vente du General Merlin, June 14, 1839, INHA, mfilm 35-1839-06-14; Catalogue de vente de la Comtesse Merlin, May 18, 28, 1852, BAD, M1004 and NG. All are annotated copies.

Stay in Stuttgart: Mercedes to M. Delapalme, September 30, 1839, FC, p. 330.

Baden/Stuttgart articles: *Journal des Débats*, August 10, 1839; "Courrier de Paris," *La Presse*, August 31, 1839; *Revue de Paris*, vol. 14 (1840), p. 297.

Merced Toledo: Settlement, December 17, 1839, ANC, Escribanía de Daumy, Leg. 416, N.3; Merced Toledo v. Count de Casa-Barreto, 1841–1845, Escribanía de Guerra, Leg. 239, No. 3932.

Letters allowed Custine: Anka Muhlstein, *A Taste for Freedom: The Life of Astolphe de Custine*, pp. 248–249.

Custine's travel writing: George F. Kennan, "Introduction," in *Empire of the Czar, A Journey through Eternal Russia*; Muhlstein, pp. 247–258, 267–283.

Details from Comtesse Merlin, "L'Esclavage aux Colonies Espagnols," *Revue des Deux Mondes*, June 1, 1841, unless otherwise stated.

British government: Mercedes to Dr. Koreff, October 16, 1846, BIDF, Ms Lov H 1436/Fol. 13–381/Fol. 323–324 bis.

Mercedes used Monte-Hermoso: Marques de Cárdenas de Monte-Hermoso and sugar millowners, AGI ESTADO, 7, N.5.

1817 Royal Decree: R.C. Prohibiendo el tráfico de esclavos con África 19 diciembre 1817, Manuel Lucena Salmoral, *Regulación de la Esclavitud Negra en las Colonias de América Española (1503–1886)*, p. 296.

Many landowners: Thomas, *Cuba*, p. 206. Thomas argues that the 1843 revolts and the 1844 Escalera Conspiracy shocked many into finally considering an end to the trade.

Fragments of correspondence: Mercedes to Chasles, lundi soir, and n.d. "Notre Code," BHVP-PC.

Above all do not permit: Mercedes to Chasles, n.d. beginning "Notre Code," BHVP-PC.

Other journals: "Variété," *La Presse*, June 15, 1841; "De l'Esclavage à Cuba," *Le Voleur*, June 30, 1841; Felix Milliroux, *Demerary, Transition de l'Esclavage a la Liberté*.

German reception and immigrants: Mercedes to Chasles, July 11, 1841, August 11 [1841], FC, pp. 206–208, 217.

Spanish pamphlet: *Los Esclavos en las Colonias Españolas*.

Reopened her salon: "Chronique du Grand Monde," *La Sylphide*, February 27, March 6, 1841, pp. 160, 124; "Courrier de Paris," *La Presse*, May 17, 1841; "Chronique–Salon," *La Mode*, March 20, 1841, p. 373; "Chronique," *Court Magazine and Monthly Critic* (London), May 1, 1841, p. 145.

Meet in Baden: Mercedes to Anna, June 29, 1841, FC, p. 332.

Prince Jérôme and relationship incomplete: Mercedes to Chasles, July 26, 28, August 9, 1841, FC, pp. 212–216.

Saco and Merlin: Saco to Alfonso, July 29, October 10, 1842, José Antonio Saco, *Documentos para su Vida*, pp. 53, 58. Del Monte asked Alfonso: del

Monte to Alfonso, July 30, 1840, BNC, CM. Monte No. 19–44. Carta a José L. Alfonso. T II. 1838–1847. Saco said that he permitted Mercedes to modify his work but refused to review her writings. Still, he never wrote anything critical of her. Alfonso provided an essay on the government, April 15, 1842, BNC, C.M. Alfonso No. 9 José Luis Alfonso, Marqués de Montelo. Noticias sobre el estado politico y administrative de Cuba dirigida a la Sra. Condesa de Merlin. Abril de 1842.

Opulent lifestyle: Mercedes to Chasles, November 7, 1843, FC, p. 289.

Chasles' debts: Mercedes to Chasles, n.d. (1840, possibly later), January 8, [1842], two n.d. (possibly April 1842), November 18, [1842], late November, November 30, December 3, 7, 1842, FC, pp. 201–200, 242–244, 260–268. "Labyrinthine," p. 260; Pichois, p. 462.

Financial woes: Mercedes to Chasles, Metz 29th [September 29, 1843], dated 25 [October 25, 1843], October 1, 5, n.d., 9, 10, n.d., 20, 20, 30, November 14, [1843], November 1, 3, 4, 7, 12, 24, 1843, FC, pp. 226–229, 240–242, 254–257, 269–290. Quote p. 288. Note: FC dated several undated letters either 1841/1842 but upon closer examination of the content, these letters clearly and logically form part of series from Sept.–Nov. 1843. I have therefore redated them.

Completing Havana: August 11 [1841], January 8 [1842], June 1 [1842], n.d., n.d. Dissay 1842, October 15, (twice), 27, n.d., November 6, n.d., 14, 17, 18, fin, 30, December 7, 1842, October 1, 10, 22, November 3, 4, 24, 1843, November 14 [1843—redated], n.d., n.d. [1844], FC pp. 217, 242–243, 245–270, 274–276, 280–282, 284–287, 290–293. Two undated fragments re: agriculture, paseo Tacón, and outline of topics, BHVP-PC.

Subscription failure: Mercedes to Chasle, November 14 [redated 1843], FC, pp. 254–257.

O'Farrill's attempts: Félix Tanco to del Monte, April 22, 1843, del Monte, *Centón Epistolario*, vol. 7, pp. 177–178.

Cassagnac's subscription: Elborg Forster and Robert Forster, *Sugar and Slavery, Family and Race—Letters and Diary of Pierre Dessalles*, p. 156. Interestingly, Cassagnac's brother-in-law Rosemund de Beauvallon also published a Cuba book—suspiciously using descriptions similar to Mercedes'—even mistakenly calling uncle Juanito the Count of Montalvo as Mercedes had done.

The selection of letters is discussed in Salvador Bueno, *Ensayos sobre Cubanos*, pp. 54–57. The ten letters were those serialized in *La Presse*.

French press: *L'illustration*, March 16, 1844, quoted in FC, pp. 168–169, *La Sylphide* series 2, vol. 4 (1841) p. 124; Saint-Priest: quoted in Marie-Louise Pailleron, *François Buloz et ses Amies*, pp. 214–215. Also see "La Havane," *L'Artiste*, series 3, vol. 5 (February 18, 1844) pp. 107–109; "La Havane," *Le Constitutionnel*, June 13, 1844, pp. 1–2; "Publicaciones Importantes," *Revista de Madrid*, Época 2, vol. 2 (1844), pp. 69–84.

Women of Havana: "Cartas Dirigidas a Jorge Sand," *Diario de la Habana*, September 10–12, 1843; "Cartas a Chucha—Las Mugeres [*sic*] de La Habana," September 21, 24, and 28, 1843, *El Faro Industrial de la Habana*. Interestingly, Mercedes' account had very strong similarities to some of the descriptions of women by F. Gaillardet in a series of articles in *La Presse*, August 9 and 20, 1838—whose author in turn references Mercedes' own memoirs.

Tanco's attack: Félix Tanco, *Refutación a Viage* [*sic*] *a la Habana por Verafilo*.

Cuban *costumbristas*: Mercedes to Chasles, dated 25 [October 25, 1843], November 3, 4, 1843, FC, pp. 226–228, 284–287. Request to cite: Mercedes to Chasles, n.d., FC, pp. 252–253.

Luz's defense: "Fairplay," *El Faro Industrial de la Habana*, April 27, 30, 1844, reprinted in Luz y Caballero, *Escritos Literarios*, pp. 107–116.

Escalera Conspiracy: A slave woman supposedly informed on the conspiracy and the colonial government preempted by ordering mass arrests. The ex-slave and renowned poet Placido (who had written one of the poems to Mercedes and owed his freedom to del Monte's circle) was among those executed. Escalera name comes from torture method of whipping on a ladder (escalera). See Thomas, *Cuba* and letters addressed to del Monte in *Centón Epistolario*, vol. 6.

Mercedes warmly welcomed: Mercedes to del Monte, June 17, 1844, *Centón Epistolario*, vol. 6, p. 69.

Del Monte explained: Del Monte to Alexander Everett, July 31, 1844, Enildo A. Garcia, "Cartas de Domingo del Monte a Alexander Everett," pp. 135–138.

Hugh Thomas: Hugh Thomas, "Prologue," in Maria Luisa Lobo Montalvo, *Havana, History and Architecture of a Romantic City*. He also cites her in *Cuba* and *The Slave Trade*.

CHAPTER 17: *Finale*

1844 carnival ball: "Courrier de Paris," *La Presse*, March 3, 1844; Roths-child: *La Chronique* 1843–1844, vol. 4, p. 394, quoted in FC, p. 112.

Mercedes' concerts: Two programs survive in a remarkable Engagements Album belonging to the Tudors, a wealthy English couple in Paris. *Mr. and Mrs. Tudor's Engagement Album*, MOMH.

Failure to pay: Mercedes to Chasles, October 12, 1846, BHVP-PC.

Nazareno dispute: ANC Nazareno Lawsuit. Original valuation: ANC Pro-tocolo Notarial de José Ortega, 1820, Escritura Folio 6556/v. All fig-ures rounded.

Aunt O'Farrill's fortune: François Merlin to Quico, submitted April 30, 1841, ANC Nazareno Lawsuit.

Mercedes' reason: Mérimée to Montijo, December 20, 1845, Mérimée, *Lettres*, vol. 1, pp. 140–142. Date of Spain trip based on letters from Mercedes to Chasles and Blaze de Bury.

Osuna: Mercedes to Osuna, June 20, 1844, AHN-SN, Diversos-Titulos_familias, 3538 Leg. 2, Exp. 26; Certificate: December 31, 1844, AHN-SN Osuna, CT. 533. D. 4.

Martínez de la Rosa: Numerous letters to/from Chasles, Balzac, Mérimée attest to friendship.

Montijo hospitality: Mérimée to Montijo, April 2, 1841, Mérimée, *Lettres*, vol. 1, p. 42.

Petitioner: Mercedes to Chasles, October 25, 1845, FC, pp. 297–298.

Somosierra: Ibid.

Bullfight: Mercedes to Blaze de Bury, 1845, quoted in Pailleron, pp. 215–217.

Letters to Buloz: Ibid., pp. 215–217.

Concert in Madrid: *La Postdata*, November 19, 1845; *Morning Post* (London), November 24, 1845.

Avellaneda literary: *El Espectador*, October 25, 1845; Mercedes to Avellaneda, October 31, [1845], Domingo Figarola Caneda, *Gertrudis Gómez de Avellanada*, p. 156; Mercedes to Avellaneda, June 20, 1846, ibid., p. 157 and n.

Bitter fruits: Mercedes to Chasles, October 25, 1845, FC, p. 297.

Mérimée's comments: Mérimée to Montijo, April 2, 1841, March 18, 25, 1843, April 29, 1843, November 11, 1843, June 2, 1844, April 26, December 20,

27, 1845, January 17, 1846, Mérimée, *Lettres*, vol. 1, pp. 40–42, 57–60, 63–64, 71, 98–99, 127–129, 140–144, 150–151. Mérimée to Mercedes, June 3, 1844, BIDF, Ms Lov B 396/f133–134.

Giuditta: "Les Académies de Femmes en France par une vieille Saint-Simonienne," *La Revue des Revues*, December 15, 1899, pp. 557–574; Heinrich Heine, *The Romantic School and Other Essays*, pp. 284–286.

Les Lionnes: Mercedes to Chasles, October 1, 5, 22, 1843, FC, pp. 269–272, 280–283. "Lola," *La Presse*, October 15–18, 1844.

L'Expiation: Anténor Joly to Mercedes, February 4, 1847, BIDF, Ms 7913–4; Mercedes to Joly, September 21, 1846; Mercedes to Chasles, October 12, 1846, November 22 [1846], BHVP-PC; Mercedes to Chasles, September 9, n.d., 1846; Mercedes to Joly, October 1, 1846 [FC incorrectly has addressed to Chasles], December 28, 1846 [FC incorrectly has addressed to Paul Permain, who published an edition in 1852] FC, pp. 299–300, 306, 340–341. Annotated manuscript/outline in BHVP-PC.

Limping: Mérimée to Montijo, March 7, 1846, Mérimée, *Lettres*, vol. 1, pp. 156–158.

New musicians: "Nouvelles Diverses," *Le Ménstrel*, April 26, 1846; "Un peu de tout," *La Presse Musicale*, November 26, 1846; Balzac to Madame Hanska, February 4,1846, Honoré de Balzac, *Lettres à Madame Hanska*, vol. 3, p. 161. Balzac mentions the card game *lansquenet* numerous times 1845–1846.

Mercedes' health: Mercedes to Dr. Koreff, October 16, 1846, BIDF Ms Lov H 1436/Fol. 13–381/Fol. 323–324 bis; Mercedes to Chasles, September 17, 1847, FC, pp. 307–308; Alex Reumont, MD, *The Mineral Springs of Aix-la-Chapelle and of Borcette*, pp. 29–34.

Unfortunate to plan: Mercedes to Chasles, September 17, 1847, FC, pp. 307–308.

Opened her heart: Mercedes to Chasles, December 5, 15, 1847, FC, pp. 308–310.

Teresa not in Paris: Mercedes to Chasles, January 27, 1847, BHVP-PC.

Refuge at Saint-Gratien: Muhlstein, p. 161.

Emotional affairs: Two undated letters, FC, pp. 300–301, 305–306.

Custine and Mercedes: Mercedes to Chasles, Monday [1849], FC, p. 311 and note; Muhlstein, pp. 356–357; Custine to Balzac, June 29, 1846, Honoré de Balzac, *Correspondance*, vol. 5, pp. 130–133. Custine was a complex man; his fairly open homosexual lifestyle was unprecedented in the era. He lived in Saint-Gratien with his longtime companion Edward Sainte-Barbe and occasionally other lovers. In his rather pompous *Mémoires* (pp. 309–311), Chasles described Custine as unfortunate and claimed that Mercedes was repelled by his touch, although she saw a profound sadness within him. Yet Mercedes stayed close to Custine all her life. See Muhlstein for a sympathetic look at Custine.

Mercedes' final trip: "Southampton," *Times* (London), September 3, 1849; "Entradas Puerto," *Gaceta de la Habana*, September 30, 1849; "Ramillete," ibid., October 7, 1849; "Vapor de Europa," *Faro Industrial de la Habana*, September 30/October 1, 1849.

Italian singers: "Folletín," *Faro Industrial de la Habana*, October 13, 16, 21, November 1, 1849; "Folletín, Baile en Palacio," ibid., November 21, 1849; "Fiesta del Conde de Peñalver," ibid., December 21, 1849.

Ohio: "Salidas Puerto," *Faro Industrial de la Habana*, April 21, 1850; *Ohio* Manifest, April 24, 1850, New York Passenger Lists 1820–1857, Ancestry. com; "Passengers by the *America*," *Manchester Times*, May 15, 1850.

Quico's son: "Isla de Cuba," *El Popular*, November 3, 1849.

Contract: Protocolo de Gabriel Ramírez. Año 1849. Tomo II. Folio 1616–1617.

Marriage: March 16, 1850, Santa Cruz entry, Jaruco.

Gonzalo's return: Inventory by French Consul, 1888, ANC, Escribanía de Varios, Leg. 622, No. 10065.

Parish priest: Baron Fruchard, quoted in FC, p. 62.

Faithful friends and Chasles: Mercedes to Chasles, January 30, 1851, FC, pp. 312–313; Mercedes to Chasles, April 2, 1851, BHVP-PC; Gronow, pp. 84–86.

Summer rental: Mercedes to M. Bouteiller, April 26, 1851, FC, pp. 343–344; Mercedes to Chasles, June 4, September 20, 1851, BHVP-PC.

Music and philanthropy: Gronow, pp. 84–85; "Concert au profit de l'oeuvre des sourds-muets de France," *La Presse*, February 9, 1851.

Gottschalk: Serafín Ramírez, *La Habana Artística*, p. 41. According to Ramírez, Gottschalk profoundly admired her.

Flavia: "Flavia," *La España*, November 13–December 10, 1850.

All details of Mercedes' estate: Comtesse Merlin Succession, ANF, MC/ ET/XCIII/646. Apartment auction: "Notice d'un joli mobilier," May 17–19, 1852 (postponed to May 28), BNF; Art sale: Catalogue de vente Comtesse Merlin, May 18, 1852, BAD, M1004; NG. Reason for postponement noted on NG catalogue. The INHA holds an unannotated catalogue showing May 28, 1852 date.

Karr, journalist/writer whose famous quote was *plus ça change plus c'est la meme chose.*

Mercedes' funeral: *La France Musicale*, April 4, 1852, quoted in FC p. 71; *La Presse*, April 2, 1852; Chasles' sketch: *Le Convoi de Mme Merlin*, BHVP-PC. Her death was also mentioned in Cuba and Spain.

Mercedes' final tomb: Mairie de Paris, Service des Cimetiers (Conservateurs de Père-Lachaise) to author, February 9, 2012.

Information regarding the removal: Monsieur Domenico Gabrielli Veneto to author, May 26, 2012; M. Gabrielli Veneto is author of *Dictionnaire Historique du Père-Lachaise* (2002).

SELECTED BIBLIOGRAPHY

Abrantès, Duchesse d'. *Histoire des Salons de Paris*. 6 vols. Paris: Ladvocat, 1837–1838.

————. *Mémoires de Madame la Duchesse d'Abrantès ou Souvenirs Historiques*. 18 vols. Paris: Ladvocat, 1832.

————. *Souvenirs d'une Ambassade et d'un Séjour en Espagne et Portugal 1808–1811*. 2 vols. Brussels: Hauman, Cattoir et Comp:, 1838.

Agoult, Comtesse d'. *Mes Souvenirs (1806–1833)*. Paris: Calmann-Lévy, 1880.

Albert, Paul. *Une Famille Lorraine: Les Merlin de Thionville*. Metz: Coopérative d'édition et d'impression, 1949.

Almanach des 25,000 adresses des principaux habitans [sic] *de Paris*. Paris: 1817, 1820, 1846.

Annuaire Historique et Biographique des souverains, des chefs et membres des maisons princières. Vol. 1. Paris: Archives Historiques, 1844.

Apponyi, Rodolphe, Comte. *Vingt-Cinq Ans à Paris*. 3 vols. Paris: Plon-Nourrit, 1913–1914.

Arango, Rubén C. *La Sacarocracia: Historia de la Aristocracia Azucarera Cubana*. Miami: Ego Group, 2006.

Armstrong, Martin. *The Spanish Circus*. London: Collins, 1937.

Arrate, José Martín Félix de. *Llave del Nuevo Mundo*. Edited by Julio J. Le Riverend. Mexico: Fondo de Cultura Económica, 1949.

Artola, Miguel. *Los Afrancesados*. Madrid: Alianza Editorial, 2008.

Azanza, Miguel de, and Gonzalo O'Farrill. *Memoria de D. Miguel José de Azanza y D. Gonzalo O´Farrill sobre los hechos que justifican su conducta política*. Paris: P.N. Rougeron, 1815.

Badaracco, Claire M. "The Cuba Journal of Sophia Peabody Hawthorne." PhD Dissertation. Rutgers University, 1978.

Balzac, Honoré de. *A Marriage Settlement*. Edited by George Saintsbury. Translated by Clara Bell. London: J. M. Dent and Co., 1897.

————. *Béatrix*. In *Œuvres Complète*. Vol. 4. Paris: Calmann-Lévy, n.d.

————. *Correspondance*. Edited by Roger Pierrot. Paris: Editions Garnier Frères, 1969.

————. *Juana (Les Maranas)*. e-book edition. Translated by Katharine Prescott Wormesley. Boston: Roberts Bros, 1896.

————. *La Fille aux Yeux d'Or*. In *Oeuvres Complètes*. Vol. 9. edited by Guy Le Prat. Paris: La Société d'Etudes Balzaciennes, 1959.

————. *Lettres à Madame Hanska*. Edited by Roger Pierrot. Paris: Editions du Delta, 1969.

Barras de Aragón, Francisco de las. "Noticias y Documentos de la Expedición del Conde de Mompox a la Isla de Cuba." *Anuario de Estudios Americanos* 9 (1952).

Barreiro, P. "Documentos Relativos a la Expedición del Conde de Mopox a la Isla de Cuba durante los años 1796 a 1802." *Revista de la Academia de Ciencia de Madrid* 30 (1933): 107–121.

Bassanville, Comtesse de. *Les Salons d'Autrefois; Souvenirs Intimes*. 4 vols. Paris: Broussois, n.d.

Bearne, Catherine. *A Royal Quartette*. London: T. F. Unwin, 1908.

Beerman, Eric. "El Conde de Aranda y la Tertulía Madrileña (1788–90) de la Viuda de Bernardo de Gálvez." *In El Conde de Aranda y su Tiempo*, vol. 2, edited by José Antonio Ferrer Benomeli, Esteban Sarasa Sánchez & Eliseo Serrano Martín, 349–362. Zaragoza: Institución Fernando el Cátolico, 2000.

Bernard, Charles de. *Nouvelles et Mélanges*. Paris: Michel Lévy Frères, 1854.

Bigarré, Auguste-Julien. *Mémoires du Général Bigarré, Aide de Camp du Roi Joseph*. Paris: Ernest Kolb, 1907.

Blaze de Bury, Henri. *Alexandre Dumas, Sa Vie, Son Temps; Son Œuvre.* Paris: Calmann-Lévy, 1885.

Bocher, Charles. *Mémoires (1816–1907).* Paris: Ernest Flammarion, 1907.

Bonaparte, Joseph, and Albert Du Casse. *Mémoires et Correspondance Politique et Militaire du Roi Joseph.* 10 vols. Paris: Perrotin, 1853–1854.

Boubée, Théodore. *Mémoire sur le Traitement de la Goutte et des Rheumatism par le Sirop Anti-Goutteux.* Paris: Claye, Tailleferet et Cie, 1847.

Bueno, Salvador. *Cuba, crucero del mundo.* Havana: Editorial Pablo de la Torriente, 1980.

————. *Ensayos sobre Cubanos.* Havana: Ediciones Unión, 1994.

————. *Leyendas Cubanas.* Havana: Editorial Arte y Literatura, 1978.

Bulletin des Lois du Royaume de France, Series 8, Règne de Charles X. Vols. 1–2. Paris: Imprimerie Royale, 1825.

Chasles, Philarète. *Mémoires.* 2 vols. Paris: Charpentier, 1876.

Clayton, Ellen Creathorne. *Queens of Song.* New York: Harper and Brothers, 1864.

Clune, John James. "A Cuban Convent in the Age of Enlightenment: The Observant Franciscan Community of Santa Clara of Havana 1768–1808." *The Americas* 57, no. 3 (January 2001): 309–327.

Cornide, María Teresa. *De la Habana, de Siglos y de Familias.* Habana: Editorial de Ciencias Sociales, 2008.

Custine, Astolphe de, Marquis. *Empire of the Czar: A Journey through Eternal Russia (La Russie en 1839).* New York: Doubleday, 1989.

————. *L'Espagne sous Ferdinand VII.* 4 vols. Paris: Ladvocat, 1838.

Cuza Male, Belkis. "Viaje a la Habana: La Condesa de Merlin." *Linden Lane Magazine* 2, no. 1 (January/March 1983): 11–12.

Dash, Comtesse. *Mémoires des Autres: Souvenirs Anecdotiques sur le Règne de Louis-Philippe.* Paris: Librairie Illustrée, n.d.

Del Monte, Domingo. *Centón Epistolario.* Edited by Domingo Figarola Caneda, Joaquín Llaverías Martínez, and Manuel I. Mesa Rodríguez. 7 vols. Havana: El Siglo XX, 1923–1957.

————. *Ensayos Críticos de Domingo del Monte.* Edited by Salvador Bueno. Havana: Pablo de la Torriente, 2000.

————. "Mes Douze Premières Années/Mis Doce Primeros Años." *Revista y Repertorio Bimestre de la Isla de Cuba* 1, no. 3 (September–October 1831): 346–360.

Diana, Manuel Juan. *Memoria Histórica-Artística del Teatro Real de Madrid.* Madrid: Imprenta Nacional, 1850.

Dumas, Alexandre. *La Salle d'Armes—Pauline.* Paris: Dumont, 1838.

Duvergier, J. B. *Collection Complète des Lois, Décrets, Ordonnances, Réglemens et Avis du Conseil d'Etat.* Vol. 20. Paris: A. Guyot et Scribe, 1827.

Egorova, Olga V. "Agustín de Betancourt y la Primera Máquina de Vapor en Cuba." *Opus Habana* 12, no. 2 (March–August 2009).

Esdaile, Charles. *The Peninsular War.* London: Penguin, 2003.

Esquivel y Castañeda, Manuel. "Memorias Inéditas del Alférez de Fragata D. Manuel Esquivel y Castañeda." *Boletín de la Real Academia de la Historia* 52, no. 5 (May 1908): 377–395.

Etienne, Pascal, ed. *Le Faubourg Poissonnière: Architecture, Élégance et Décor.* Paris: Délégation à l'Action Artistique de la Ville de Paris, 1986.

Everett, Alexander H. "La Havane." *The Southern Quarterly Review* 7 (January 1845): 153–197.

Fernández García, Matías. *Parroquias Madrileñas de San Martín y San Pedro el Real.* Madrid: Caparrós Editoras, 2004.

Fétis, F. J. *Biographie Universelle des Musiciens et Bibliographie Générale de la Musique.* Vol. 4. Brussels: Melire, Cans et Cie, 1837.

Figarola Caneda, Domingo. *Gertrudis Gómez de Avellaneda: Bibliografía e Iconografía.* Madrid: Sociedad General Española de Librería, 1929.

————. *La Condesa de Merlin (María de la Merced Santa Cruz y Montalvo): estudio Bibliográfico e Iconográfico.* Paris: Editions Excelsior, 1928.

Figueroa, Agustín de. *La Condesa de Merlin, Musa del Romanticismo.* Madrid: Imprenta de Juan Pueyo, 1934.

Forster, Elborg, and Robert Forster. *Sugar and Slavery, Family and Race: The Letters and Diary of Pierre Dessalles.* Baltimore: The Johns Hopkins University Press, 1996.

Galignani's New Paris Guide. Paris: A. and W. Galignani & Co., 1839, 1883.

García del Pino, Cesar, and Alicia Melis. *Documentos para la Historia Colonial de Cuba: Siglos XVI, XVII, XVIII, XIX.* Havana: Editorial de Ciencias Sociales, 1988.

García, Enildo A. "Cartas de Domingo del Monte." *Revista de Literatura Cubana* 7, no. 13 (1989): 105–147.

Gatley, Charles Neilson. *A Bird of Curious Plumage: The Life of Princess Cristina di Belgiojoso.* London: Constable, 1971.

Gay, Sophie. *Salons Célèbres.* Paris: Michel Lévy et Frères, 1864.

Geoffroy de Grandmaison, Charles-Alexandre. *L'Espagne et Napoléon.* 3 vols. Paris: Librairie Plon, 1908–1931.

González del Valle, Francisco. "Luz, Saco y Del Monte ante la Esclavitud Negra: Cinco Cartas Inéditas de Félix Tanco y Bosmeniel." *Revista Bimestre Cubana* 47 (1941): 190–196.

González-Ripoll Navarro, María Dolores. *Cuba, Isla de los Ensayos: Cultura y Sociedad (1750–1815).* Madrid: Consejo Superior de Investigaciones Cientificas, 1999.

González-Ripoll Navarro, María Dolores, and Izaskun Alvarez Cuartero. *Francisco Arango y la Invención de la Cuba Azucarera.* Salamanca: Ediciones Universidad de Salamanca, 2009.

Gourdon de Genouillac, Henri. *Paris à travers les Siècles.* Vol. 3. Paris: F. Roy, 1880.

Granier de Cassagnac, Adolphe. *Le Secret du Chevalier de Médrane.* Paris: E. Dentu, 1877.

_____. *Voyage sux Antilles.* 2 vols. Paris: Dauvin et Fontaine, 1842–1844.

Gronow, Captain R. H. *Celebrities of London and Paris.* London: Smith, Elder & Co., 1865.

Heine, Heinrich. *The Romantic School and Other Essays.* Edited by Jost Hermand and Robert C. Holub. New York: Continuum, 2002.

Higueras, María Dolores and José Guío y Sánchez. *Cuba Ilustrada: Real Comisión de Guantánamo 1796–1808.* 2 vols. Barcelona: Lunwerg Editores, 1991.

Holland, Elizabeth, Lady. *The Spanish Journal of Elizabeth, Lady Holland.* London: Longman, Green and Co., 1910.

Holland, Henry Richard, Lord. *Foreign Reminiscences.* London: Longman, Brown, Green and Longman, 1850.

Houssaye, Henry. *1815: La Première Restauration.* 22nd ed. Paris: Perrin, 1896.

_____. *1815: La Seconde Abdication.* 4th ed. Paris: Perrin, 1905.

Howison, James. *Foreign Scenes and Travelling Recreations*. 2 vols. Edinburgh: Oliver and Boyd, 1825.

Hugo, Joseph Léopold. *Mémoires du Général Hugo*. 3 vols. Paris: Ladvocat, 1823.

Humboldt, Alexander von. *The Island of Cuba, A Political Essay (with The Nature of Slavery)*. Translated by J. S. Thrasher and Shelley L. Frisch. Princeton, New Jersey: Markus Weiner Publishers, 2001.

Jack, Belinda. *George Sand: A Woman's Life Writ Large*. London: Vintage, 1999.

Jameson, Robert Francis. *Letters from Havana, during the Year 1820*. London: John Miller, 1820.

Johnson, Sherry. *The Social Transformation of Eighteenth-Century Cuba*. Gainesville: University Press of Florida, 2001.

Kale, Steven. *French Salons: High Society and Political Sociability from the Old Regime to the Revolution of 1848*. Baltimore: The Johns Hopkins University Press, 2004.

Kany, Charles E. *Life and Manners in Madrid 1750–1800*. Berkeley: University of California Press, 1932.

"La Condesa de Merlin." *La Cartera Cubana* 2, no. 1 (February 1839): 99–102.

La Forest, Antoine-René-Charles-Maturin de, and Charles-Alexandre Geoffroy de Grandmaison. *Correspondance du Comte de La Forest, Ambassadeur de France en Espagne 1808–1813*. 7 vols. Paris: Société d'Histoire Contemporaine, 1905–1913.

Lamas, Waldo, and Osvaldo Valdés de la Paz. *Historia del Convento de Santa Clara de Asís*. Havana: Montalvo, Cárdenas, 1922.

Lastra, Joaquín de la. "Teresa Montalvo: Una Habanera en la Corte de España." *Revista Bimestre Cubana* 48, no. 1 (Julio-Agosto 1941): 73–88.

Lavín, Arturo G. "El Palacio de los Condes de San Juan de Jaruco, Muralla 109." *Revista de la Biblioteca Nacional* (July–September 1951): 45–70.

Lavrín, Asunción. "Ecclesiastical Reform of Nunneries in New Spain in the Eighteenth Century." *The Americas* 22, no. 12 (October 1965): 182–203.

Le Livre Noir de MM Delavau et Franchet. Paris: Moutardier, 1829.

Lipschultz, Ilse Hempel. *Spanish Painting and the French Romantics*. Cambridge, MA: Harvard University Press, 1972.

Lobo Montalvo, Maria Luisa. *Havana: History and Architecture of a Romantic City*. New York: The Monacelli Press, 2000.

Lucena Salmoral, Manuel. *Regulación de la Esclavitud Negra en las Colonias de América Española* (1503–1886). Madrid: Universidad de Alcalá, 2005.

Lucotte, Jules-Alexis. *Notice Historique sur le Lt. Général Comte Lucotte*. Epernay: Imprimerie Noel-Boucort, 1866.

Luz y Caballero, José de la. *De la Vida Íntima*. Edited by Elias Entralgo. 2 vols. Havana: Editorial de la Universidad de la Habana, 1945–1949.

———. *Escritos Literarios*. Edited by Raimundo Lazo. Havana: Editorial de la Universidad de la Habana, 1946.

Madison, James. *The Papers of James Madison: Secretary of State Series*. Vol. 4 (8 October–15 May 1803). Edited by Mary A. Hackett Charlottesville: University Press of Virginia, 1986.

María Luisa, and Manuel Godoy. *Cartas Confidenciales de la Reina María Luisa y de don Manuel Godoy*. Edited by Carlos Pereyra. Madrid: M. Aguilar, 1935.

Marrero, Levi. *Cuba: Economía y Sociedad*. 15 vols. Madrid: Playor, 1974–1992.

Martineaud, J. P. *Une Histoire de l'Hôpital Lariboisière*. Paris: L'Harmattan, 1998.

Martínez, Manuel, Fray. *Los Famosos Traidores: Refugiados en Francia Convencidos de sus Crímenes y Justificación del Real Decreto de 30 de Mayo*. Madrid: Imprenta Real, 1814.

Martin-Fugier, Anne. *La Vie Elégante ou la Formation du Tout-Paris 1815–1848*. Paris: Perrin, 2011.

Martín-Valdepeñas Yagüe, Elisa. "Afrancesadas y Patriotas: la Junta de Honor y Mérito Real Sociedad Económica Matritense de Amigos del País." Chap. 12 in *Heroínas y Patriotas: Mujeres de 1808*. Edited by Irene Castello, Gloria Espigado, and María Cruz Romeo, 343–370. Madrid: Cátedra, 2009.

———. "Ilustracíon, Jacobismo y Afrancesamiento: Ana Rodríguez de Carasa (1763–1816)." *Cuadernos de Estudios del Siglo XVII*, no. 18 (2008): 33–80.

Méndez Rodenas, Adriana. *Gender and Nationalism in Colonial Cuba: The Travels of Santa Cruz y Montalvo, Condesa de Merlin*. Nashville: Vanderbilt University Press, 1998.

Mérimée, Prosper. *Lettres de Prosper Mérimée à la Comtesse de Montijo.* Edited by Gabriel Hanotaux. 2 vols. Paris: Edition Privée, 1930.

Merlin, Roger. *Merlin de Thionville.* 2 vols. Paris: Librairie Félix Alcan, 1927.

Mesonero Romanos, Ramón. *Memorias de un Setentón.* Vol. 5, in Obras de Don Ramón Mesonero Romanos. Edited by Carlos Seco Serrano. Madrid: Atlas, 1967.

Milliroux, Félix. *Demerary: Transition de l'Esclavage à la Liberté.* Paris: H. Fournier, 1843.

Miot de Melito, André-François, Comte. *Mémoires du Comte Miot de Melito.* Edited by General Fleischmann. 3 vols. Paris: Michel Lévy Frères, 1858.

————. *Memoirs of Count Miot de Melito.* Edited by General Fleischmann. Translated by Cashel Hoey and John Lillie. 2 vols. London: Sampson Low, Marston, Searle and Rivington, 1881.

Montoto, Santiago. Catálogo de los Fondos Cubanos del Archivo de Indias: Compañía Ibero Americana de Publicaciones, S.A. Colección de Documentos Inéditos Para la Historia de Hispano-América. Madrid: Co. Ibero-Americana de Publ, 1930.

Moreno Fraginals, Manuel. *El Ingenio, Complejo Económico Social Cubano del Azúcar.* Havana: Comisión Nacional Cubana de la UNESCO, 1964.

Muhlstein, Anka. *A Taste for Freedom: The Life of Astolphe de Custine.* Translated by Teresa Waugh. New York: Helen Marx Books, 1999.

Mullié, M. C. *Biographie des Célébrités Militaires des Armées de Terre et de Mer 1789–1850.* 2 vols. Paris: Poignavant, 1852.

Muriel, Andrés. *Notice sur D. Gonzalo O'Farrill Lieutenant-Général des Armées de SM le Roi d'Espagne—Son Ancien Ministre de la Guerre.* Paris: Bure Frères, 1831.

Nieto y Cortadellas, Rafael. *Dignidades Nobiliarias en Cuba.* Madrid: Imprenta Arba, 1954.

O'Farrill, Gonzalo. *A D. Pedro Sáenz de Santa María y Carassa, Carta de su Padre Político D. Gonzalo O'Farrill Sobre la Vida y Buenos Ejemplos de su Madre.* Paris: 1817.

Oman, Charles. *A History of the Peninsular War.* Vol. 5. Oxford: Clarendon Press, 1914.

Pailleron, Marie-Louise. *François Buloz et Ses Amis: Les Derniers Romantiques.* Paris: Perrin, 1923.

Pérez de la Riva, Juan. *Correspondecia Reservada del Capitan General D. Miguel de Tacón*. Havana: Biblioteca Nacional José Martí, 1963.

Pérez, Rafael. *Madrid en 1808, El Relato de un Actor*. Edited by Joaquín Alvarez Barrientos, Ana Isabel Fernández, and Ascensión Aguerri. Madrid: Dirección General de Archivos, Museos y Bibliotecas, 2008.

Pérez-Beato, Manuel. *Habana Antigua*. Vol. 1. Havana: Seoane, Fernández y Ca., 1936.

Pezuela, Jacobo de la. *Diccionario Geográfico, Estadístico e Histórico de la Isla de Cuba*. Madrid: Imprenta del Establecimiento de Mellado, 1863–1864.

_____. *Ensayo Histórico de la Isla de Cuba*. New York: Imp. Española de R. Rafael, 1842.

Pichois, Claude. *Philarète Chasles et la Vie Littéraire au Temps du Romantisme*. 2 vols. Paris: Librairie José Corti, 1965.

Queipo de Llano, José María, Conde de Toreno. *Historia del Levantamiento, Guerra y Revolución de España*. Madrid: Imprenta de Don Tomás Jordan, 1835.

Quérard, J-M. *La France Littéraire ou Dictionnaire Bibliographique*. Vol. 11. Paris: L'Editeur, 1854–1857.

Quintana, Manuel José. *Obras Inéditas del Excmo. Señor Manuel José Quintana*. Madrid: Medina y Navarro Editores, 1872.

Quiroz, Alfonso W. "The Scientist and the Patrician: Reformism in Cuba." *Alexander von Humboldt: From the Americas to the Cosmos*. New York: Bildner Center for Western Hemisphere Studies, CUNY, 2004.

Ramírez, Serafín. *La Habana Artística*. Havana: Imprenta del EM de la Capitanía General, 1891.

Rapetti, Pierre-Nicolas. *La Défection de Marmont en 1814*. Paris: Poulet-Malassis et de Broise, 1858.

Reumont, Alex. *The Mineral Springs of Aix-la-Chapelle and of Borcette*. London: Williams and Norgate, 1861.

Robb, Graham. *Balzac: A Biography*. London: Picador, 1994.

Rodríguez Fuentes, Lyding. "Santa Clara de Asís—El Esplendor de un Convento para Doncellas de Elite." *Revolución y Cultura*, No. 2 (April–June 2005): 28–33.

Roig de Leuchsenring, Emilio. *La Habana: Apuntes Históricos de la Oficina del Historiador de la Ciudad*. Havana: Editora del Consejo Nacional de Cultura, 1963.

Rosaín, Domingo. *Necrópolis de la Habana: Historia de los Cementerios de Esta Ciudad.* Havana: Imprenta "El Trabajo," 1875.

Rosemond de Beauvallon, J-B. *L'Ile de Cuba.* Vol. 1. Paris: Dauvin et Fontaine; Garnier Frères, 1844.

Saco, José Antonio. *Documentos para su Vida.* Edited by Domingo Figarola Caneda. Havana: El Siglo XX, 1921.

Sagra, Ramón de la. *Historia Económica-Política y Estadística de la Isla de Cuba.* Havana: Impr. de las viudas de Arazoza y Soler, 1831.

Sand, George. *Correspondance.* Vol. 3 (July 1835–April 1837). Edited by George Lubin. Paris: Editions Garnier Frères, 1967.

Santa Cruz y Mallén, Francisco Xavier, Conde de Jaruco. *Historia de Familias Cubanas.* 6 vols. Havana: Editorial Hercules, 1940–1950.

Santa Cruz y Montalvo, Mercedes, Comtesse Merlin. *La Havane.* 3 vols. Paris: Amyot, 1844.

———. *Les Lionnes de Paris.* 2 vols. Paris: Amyot, 1845

———. *Lola et Maria.* Paris: L. de Potter, 1845.

———. *Los Esclavos de Las Colonias Españolas.* Madrid: Imprenta de Alegria y Charlain, 1841.

———. *Madame Malibran.* 2 vols. Brussels: Société Typographique Belge—Wahlen et Cie, 1838.

———. *Souvenirs et Mémoires de Madame la Comtesse Merlin.* 4 vols. Paris: Charpentier, 1836.

———. *Viaje a la Habana.* Madrid: Imprenta de la Sociedad Literaria y Tipografica, 1844.

Sarrablo Aguareles, Eugenio. "La Fundación de Jaruco en Cuba y los Primeros Condes de este Título." *Anuario de Estudios Americanos* 8 (1951): 443–501.

Saunders, Mary F. *Honoré de Balzac—His Life and Writings.* London: John Murray, 1904.

Séché, Léon. *Alfred de Musset.* Paris: Société du Mercure de France, 1907.

Suárez de Tangil y de Angulo, Fernando, Conde de Vallellano. *Nobiliario Cubano o las Grandes Familias Isleñas.* Madrid: F. Beltrán, 1929.

Tanco y Bosmeniel, Félix Manuel. *Refutación al Folleto Intitulado Viage a la Habana por la Condesa de Merlin Publicada por el Diario por Verafilo.* Havana: Imprenta del Gobierno y Capitanía General, 1844.

Thiébault, Paul, Général Baron. *Mémoires du Général Baron Thiébault.* 5 vols. Paris: E. Plon, Nourrit et Cie, 1893–1895.

Thomas, Hugh. *Cuba or the Pursuit of Freedom.* New York: De Capo Press, 1998.

————. *The Slave Trade: The History of the Atlantic Slave Trade 1440–1870.* London: Picador, 1997.

Torre, José María de la. *Lo Que Fuimos y lo Que Somos: o La Habana Antigua y Moderna.* Havana: Imprenta de Spencer, 1857.

Valmont, Lina. "Tras los Vetustos Muros...Crónica Atribuida a Alejo Carpentier Sobre el Convento de Santa Clara." *Opus Habana* 10, no. 2 (November–January 2007): 4–15.

Vásquez, Carmen. "Histoire de Soeur Inès de la Condesa de Merlin, Relato de una Mujer Crítica de su Época." *La Torre Revista de la Universidad de Puerto Rico* 6, no. 21 (January–March 1992): 85–103.

Venegas Fornias, Carlos. "Un Conde Habanero en el Siglo de las Luces." *Revolución y Cultura*, no. 2 (April–June 2005): 24–27.

Villa-Urrutia, Wenceslao Ramírez de, Marqués de. *Fernando VII, Rey Constitucional: Historia Diplomática de España 1820–1823.* Madrid: F. Beltrán, 1922.

————. "La Condesa de Merlin." *Revista Bimestre* Cubana 27 (n.d.): 362–370.

————. *La Reina María Luisa, esposa de Carlos IV: Mujeres de Antaño.* Madrid: F. Beltrán, 1927.

Villaverde, Cirilo. *Cecilia Valdés.* 2 vols. New York: Anaya Book Company, 1971.

Wellesley, Arthur, Duke of Wellington. *The Dispatches of Field Marshal the Duke of Wellington.* Edited by John Gurwood. Vol. 11. London: John Murray, 1838.

Zambrana, Antonio. *El Negro Francisco.* Havana: Editorial Letras Cubanas, 1979.

Zamoyski, Adam. *Chopin: Prince of the Romantics.* London: Harper Press, 2011.

INDEX